M000113119

Advanced Natural Language Processing with TensorFlow 2

Build effective real-world NLP applications using NER, RNNs, seq2seq models, Transformers, and more

Ashish Bansal

BIRMINGHAM - MUMBAI

Advanced Natural Language Processing with TensorFlow 2

Copyright © 2021 Packt Publishing

All rights reserved. No part of this book may be reproduced, stored in a retrieval system, or transmitted in any form or by any means, without the prior written permission of the publisher, except in the case of brief quotations embedded in critical articles or reviews.

Every effort has been made in the preparation of this book to ensure the accuracy of the information presented. However, the information contained in this book is sold without warranty, either express or implied. Neither the author, nor Packt Publishing or its dealers and distributors, will be held liable for any damages caused or alleged to have been caused directly or indirectly by this book.

Packt Publishing has endeavored to provide trademark information about all of the companies and products mentioned in this book by the appropriate use of capitals. However, Packt Publishing cannot guarantee the accuracy of this information.

Producer: Tushar Gupta

Acquisition Editor – Peer Reviews: Divya Mudaliar

Content Development Editor: Alex Patterson

Technical Editor: Gaurav Gavas

Project Editor: Mrunal Dave

Proofreader: Safis Editing

Indexer: Rekha Nair

Presentation Designer: Sandip Tadge

First published: February 2021

Production reference: 1290121

Published by Packt Publishing Ltd.
Livery Place
35 Livery Street
Birmingham B3 2PB, UK.

ISBN 978-1-80020-093-7

www.packt.com

packt.com

Subscribe to our online digital library for full access to over 7,000 books and videos, as well as industry leading tools to help you plan your personal development and advance your career. For more information, please visit our website.

Why subscribe?

- Spend less time learning and more time coding with practical eBooks and Videos from over 4,000 industry professionals
- Learn better with Skill Plans built especially for you
- Get a free eBook or video every month
- Fully searchable for easy access to vital information
- Copy and paste, print, and bookmark content

Did you know that Packt offers eBook versions of every book published, with PDF and ePub files available? You can upgrade to the eBook version at www.Packt.com and as a print book customer, you are entitled to a discount on the eBook copy. Get in touch with us at customercare@packtpub.com for more details.

At www.Packt.com, you can also read a collection of free technical articles, sign up for a range of free newsletters, and receive exclusive discounts and offers on Packt books and eBooks.

Contributors

About the author

Ashish Bansal is the Director of Recommendations at Twitch, where he works on building scalable recommendation systems across a variety of product surfaces, connecting content to people. He has worked on recommendations systems at multiple organizations, most notably Twitter, where he led Trends and Events recommendations, and at Capital One, where he worked on B2B and B2C products. Ashish was also a co-founder of GALE Partners, a full-service digital agency in Toronto, and spent over 9 years at SapientNitro, a leading digital agency.

In many years of work building hybrid recommendation systems balancing collaborative filtering signals with content-based signals, he has spent a lot of time building NLP systems for extracting content signals. In digital marketing, he built systems to analyze coupons, offers, and subject lines. He has worked on messages, tweets, and news articles among other types of textual data and applying cutting edge NLP techniques.

He has over 20 years of experience, with over a decade building ML and Deep Learning systems. Ashish is a guest lecturer at IIT BHU teaching Applied Deep Learning. He has a bachelor's in technology from IIT BHU, and an MBA in marketing from Kellogg School of Management.

My father, Prof. B. B. Bansal, said that the best way to test understanding of a subject is to explain it to someone else. This book is dedicated to him, and my Gurus – my mother, my sister, who instilled the love of reading, and my wife, who taught me consider all perspectives. I would like to mention Aditya sir, who instilled the value of hard work, which was invaluable in writing this book while balancing a full-time job and family. I would like to mention Ajeet, my manager at Twitter, and Omar, my manager at Twitch, for their support during the writing of this book. Ashish Agrawal and Subroto Chakravorty helped me tide over issues in code.

I would like to thank the technical reviewers for ensuring the quality of the book and the editors for working tirelessly on the book. Tushar Gupta, my acquisitions editor, was instrumental in managing the various challenges along the way. Alex – your encouraging comments kept my morale high!

About the reviewers

Tony Mullen is an Associate Teaching Professor at The Khoury College of Computer Science at Northeastern University in Seattle. He has been involved in language technology for over 20 years and holds a master's degree in Linguistics from Trinity College, Dublin, and a PhD in natural language processing from the University of Groningen. He has published papers in the fields of sentiment analysis, named entity recognition, computer-assisted language learning, and ontology development, among others. Recently, in addition to teaching and supervising graduate computer science, he has been involved in NLP research in the medical domain and consulted for a startup in language technology.

Kumar Shridhar is an NLP researcher at ETH Zürich and founder of NeuralSpace. He believes that an NLP system should comprehend texts as humans do. He is working towards the design of flexible NLP systems making them more robust and interpretable. He also believes that NLP systems should not be restricted to few languages, and with NeuralSpace he is extending NLP capabilities to low-resource languages.

Table of Contents

Preface

2017 was a watershed moment for **Natural Language Processing (NLP)**, with Transformer-and attention-based networks coming to the fore. The past few years have been as transformational for NLP as AlexNet was for computer vision in 2012. Tremendous advances in NLP have been made, and we are now moving from research labs into applications.

These advances span the domains of **Natural Language Understanding (NLU)**, **Natural Language Generation (NLG)**, and **Natural Language Interaction (NLI)**. With so much research in all of these domains, it can be a daunting task to understand the exciting developments in NLP.

This book is focused on cutting-edge applications in the fields of NLP, language generation, and dialog systems. It covers the concepts of pre-processing text using techniques such as tokenization, **parts-of-speech (POS)** tagging, and lemmatization using popular libraries such as Stanford NLP and spaCy. **Named Entity Recognition (NER)** models are built from scratch using **Bi-directional Long Short-Term Memory networks (BiLSTMs)**, **Conditional Random Fields (CRFs)**, and Viterbi decoding. Taking a very practical, application-focused perspective, the book covers key emerging areas such as generating text for use in sentence completion and text summarization, multi-modal networks that bridge images and text by generating captions for images, and managing the dialog aspects of chatbots. It covers one of the most important reasons behind recent advances of NLP – transfer learning and fine tuning. Unlabeled textual data is easily available but labeling this data is costly. This book covers practical techniques that can simplify the labeling of textual data.

By the end of the book, I hope you will have advanced knowledge of the tools, techniques, and deep learning architectures used to solve complex NLP problems. The book will cover encoder-decoder networks, **Long Short-Term Memory networks (LSTMs)** and BiLSTMs, CRFs, BERT, GPT-2, GPT-3, Transformers, and other key technologies using TensorFlow.

Advanced TensorFlow techniques required for building advanced models are also covered:

- Building custom models and layers
- Building custom loss functions
- Implementing learning rate annealing
- Using `tf.data` for loading data efficiently
- Checkpointing models to enable long training times (usually several days)

This book contains working code that can be adapted to your own use cases. I hope that you will even be able to do novel state-of-the-art research using the skills you'll gain as you progress through the book.

Who this book is for

This book assumes that the reader has some familiarity with the basics of deep learning and the fundamental concepts of NLP. This book focuses on advanced applications and building NLP systems that can solve complex tasks. All kinds of readers will be able to follow the content of the book, but readers who can benefit the most from this book include:

- Intermediate **Machine Learning** (**ML**) developers who are familiar with the basics of supervised learning and deep learning techniques
- Professionals who already use TensorFlow/Python for purposes such as data science, ML, research, analysis, etc., and can benefit from a more solid understanding of advanced NLP techniques

What this book covers

Chapter 1, Essentials of NLP, provides an overview of various topics in NLP such as tokenization, stemming, lemmatization, POS tagging, vectorization, etc. An overview of common NLP libraries like spaCy, Stanford NLP, and NLTK, with their key capabilities and use cases, will be provided. We will also build a simple classifier for spam.

Chapter 2, Understanding Sentiment in Natural Language with BiLSTMs, covers the NLU use case of sentiment analysis with an overview of **Recurrent Neural Networks** (**RNNs**), LSTMs, and BiLSTMs, which are the basic building blocks of modern NLP models. We will also use `tf.data` for efficient use of CPUs and GPUs to speed up data pipelines and model training.

Chapter 3, Named Entity Recognition (NER) with BiLSTMs, CRFs, and Viterbi Decoding, focuses on the key NLU problem of NER, which is a basic building block of task-oriented chatbots. We will build a custom layer for CRFs for improving the accuracy of NER and the Viterbi decoding scheme, which is often applied to a deep model to improve the quality of the output.

Chapter 4, Transfer Learning with BERT, covers a number of important concepts in modern deep NLP such as types of transfer learning, pre-trained embeddings, an overview of Transformers, and BERT and its application in improving the sentiment analysis task introduced in *Chapter 2, Understanding Sentiment in Natural Language with BiLSTMs.*

Chapter 5, Generating Text with RNNs and GPT-2, focuses on generating text with a custom character-based RNN and improving it with Beam Search. We will also cover the GPT-2 architecture and touch upon GPT-3.

Chapter 6, Text Summarization with Seq2seq Attention and Transformer Networks, takes on the challenging task of abstractive text summarization. BERT and GPT are two halves of the full encoder-decoder model. We put them together to build a seq2seq model for summarizing news articles by generating headlines for them. How ROUGE metrics are used for the evaluation of summarization is also covered.

Chapter 7, Multi-Modal Networks and Image Captioning with ResNets and Transformers, combines computer vision and NLP together to see if a picture is indeed worth a thousand words! We will build a custom Transformer model from scratch and train it to generate captions for images.

Chapter 8, Weakly Supervised Learning for Classification with Snorkel, focuses on a key problem – labeling data. While NLP has a lot of unlabeled data, labeling it is quite an expensive task. This chapter introduces the snorkel library and shows how massive amounts of data can be quickly labeled.

Chapter 9, Building Conversational AI Applications with Deep Learning, combines the various techniques covered throughout the book to show how different types of chatbots, such as question-answering or slot-filling bots, can be built.

Chapter 10, Installation and Setup Instructions for Code, walks through all the instructions required to install and configure a system for running the code supplied with the book.

To get the most out of this book

- It would be a good idea to get a background on the basics of deep learning models and TensorFlow.

- The use of a GPU is highly recommended. Some of the models, especially in the later chapters, are pretty big and complex. They may take hours or days to fully train on CPUs. RNNs are very slow to train without the use of GPUs. You can get access to free GPUs on Google Colab, and instructions for doing so are provided in the first chapter.

Download the example code files

The code bundle for the book is hosted on GitHub at `https://github.com/PacktPublishing/Advanced-Natural-Language-Processing-with-TensorFlow-2`. We also have other code bundles from our rich catalog of books and videos available at `https://github.com/PacktPublishing/`. Check them out!

Download the color images

We also provide a PDF file that has color images of the screenshots/diagrams used in this book. You can download it here: `https://static.packt-cdn.com/downloads/9781800200937_ColorImages.pdf`.

Conventions used

There are a number of text conventions used throughout this book.

`CodeInText`: Indicates code words in text, database table names, folder names, filenames, file extensions, pathnames, dummy URLs, user input, and Twitter handles. For example: "In the `num_capitals()` function, substitutions are performed for the capital letters in English."

A block of code is set as follows:

```
en = snlp.Pipeline(lang='en')
def word_counts(x, pipeline=en):
  doc = pipeline(x)
  count = sum([len(sentence.tokens) for sentence in doc.sentences])
  return count
```

When we wish to draw your attention to a particular part of a code block, the relevant lines or items are set in bold:

```
en = snlp.Pipeline(lang='en')
def word_counts(x, pipeline=en):
  doc = pipeline(x)
  count = sum([len(sentence.tokens) for sentence in doc.sentences])
  return count
```

Any command-line input or output is written as follows:

```
!pip install gensim
```

Bold: Indicates a new term, an important word, or words that you see on the screen, for example, in menus or dialog boxes, also appear in the text like this. For example: "Select **System info** from the **Administration** panel."

Warnings or important notes appear like this.

Tips and tricks appear like this.

Get in touch

Feedback from our readers is always welcome.

General feedback: If you have questions about any aspect of this book, mention the book title in the subject of your message and email Packt at customercare@packtpub.com.

Errata: Although we have taken every care to ensure the accuracy of our content, mistakes do happen. If you have found a mistake in this book, we would be grateful if you could report this to us. Please visit www.packtpub.com/support/errata, select your book, click on the **Errata Submission Form** link, and enter the details.

Piracy: If you come across any illegal copies of our works in any form on the Internet, we would be grateful if you would provide us with the location address or website name. Please contact us at copyright@packtpub.com with a link to the material.

If you are interested in becoming an author: If there is a topic that you have expertise in and you are interested in either writing or contributing to a book, please visit http://authors.packtpub.com.

Reviews

Please leave a review. Once you have read and used this book, why not leave a review on the site that you purchased it from? Potential readers can then see and use your unbiased opinion to make purchase decisions, we at Packt can understand what you think about our products, and our authors can see your feedback on their book. Thank you!

For more information about Packt, please visit packtpub.com.

1
Essentials of NLP

Language has been a part of human evolution. The development of language allowed better communication between people and tribes. The evolution of written language, initially as cave paintings and later as characters, allowed information to be distilled, stored, and passed on from generation to generation. Some would even say that the hockey stick curve of advancement is because of the ever-accumulating cache of stored information. As this stored information trove becomes larger and larger, the need for computational methods to process and distill the data becomes more acute. In the past decade, a lot of advances were made in the areas of image and speech recognition. Advances in **Natural Language Processing** (**NLP**) are more recent, though computational methods for NLP have been an area of research for decades. Processing textual data requires many different building blocks upon which advanced models can be built. Some of these building blocks themselves can be quite challenging and advanced. This chapter and the next focus on these building blocks and the problems that can be solved with them through simple models.

In this chapter, we will focus on the basics of pre-processing text and build a simple spam detector. Specifically, we will learn about the following:

- The typical text processing workflow
- Data collection and labeling
- Text normalization, including case normalization, text tokenization, stemming, and lemmatization
    - Modeling datasets that have been text normalized
    - Vectorizing text
    - Modeling datasets with vectorized text

Let's start by getting to grips with the text processing workflow most NLP models use.

A typical text processing workflow

To understand how to process text, it is important to understand the general workflow for NLP. The following diagram illustrates the basic steps:

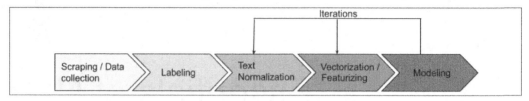

Figure 1.1: Typical stages of a text processing workflow

The first two steps of the process in the preceding diagram involve collecting labeled data. A supervised model or even a semi-supervised model needs data to operate. The next step is usually normalizing and featurizing the data. Models have a hard time processing text data as is. There is a lot of hidden structure in a given text that needs to be processed and exposed. These two steps focus on that. The last step is building a model with the processed inputs. While NLP has some unique models, this chapter will use only a simple deep neural network and focus more on the normalization and vectorization/featurization. Often, the last three stages operate in a cycle, even though the diagram may give the impression of linearity. In industry, additional features require more effort to develop and more resources to keep running. Hence, it is important that features add value. Taking this approach, we will use a simple model to validate different normalization/vectorization/ featurization steps. Now, let's look at each of these stages in detail.

Data collection and labeling

The first step of any **Machine Learning** (**ML**) project is to obtain a dataset. Fortunately, in the text domain, there is plenty of data to be found. A common approach is to use libraries such as scrapy or Beautiful Soup to scrape data from the web. However, data is usually unlabeled, and as such can't be used in supervised models directly. This data is quite useful though. Through the use of transfer learning, a language model can be trained using unsupervised or semi-supervised methods and can be further used with a small training dataset specific to the task at hand. We will cover transfer learning in more depth in *Chapter 3, Named Entity Recognition (NER) with BiLSTMs, CRFs, and Viterbi Decoding*, when we look at transfer learning using BERT embeddings.

In the labeling step, textual data sourced in the data collection step is labeled with the right classes. Let's take some examples. If the task is to build a spam classifier for emails, then the previous step would involve collecting lots of emails. This labeling step would be to attach a *spam* or *not spam* label to each email. Another example could be sentiment detection on tweets. The data collection step would involve gathering a number of tweets. This step would label each tweet with a label that acts as a ground truth. A more involved example would involve collecting news articles, where the labels would be summaries of the articles. Yet another example of such a case would be an email auto-reply functionality. Like the spam case, a number of emails with their replies would need to be collected. The labels in this case would be short pieces of text that would approximate replies. If you are working on a specific domain without much public data, you may have to do these steps yourself.

Given that text data is generally available (outside of specific domains like health), labeling is usually the biggest challenge. It can be quite time consuming or resource intensive to label data. There has been a lot of recent focus on using semi-supervised approaches to labeling data. We will cover some methods for labeling data at scale using semi-supervised methods and the **snorkel** library in *Chapter 7, Multi-modal Networks and Image Captioning with ResNets and Transformer*, when we look at weakly supervised learning for classification using Snorkel.

There is a number of commonly used datasets that are available on the web for use in training models. Using transfer learning, these generic datasets can be used to prime ML models and then you can use a small amount of domain-specific data to fine-tune the model. Using these publicly available datasets gives us a few advantages. First, all the data collection has been already performed. Second, labeling has already been done. Lastly, using such a dataset allows the comparison of results with the state of the art; most papers use specific datasets in their area of research and publish benchmarks. For example, the **Stanford Question Answering Dataset** (or **SQuAD** for short) is often used as a benchmark for question-answering models. It is a good source to train on as well.

Collecting labeled data

In this book, we will rely on publicly available datasets. The appropriate datasets will be called out in their respective chapters along with instructions on downloading them. To build a spam detection system on an email dataset, we will be using the SMS Spam Collection dataset made available by University of California, Irvine. This dataset can be downloaded using instructions available in the tip box below. Each SMS is tagged as "SPAM" or "HAM," with the latter indicating it is not a spam message.

University of California, Irvine, is a great source of machine learning datasets. You can see all the datasets they provide by visiting `http://archive.ics.uci.edu/ml/datasets.php`. Specifically for NLP, you can see some publicly available datasets on `https://github.com/niderhoff/nlp-datasets`.

Before we start working with the data, the development environment needs to be set up. Let's take a quick moment to set up the development environment.

Development environment setup

In this chapter, we will be using Google Colaboratory, or Colab for short, to write code. You can use your Google account, or register a new account. Google Colab is free to use, requires no configuration, and also provides access to GPUs. The user interface is very similar to a Jupyter notebook, so it should seem familiar. To get started, please navigate to `colab.research.google.com` using a supported web browser. A web page similar to the screenshot below should appear:

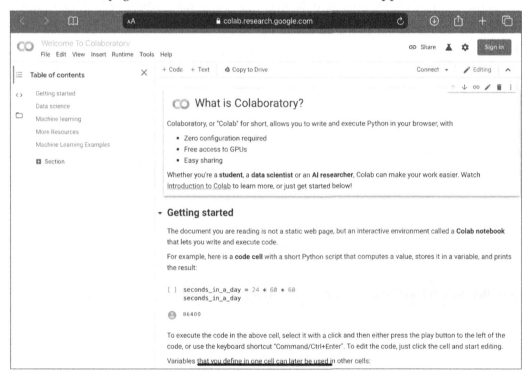

Figure 1.2: Google Colab website

The next step is to create a new notebook. There are a couple of options. The first option is to create a new notebook in Colab and type in the code as you go along in the chapter. The second option is to upload a notebook from the local drive into Colab. It is also possible to pull in notebooks from GitHub into Colab, the process for which is detailed on the Colab website. For the purposes of this chapter, a complete notebook named SMS_Spam_Detection.ipynb is available in the GitHub repository of the book in the chapter1-nlp-essentials folder. Please upload this notebook into Google Colab by clicking **File | Upload Notebook**. Specific sections of this notebook will be referred to at the appropriate points in the chapter in tip boxes. The instructions for creating the notebook from scratch are in the main description.

Click on the **File** menu option at the top left and click on **New Notebook**. A new notebook will open in a new browser tab. Click on the notebook name at the top left, just above the **File** menu option, and edit it to read SMS_Spam_Detection. Now the development environment is set up. It is time to begin loading in data.

First, let us edit the first line of the notebook and import TensorFlow 2. Enter the following code in the first cell and execute it:

```
%tensorflow_version 2.x
import tensorflow as tf
import os
import io

tf.__version__
```

The output of running this cell should look like this:

```
TensorFlow 2.x is selected.
'2.4.0'
```

This confirms that version 2.4.0 of the TensorFlow library was loaded. The highlighted line in the preceding code block is a magic command for Google Colab, instructing it to use TensorFlow version 2+. The next step is to download the data file and unzip to a location in the Colab notebook on the cloud.

 The code for loading the data is in the *Download Data* section of the notebook. Also note that as of writing, the release version of TensorFlow was 2.4.

This can be done with the following code:

```
# Download the zip file
path_to_zip = tf.keras.utils.get_file("smsspamcollection.zip",
origin="https://archive.ics.uci.edu/ml/machine-learning-
databases/00228/smsspamcollection.zip",
                    extract=True)


# Unzip the file into a folder
!unzip $path_to_zip -d data
```

The following output confirms that the data was downloaded and extracted:

```
Archive:  /root/.keras/datasets/smsspamcollection.zip
  inflating: data/SMSSpamCollection
  inflating: data/readme
```

Reading the data file is trivial:

```
# Let's see if we read the data correctly
lines = io.open('data/SMSSpamCollection').read().strip().split('\n')
lines[0]
```

The last line of code shows a sample line of data:

```
'ham\tGo until jurong point, crazy.. Available only in bugis n great
world'
```

This example is labeled as not spam. The next step is to split each line into two columns – one with the text of the message and the other as the label. While we are separating these labels, we will also convert the labels to numeric values. Since we are interested in predicting spam messages, we can assign a value of 1 to the spam messages. A value of 0 will be assigned to legitimate messages.

 The code for this part is in the *Pre-Process Data* section of the notebook.

Please note that the following code is verbose for clarity:

```
spam_dataset = []
for line in lines:
  label, text = line.split('\t')
```

```
  if label.strip() == 'spam':
    spam_dataset.append((1, text.strip()))
  else:
    spam_dataset.append(((0, text.strip()))))
print(spam_dataset[0])
```

```
(0, 'Go until jurong point, crazy.. Available only in bugis n great
world la e buffet... Cine there got amore wat...')
```

Now the dataset is ready for further processing in the pipeline. However, let's take a short detour to see how to configure GPU access in Google Colab.

Enabling GPUs on Google Colab

One of the advantages of using Google Colab is access to free GPUs for small tasks. GPUs make a big difference in the training time of NLP models, especially ones that use **Recurrent Neural Networks (RNNs)**. The first step in enabling GPU access is to start a runtime, which can be done by executing a command in the notebook. Then, click on the **Runtime** menu option and select the **Change Runtime** option, as shown in the following screenshot:

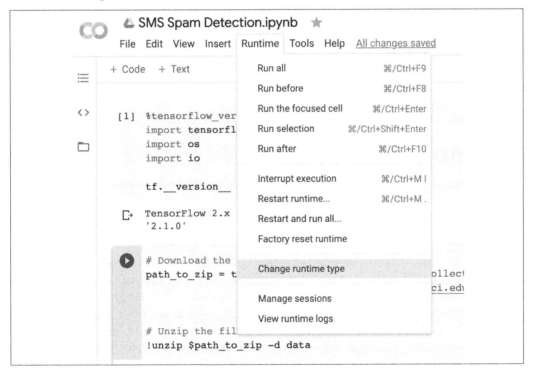

Figure 1.3: Colab runtime settings menu option

Next, a dialog box will show up, as shown in the following screenshot. Expand the **Hardware Accelerator** option and select **GPU**:

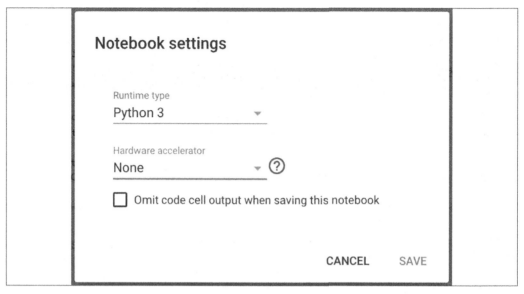

Figure 1.4: Enabling GPUs on Colab

Now you should have access to a GPU in your Colab notebook! In NLP models, especially when using RNNs, GPUs can shave a lot of minutes or hours off the training time.

For now, let's turn our attention back to the data that has been loaded and is ready to be processed further for use in models.

Text normalization

Text normalization is a pre-processing step aimed at improving the quality of the text and making it suitable for machines to process. Four main steps in text normalization are case normalization, tokenization and stop word removal, **Parts-of-Speech (POS)** tagging, and stemming.

Case normalization applies to languages that use uppercase and lowercase letters. All languages based on the Latin alphabet or the Cyrillic alphabet (Russian, Mongolian, and so on) use upper- and lowercase letters. Other languages that sometimes use this are Greek, Armenian, Cherokee, and Coptic. In case normalization, all letters are converted to the same case. It is quite helpful in semantic use cases. However, in other cases, this may hinder performance. In the spam example, spam messages may have more words in all-caps compared to regular messages.

Another common normalization step removes punctuation in the text. Again, this may or may not be useful given the problem at hand. In most cases, this should give good results. However, in some cases, such as spam or grammar models, it may hinder performance. It is more likely for spam messages to use more exclamation marks or other punctuation for emphasis.

 The code for this part is in the *Data Normalization* section of the notebook.

Let's build a baseline model with three simple features:

- Number of characters in the message
- Number of capital letters in the message
- Number of punctuation symbols in the message

To do so, first, we will convert the data into a pandas DataFrame:

```
import pandas as pd
df = pd.DataFrame(spam_dataset, columns=['Spam', 'Message'])
```

Next, let's build some simple functions that can count the length of the message, and the numbers of capital letters and punctuation symbols. Python's regular expression package, re, will be used to implement these:

```
import re
def message_length(x):
  # returns total number of characters
  return len(x)


def num_capitals(x):
  _, count = re.subn(r'[A-Z]', '', x) # only works in english
  return count


def num_punctuation(x):
  _, count = re.subn(r'\W', '', x)
  return count
```

In the num_capitals() function, substitutions are performed for the capital letters in English. The count of these substitutions provides the count of capital letters. The same technique is used to count the number of punctuation symbols. Please note that the method used to count capital letters is specific to English.

Additional feature columns will be added to the DataFrame, and then the set will be split into test and train sets:

```
df['Capitals'] = df['Message'].apply(num_capitals)
df['Punctuation'] = df['Message'].apply(num_punctuation)
df['Length'] = df['Message'].apply(message_length)
df.describe()
```

This should generate the following output:

	Spam	Capitals	Punctuation	Length
count	5574.000000	5574.000000	5574.000000	5574.000000
mean	0.134015	5.621636	18.942591	80.443488
std	0.340699	11.683233	14.825994	59.841746
min	0.000000	0.000000	0.000000	2.000000
25%	0.000000	1.000000	8.000000	36.000000
50%	0.000000	2.000000	15.000000	61.000000
75%	0.000000	4.000000	27.000000	122.000000
max	1.000000	129.000000	253.000000	910.000000

Figure 1.5: Base dataset for initial spam model

The following code can be used to split the dataset into training and test sets, with 80% of the records in the training set and the rest in the test set. Further more, labels will be removed from both the training and test sets:

```
train=df.sample(frac=0.8,random_state=42)
test=df.drop(train.index)

x_train = train[['Length', 'Capitals', 'Punctuation']]
y_train = train[['Spam']]

x_test = test[['Length', 'Capitals', 'Punctuation']]
y_test = test[['Spam']]
```

Now we are ready to build a simple classifier to use this data.

Modeling normalized data

Recall that modeling was the last part of the text processing pipeline described earlier. In this chapter, we will use a very simple model, as the objective is to show different basic NLP data processing techniques more than modeling. Here, we want to see if three simple features can aid in the classification of spam. As more features are added, passing them through the same model will help in seeing if the featurization aids or hampers the accuracy of the classification.

The *Model Building* section of the workbook has the code shown in this section.

A function is defined that allows the construction of models with different numbers of inputs and hidden units:

```
# Basic 1-layer neural network model for evaluation
def make_model(input_dims=3, num_units=12):
  model = tf.keras.Sequential()

  # Adds a densely-connected layer with 12 units to the model:
  model.add(tf.keras.layers.Dense(num_units,
                                   input_dim=input_dims,
                                   activation='relu'))

  # Add a sigmoid layer with a binary output unit:
  model.add(tf.keras.layers.Dense(1, activation='sigmoid'))

  model.compile(loss='binary_crossentropy', optimizer='adam',
               metrics=['accuracy'])
  return model
```

This model uses binary cross-entropy for computing loss and the Adam optimizer for training. The key metric, given that this is a binary classification problem, is accuracy. The default parameters passed to the function are sufficient as only three features are being passed in.

We can train our simple baseline model with only three features like so:

```
model = make_model()
model.fit(x_train, y_train, epochs=10, batch_size=10)
```

```
Train on 4459 samples
Epoch 1/10
4459/4459 [==============================] - 1s 281us/sample - loss:
0.6062 - accuracy: 0.8141
Epoch 2/10
...
Epoch 10/10
4459/4459 [==============================] - 1s 145us/sample - loss:
0.1976 - accuracy: 0.9305
```

This is not bad as our three simple features help us get to 93% accuracy. A quick check shows that there are 592 spam messages in the test set, out of a total of 4,459. So, this model is doing better than a very simple model that guesses everything as not spam. That model would have an accuracy of 87%. This number may be surprising but is fairly common in classification problems where there is a severe class imbalance in the data. Evaluating it on the training set gives an accuracy of around 93.4%:

```
model.evaluate(x_test, y_test)
```

```
1115/1115 [==============================] - 0s 94us/sample - loss:
0.1949 - accuracy: 0.9336
[0.19485870356516988, 0.9336323]
```

Please note that the actual performance you see may be slightly different due to the data splits and computational vagaries. A quick verification can be performed by plotting the confusion matrix to see the performance:

```
y_train_pred = model.predict_classes(x_train)
# confusion matrix
tf.math.confusion_matrix(tf.constant(y_train.Spam),
                         y_train_pred)

<tf.Tensor: shape=(2, 2), dtype=int32, numpy=
array([[3771,   96],
       [ 186,  406]], dtype=int32)>
```

	Predicted Not Spam	Predicted Spam
Actual Not Spam	3,771	96
Actual Spam	186	406

This shows that 3,771 out of 3,867 regular messages were classified correctly, while 406 out of 592 spam messages were classified correctly. Again, you may get a slightly different result.

To test the value of the features, try re-running the model by removing one of the features, such as punctuation or a number of capital letters, to get a sense of their contribution to the model. This is left as an exercise for the reader.

Tokenization

This step takes a piece of text and converts it into a list of tokens. If the input is a sentence, then separating the words would be an example of tokenization. Depending on the model, different granularities can be chosen. At the lowest level, each character could become a token. In some cases, entire sentences of paragraphs can be considered as a token:

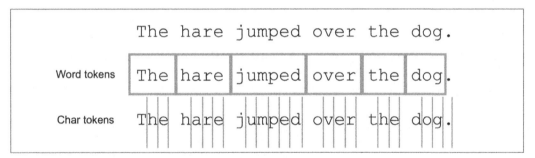

Figure 1.6: Tokenizing a sentence

The preceding diagram shows two ways a sentence can be tokenized. One way to tokenize is to chop a sentence into words. Another way is to chop into individual characters. However, this can be a complex proposition in some languages such as Japanese and Mandarin.

Segmentation in Japanese

Many languages use a word separator, a space, to separate words. This makes the task of tokenizing on words trivial. However, there are other languages that do not use any markers or separators between words. Some examples of such languages are Japanese and Chinese. In such languages, the task is referred to as *segmentation*.

Specifically, in Japanese, there are mainly three different types of characters that are used: *Hiragana*, *Kanji*, and *Katakana*. Kanji is adapted from Chinese characters, and similar to Chinese, there are thousands of characters. Hiragana is used for grammatical elements and native Japanese words. Katakana is mostly used for foreign words and names. Depending on the preceding characters, a character may be part of an existing word or the start of a new word. This makes Japanese one of the most complicated writing systems in the world. Compound words are especially hard. Consider the following compound word that reads *Election Administration Committee*:

選挙管理委員会

This can be tokenized in two different ways, outside of the entire phrase being considered one word. Here are two examples of tokenizing (from the Sudachi library):

選挙/管理/委員会 (Election / Administration / Committee)

選挙/管理/委員/会 (Election / Administration / Committee / Meeting)

Common libraries that are used specifically for Japanese segmentation or tokenization are MeCab, Juman, Sudachi, and Kuromoji. MeCab is used in Hugging Face, spaCy, and other libraries.

 The code shown in this section is in the *Tokenization and Stop Word Removal* section of the notebook.

Fortunately, most languages are not as complex as Japanese and use spaces to separate words. In Python, splitting by spaces is trivial. Let's take an example:

```
Sentence = 'Go until Jurong point, crazy.. Available only in bugis n
great world'
sentence.split()
```

The output of the preceding split operation results in the following:

```
['Go',
 'until',
 'jurong',
 'point,',
 'crazy..',
 'Available',
 'only',
 'in',
```

```
'bugis',
'n',
'great',
'world']
```

The two highlighted lines in the preceding output show that the naïve approach in Python will result in punctuation being included in the words, among other issues. Consequently, this step is done through a library like StanfordNLP. Using `pip`, let's install this package in our Colab notebook:

```
!pip install stanfordnlp
```

The StanfordNLP package uses PyTorch under the hood as well as a number of other packages. These and other dependencies will be installed. By default, the package does not install language files. These have to be downloaded. This is shown in the following code:

```
Import stanfordnlp as snlp
en = snlp.download('en')
```

The English file is approximately 235 MB. A prompt will be displayed to confirm the download and the location to store it in:

```
Using the default treebank "en_ewt" for language "en".
Would you like to download the models for: en_ewt now? (Y/n)
Y
```

Figure 1.7: Prompt for downloading English models

Google Colab recycles the runtimes upon inactivity. This means that if you perform commands in the book at different times, you may have to re-execute every command again from the start, including downloading and processing the dataset, downloading the StanfordNLP English files, and so on. A local notebook server would usually maintain the state of the runtime but may have limited processing power. For simpler examples as in this chapter, Google Colab is a decent solution. For the more advanced examples later in the book, where training may run for hours or days, a local runtime or one running on a cloud **Virtual Machine (VM)** would be preferred.

This package provides capabilities for tokenization, POS tagging, and lemmatization out of the box. To start with tokenization, we instantiate a pipeline and tokenize a sample text to see how this works:

```
en = snlp.Pipeline(lang='en', processors='tokenize')
```

The `lang` parameter is used to indicate that an English pipeline is desired. The second parameter, `processors`, indicates the type of processing that is desired in the pipeline. This library can also perform the following processing steps in the pipeline:

- `pos` labels each token with a POS token. The next section provides more details on POS tags.

- `lemma`, which can convert different forms of verbs, for example, to the base form. This will be covered in detail in the *Stemming and lemmatization* section later in this chapter.

- `depparse` performs dependency parsing between words in a sentence. Consider the following example sentence, "Hari went to school." *Hari* is interpreted as a noun by the POS tagger, and becomes the governor of the word *went*. The word *school* is dependent on *went* as it describes the object of the verb.

For now, only tokenization of text is desired, so only the tokenizer is used:

```
tokenized = en(sentence)
len(tokenized.sentences)
```

```
2
```

This shows that the tokenizer correctly divided the text into two sentences. To investigate what words were removed, the following code can be used:

```
for snt in tokenized.sentences:
  for word in snt.tokens:
    print(word.text)
  print("<End of Sentence>")
```

```
Go
until
jurong
point
,
crazy
..
<End of Sentence>
Available
only
in
bugis
n
```

```
great
world
<End of Sentence>
```

Note the highlighted words in the preceding output. Punctuation marks were separated out into their own words. Text was split into multiple sentences. This is an improvement over only using spaces to split. In some applications, removal of punctuation may be required. This will be covered in the next section.

Consider the preceding example of Japanese. To see the performance of StanfordNLP on Japanese tokenization, the following piece of code can be used:

```
jp = snlp.download('ja')
```

This is the first step, which involves downloading the Japanese language model, similar to the English model that was downloaded and installed previously. Next, a Japanese pipeline will be instantiated and the words will be processed:

```
jp = snlp.download('ja')
jp_line = jp("選挙管理委員会")
```

You may recall that the Japanese text reads Election Administration Committee. Correct tokenization should produce three words, where first two should be two characters each, and the last word is three characters:

```
for snt in jp_line.sentences:
  for word in snt.tokens:
    print(word.text)
```

```
選挙
管理
委員会
```

This matches the expected output. StanfordNLP supports 53 languages, so the same code can be used for tokenizing any language that is supported.

Coming back to the spam detection example, a new feature can be implemented that counts the number of words in the message using this tokenization functionality.

 This word count feature is implemented in the *Adding Word Count Feature* section of the notebook.

It is possible that spam messages have different numbers of words than regular messages. The first step is to define a method to compute the number of words:

```
en = snlp.Pipeline(lang='en')
def word_counts(x, pipeline=en):
  doc = pipeline(x)
  count = sum([len(sentence.tokens) for sentence in doc.sentences])
  return count
```

Next, using the train and test splits, add a column for the word count feature:

```
train['Words'] = train['Message'].apply(word_counts)
test['Words'] = test['Message'].apply(word_counts)

x_train = train[['Length', 'Punctuation', 'Capitals', 'Words']]
y_train = train[['Spam']]

x_test = test[['Length', 'Punctuation', 'Capitals' , 'Words']]
y_test = test[['Spam']]

model = make_model(input_dims=4)
```

The last line in the preceding code block creates a new model with four input features.

PyTorch warning

When you execute functions in the StanfordNLP library, you may see a warning like this:

```
/pytorch/aten/src/ATen/native/LegacyDefinitions.
cpp:19: UserWarning: masked_fill_ received a mask
with dtype torch.uint8, this behavior is now
deprecated,please use a mask with dtype torch.bool
instead.
```

Internally, StanfordNLP uses the PyTorch library. This warning is due to StanfordNLP using an older version of a function that is now deprecated. For all intents and purposes, this warning can be ignored. It is expected that maintainers of StanfordNLP will update their code.

Modeling tokenized data

This model can be trained like so:

```
model.fit(x_train, y_train, epochs=10, batch_size=10)
Train on 4459 samples
Epoch 1/10
4459/4459 [==============================] - 1s 202us/sample - loss:
2.4261 - accuracy: 0.6961
...
Epoch 10/10
4459/4459 [==============================] - 1s 142us/sample - loss:
0.2061 - accuracy: 0.9312
```

There is only a marginal improvement in accuracy. One hypothesis is that the number of words is not useful. It would be useful if the average number of words in spam messages were smaller or larger than regular messages. Using pandas, this can be quickly verified:

```
train.loc[train.Spam == 1].describe()
```

	Spam	Capitals	Punctuation	Length	Words
count	592.0	592.000000	592.000000	592.000000	592.000000
mean	1.0	15.320946	29.086149	138.856419	29.511824
std	0.0	11.635105	7.083572	28.079980	7.474256
min	1.0	0.000000	2.000000	13.000000	3.000000
25%	1.0	7.000000	26.000000	132.000000	26.000000
50%	1.0	14.000000	30.000000	149.000000	30.000000
75%	1.0	21.000000	34.000000	157.000000	35.000000
max	1.0	128.000000	49.000000	197.000000	49.000000

Figure 1.8: Statistics for spam message features

Let's compare the preceding results to the statistics for regular messages:

```
train.loc[train.Spam == 0].describe()
```

	Spam	Capitals	Punctuation	Length	Words
count	3867.0	3867.000000	3867.000000	3867.000000	3867.000000
mean	0.0	4.018878	17.325058	71.354538	17.344194
std	0.0	10.599291	14.826644	57.755351	13.811278
min	0.0	0.000000	0.000000	2.000000	1.000000
25%	0.0	1.000000	8.000000	33.000000	8.000000
50%	0.0	2.000000	13.000000	53.000000	13.000000
75%	0.0	3.000000	23.000000	92.000000	22.000000
max	0.0	129.000000	253.000000	910.000000	209.000000

Figure 1.9: Statistics for regular message features

Some interesting patterns can quickly be seen. Spam messages usually have much less deviation from the mean. Focus on the **Capitals** feature column. It shows that regular messages use far fewer capitals than spam messages. At the 75th percentile, there are 3 capitals in a regular message versus 21 for spam messages. On average, regular messages have 4 capital letters while spam messages have 15. This variation is much less pronounced in the number of words category. Regular messages have 17 words on average, while spam has 29. At the 75th percentile, regular messages have 22 words while spam messages have 35. This quick check yields an indication as to why adding the word features wasn't that useful. However, there are a couple of things to consider still. First, the tokenization model split out punctuation marks as words. Ideally, these words should be removed from the word counts as the punctuation feature is showing that spam messages use a lot more punctuation characters. This will be covered in the *Parts-of-speech tagging* section. Secondly, languages have some common words that are usually excluded. This is called stop word removal and is the focus of the next section.

Stop word removal

Stop word removal involves removing common words such as articles (the, an) and conjunctions (and, but), among others. In the context of information retrieval or search, these words would not be helpful in identifying documents or web pages that would match the query. As an example, consider the query "Where is Google based?". In this query, *is* is a stop word. The query would produce similar results irrespective of the inclusion of *is*. To determine the stop words, a simple approach is to use grammar clues.

In English, articles and conjunctions are examples of classes of words that can usually be removed. A more robust way is to consider the frequency of occurrence of words in a corpus, set of documents, or text. The most frequent terms can be selected as candidates for the stop word list. It is recommended that this list be reviewed manually. There can be cases where words may be frequent in a collection of documents but are still meaningful. This can happen if all the documents in the collection are from a specific domain or on a specific topic. Consider a set of documents from the Federal Reserve. The word *economy* may appear quite frequently in this case; however, it is unlikely to be a candidate for removal as a stop word.

In some cases, stop words may actually contain information. This may be applicable to phrases. Consider the fragment "flights to Paris." In this case, *to* provides valuable information, and its removal may change the meaning of the fragment.

Recall the stages of the text processing workflow. The step after text normalization is vectorization. This step is discussed in detail later in the *Vectorizing text* section of this chapter, but the key step in vectorization is to build a vocabulary or dictionary of all the tokens. The size of this vocabulary can be reduced by removing stop words. While training and evaluating models, removing stop words reduces the number of computation steps that need to be performed. Hence, the removal of stop words can yield benefits in terms of computation speed and storage space. Modern advances in NLP see smaller and smaller stop words lists as more efficient encoding schemes and computation methods evolve. Let's try and see the impact of stop words on the spam problem to develop some intuition about its usefulness.

Many NLP packages provide lists of stop words. These can be removed from the text after tokenization. Tokenization was done through the StanfordNLP library previously. However, this library does not come with a list of stop words. NLTK and spaCy supply stop words for a set of languages. For this example, we will use an open source package called `stopwordsiso`.

 The *Stop Word Removal* section of the notebook contains the code for this section.

This Python package takes the list of stop words from the stopwords-iso GitHub project at `https://github.com/stopwords-iso/stopwords-iso`. This package provides stop words in 57 languages. The first step is to install the Python package that provides access to the stop words lists.

The following command will install the package through the notebook:

```
!pip install stopwordsiso
```

Supported languages can be checked with the following commands:

```
import stopwordsiso as stopwords

stopwords.langs()
```

English language stop words can be checked as well to get an idea of some of the words:

```
sorted(stopwords.stopwords('en'))
```

```
["'ll",
 "'tis",
 "'twas",
 "'ve",
 '10',
 '39',
 'a',
 "a's",
 'able',
 'ableabout',
 'about',
 'above',
 'abroad',
 'abst',
 'accordance',
 'according',
 'accordingly',
 'across',
 'act',
 'actually',
 'ad',
 'added',
...
```

Given that tokenization was already implemented in the preceding word_counts() method, the implementation of that method can be updated to include removing stop words. However, all the stop words are in lowercase. Case normalization was discussed earlier, and capital letters were a useful feature for spam detection. In this case, tokens need to be converted to lowercase to effectively remove them:

```
en_sw = stopwords.stopwords('en')

def word_counts(x, pipeline=en):
  doc = pipeline(x)
  count = 0
  for sentence in doc.sentences:
    for token in sentence.tokens:
        if token.text.lower() not in en_sw:
          count += 1
  return count
```

A consequence of using stop words is that a message such as "When are you going to ride your bike?" counts as only 3 words. When we see if this has had any effect on the statistics for word length, the following picture emerges:

	Spam	Capitals	Punctuation	Length	Words
count	592.0	592.000000	592.000000	592.000000	592.000000
mean	1.0	15.320946	29.086149	138.856419	18.464527
std	0.0	11.635105	7.083572	28.079980	6.100852
min	1.0	0.000000	2.000000	13.000000	2.000000
25%	1.0	7.000000	26.000000	132.000000	14.000000
50%	1.0	14.000000	30.000000	149.000000	19.000000
75%	1.0	21.000000	34.000000	157.000000	23.000000
max	1.0	128.000000	49.000000	197.000000	33.000000

Figure 1.10: Word counts for spam messages after removing stop words

Compared to the word counts prior to stop word removal, the average number of words has been reduced from 29 to 18, almost a 30% decrease. The 25th percentile changed from 26 to 14. The maximum has also reduced from 49 to 33.

The impact on regular messages is even more dramatic:

	Spam	Capitals	Punctuation	Length	Words
count	3867.0	3867.000000	3867.000000	3867.000000	3867.000000
mean	0.0	4.018878	17.325058	71.354538	7.911042
std	0.0	10.599291	14.826644	57.755351	7.326390
min	0.0	0.000000	0.000000	2.000000	0.000000
25%	0.0	1.000000	8.000000	33.000000	4.000000
50%	0.0	2.000000	13.000000	53.000000	6.000000
75%	0.0	3.000000	23.000000	92.000000	10.000000
max	0.0	129.000000	253.000000	910.000000	147.000000

Figure 1.11: Word counts for regular messages after removing stop words

Comparing these statistics to those from before stop word removal, the average number of words has more than halved to almost 8. The maximum number of words has also reduced from 209 to 147. The standard deviation of regular messages is about the same as its mean, indicating that there is a lot of variation in the number of words in regular messages. Now, let's see if this helps us train a model and improve its accuracy.

Modeling data with stop words removed

Now that the feature without stop words is computed, it can be added to the model to see its impact:

```
train['Words'] = train['Message'].apply(word_counts)
test['Words'] = test['Message'].apply(word_counts)

x_train = train[['Length', 'Punctuation', 'Capitals', 'Words']]
y_train = train[['Spam']]

x_test = test[['Length', 'Punctuation', 'Capitals', 'Words']]
y_test = test[['Spam']]

model = make_model(input_dims=4)

model.fit(x_train, y_train, epochs=10, batch_size=10)
```

```
Epoch 1/10
4459/4459 [==============================] - 2s 361us/sample - loss:
0.5186 - accuracy: 0.8652
Epoch 2/10
...
Epoch 9/10
4459/4459 [==============================] - 2s 355us/sample - loss:
0.1790 - accuracy: 0.9417
Epoch 10/10
4459/4459 [==============================] - 2s 361us/sample - loss:
0.1802 - accuracy: 0.9421
```

This accuracy reflects a slight improvement over the previous model:

```
model.evaluate(x_test, y_test)
```

```
1115/1115 [==============================] - 0s 74us/sample - loss:
0.1954 - accuracy: 0.9372

 [0.19537461110027382, 0.93721974]
```

 In NLP, stop word removal used to be standard practice. In more modern applications, stop words may actually end up hindering performance in some use cases, rather than helping. It is becoming more common not to exclude stop words. Depending on the problem you are solving, stop word removal may or may not help.

Note that StanfordNLP will separate words like *can't* into *ca* and *n't*. This represents the expansion of the short form into its constituents, *can* and *not*. These contractions may or may not appear in the stop word list. Implementing a more robust stop word detector is left to the reader as an exercise.

StanfordNLP uses a supervised RNN with **Bi-directional Long Short-Term Memory (BiLSTM)** units. This architecture uses a vocabulary to generate embeddings through the vectorization of the vocabulary. The vectorization and generation of embeddings is covered later in the chapter, in the *Vectorizing text* section. This architecture of BiLSTMs with embeddings is often a common starting point in NLP tasks. This will be covered and used in successive chapters in detail. This particular architecture for tokenization is considered the state of the art as of the time of writing this book. Prior to this, **Hidden Markov Model (HMM)**-based models were popular.

Depending on the languages in question, regular expression-based tokenization is also another approach. The NLTK library provides the Penn Treebank tokenizer based on regular expressions in a sed script. In future chapters, other tokenization or segmentation schemes such as **Byte Pair Encoding** (BPE) and WordPiece will be explained.

The next task in text normalization is to understand the structure of a text through POS tagging.

Part-of-speech tagging

Languages have a grammatical structure. In most languages, words can be categorized primarily into verbs, adverbs, nouns, and adjectives. The objective of this part of the processing step is to take a piece of text and tag each word token with a POS identifier. Note that this makes sense only in the case of word-level tokens. Commonly, the Penn Treebank POS tagger is used by libraries including StanfordNLP to tag words. By convention, POS tags are added by using a code after the word, separated by a slash. As an example, NNS is the tag for a plural noun. If the words goats was encountered, it would be represented as goats/NNS. In the StandfordNLP library, **Universal POS (UPOS)** tags are used. The following tags are part of the UPOS tag set. More details on mapping of standard POS tags to UPOS tags can be seen at https://universaldependencies.org/docs/tagset-conversion/en-penn-uposf.html. The following is a table of the most common tags:

Tag	Class	Examples
ADJ	**Adjective**: Usually describes a noun. Separate tags are used for comparatives and superlatives.	Great, pretty
ADP	**Adposition**: Used to modify an object such as a noun, pronoun, or phrase; for example, "Walk **up** the stairs." Some languages like English use prepositions while others such as Hindi and Japanese use postpositions.	Up, inside
ADV	**Adverb**: A word or phrase that modifies or qualifies an adjective, verb, or another adverb.	Loudly, often
AUX	**Auxiliary verb**: Used in forming mood, voice, or tenses of other verbs.	Will, can, may
CCONJ	**Co-ordinating conjunction**: Joins two phrases, clauses, or sentences.	And, but, that
INTJ	**Interjection**: An exclamation, interruption, or sudden remark.	Oh, uh, lol
NOUN	**Noun**: Identifies people, places, or things.	Office, book
NUM	**Numeral**: Represents a quantity.	Six, nine
DET	**Determiner**: Identifies a specific noun, usually as a singular.	A, an, the

PART	**Particle**: Parts of speech outside of the main types.	To, n't
PRON	**Pronoun**: Substitutes for other nouns, especially proper nouns.	She, her
PROPN	**Proper noun**: A name for a specific person, place, or thing.	Gandhi, US
PUNCT	Different punctuation symbols.	, ? /
SCONJ	**Subordinating conjunction**: Connects independent clause to a dependent clause.	Because, while
SYM	Symbols including currency signs, emojis, and so on.	$, #, % :)
VERB	**Verb**: Denotes action or occurrence.	Go, do
X	**Other**: That which cannot be classified elsewhere.	Etc, 4. (a numbered list bullet)

The best way to understand how POS tagging works is to try it out:

 The code for this section is in the *POS Based Features* section of the notebook.

```
en = snlp.Pipeline(lang='en')

txt = "Yo you around? A friend of mine's lookin."
pos = en(txt)
```

The preceding code instantiates an English pipeline and processes a sample piece of text. The next piece of code is a reusable function to print back the sentence tokens with the POS tags:

```
def print_pos(doc):
    text = ""
    for sentence in doc.sentences:
        for token in sentence.tokens:
            text += token.words[0].text + "/" + \
                    token.words[0].upos + " "
        text += "\n"
    return text
```

This method can be used to investigate the tagging for the preceding example sentence:

```
print(print_pos(pos))
```

```
Yo/PRON you/PRON around/ADV ?/PUNCT
A/DET friend/NOUN of/ADP mine/PRON 's/PART lookin/NOUN ./PUNCT
```

Most of these tags would make sense, though there may be some inaccuracies. For example, the word *lookin* is miscategorized as a noun. Neither StanfordNLP, nor a model from another package, will be perfect. This is something that we have to account for in building models using such features. There are a couple of different features that can be built using these POS. First, we can update the word_counts() method to exclude the punctuation from the count of words. The current method is unaware of the punctuation when it counts the words. Additional features can be created that look at the proportion of different types of grammatical elements in the messages. Note that so far, all features are based on the structure of the text, and not on the content itself. Working with content features will be covered in more detail as this book continues.

As a next step, let's update the word_counts() method and add a feature to show the percentages of symbols and punctuation in a message – with the hypothesis that maybe spam messages use more punctuation and symbols. Other features around types of different grammatical elements can also be built. These are left to you to implement. Our word_counts() method is updated as follows:

```
en_sw = stopwords.stopwords('en')

def word_counts_v3(x, pipeline=en):
  doc = pipeline(x)
  totals = 0.
  count = 0.
  non_word = 0.
  for sentence in doc.sentences:
    totals += len(sentence.tokens)  # (1)
    for token in sentence.tokens:
        if token.text.lower() not in en_sw:
          if token.words[0].upos not in ['PUNCT', 'SYM']:
            count += 1.
          else:
            non_word += 1.
  non_word = non_word / totals
  return pd.Series([count, non_word], index=['Words_NoPunct', 'Punct'])
```

This function is a little different compared to the previous one. Since there are multiple computations that need to be performed on the message in each row, these operations are combined and a Series object with column labels is returned. This can be merged with the main DataFrame like so:

```
train_tmp = train['Message'].apply(word_counts_v3)
train = pd.concat([train, train_tmp], axis=1)
```

A similar process can be performed on the test set:

```
test_tmp = test['Message'].apply(word_counts_v3)
test = pd.concat([test, test_tmp], axis=1)
```

A quick check of the statistics for spam and non-spam messages in the training set shows the following, first for non-spam messages:

```
train.loc[train['Spam']==0].describe()
```

	Spam	Capitals	Punctuation	Length	Words	Words_NoPunct	Punct
count	3867.0	3867.000000	3867.000000	3867.000000	3867.000000	3867.000000	3867.000000
mean	0.0	4.018878	17.325058	71.354538	7.911042	5.356866	0.147485
std	0.0	10.599291	14.826644	57.755351	7.326390	4.818043	0.097180
min	0.0	0.000000	0.000000	2.000000	0.000000	0.000000	0.000000
25%	0.0	1.000000	8.000000	33.000000	4.000000	2.000000	0.090909
50%	0.0	2.000000	13.000000	53.000000	6.000000	4.000000	0.142857
75%	0.0	3.000000	23.000000	92.000000	10.000000	7.000000	0.200000
max	0.0	129.000000	253.000000	910.000000	147.000000	54.000000	0.750000

Figure 1.12: Statistics for regular messages after using POS tags

And then for spam messages:

```
train.loc[train['Spam']==1].describe()
```

	Spam	Capitals	Punctuation	Length	Words	Words_NoPunct	Punct
count	592.0	592.000000	592.000000	592.000000	592.000000	592.000000	592.000000
mean	1.0	15.320946	29.086149	138.856419	18.464527	14.199324	0.140939
std	0.0	11.635105	7.083572	28.079980	6.100852	4.726081	0.064785
min	1.0	0.000000	2.000000	13.000000	2.000000	1.000000	0.000000
25%	1.0	7.000000	26.000000	132.000000	14.000000	11.000000	0.096774
50%	1.0	14.000000	30.000000	149.000000	19.000000	14.000000	0.137931
75%	1.0	21.000000	34.000000	157.000000	23.000000	17.000000	0.181818
max	1.0	128.000000	49.000000	197.000000	33.000000	27.000000	0.363636

Figure 1.13: Statistics for spam messages after using POS tags

In general, word counts have been reduced even further after stop word removal. Further more, the new Punct feature computes the ratio of punctuation tokens in a message relative to the total tokens. Now we can build a model with this data.

Modeling data with POS tagging

Plugging these features into the model, the following results are obtained:

```
x_train = train[['Length', 'Punctuation', 'Capitals', 'Words_NoPunct',
'Punct']]
y_train = train[['Spam']]

x_test = test[['Length', 'Punctuation', 'Capitals' , 'Words_NoPunct',
'Punct']]
y_test = test[['Spam']]

model = make_model(input_dims=5)
# model = make_model(input_dims=3)

model.fit(x_train, y_train, epochs=10, batch_size=10)
```

```
Train on 4459 samples
Epoch 1/10
4459/4459 [==============================] - 1s 236us/sample - loss:
3.1958 - accuracy: 0.6028
Epoch 2/10
...
Epoch 10/10
```

```
4459/4459 [==============================] - 1s 139us/sample - loss:
0.1788 - accuracy: 0.9466
```

The accuracy shows a slight increase and is now up to 94.66%. Upon testing, it seems to hold:

```
model.evaluate(x_test, y_test)
```

```
1115/1115 [==============================] - 0s 91us/sample - loss:
0.2076 - accuracy: 0.9426
[0.20764057086989485, 0.9426009]
```

The final part of text normalization is stemming and lemmatization. Though we will not be building any features for the spam model using this, it can be quite useful in other cases.

Stemming and lemmatization

In certain languages, the same word can take a slightly different form depending on its usage. Consider the word *depend* itself. The following are all valid forms of the word *depend*: *depends, depending, depended, dependent*. Often, these variations are due to tenses. In some languages like Hindi, verbs may have different forms for different genders. Another case is derivatives of the same word such as *sympathy, sympathetic, sympathize*, and *sympathizer*. These variations can take different forms in other languages. In Russian, proper nouns take different forms based on usage. Suppose there is a document talking about London (Лондон). The phrase *in London* (в Лондоне) spells *London* differently than *from London* (из Лондона). These variations in the spelling of *London* can cause issues when matching some input to sections or words in a document.

When processing and tokenizing text to construct a vocabulary of words appearing in the corpora, the ability to identify the root word can reduce the size of the vocabulary while expanding the accuracy of matches. In the preceding Russian example, any form of the word London can be matched to any other form if all the forms are normalized to a common representation post-tokenization. This process of normalization is called stemming or lemmatization.

Stemming and lemmatization differ in their approach and sophistication but serve the same objective. Stemming is a simpler, heuristic rule-based approach that chops off the affixes of words. The most famous stemmer is called the Porter stemmer, published by Martin Porter in 1980. The official website is https://tartarus.org/martin/PorterStemmer/, where various versions of the algorithm implemented in various languages are linked.

This stemmer only works for English and has rules including removing *s* at the end of the words for plurals, and removing endings such as *-ed* or *-ing*. Consider the following sentence:

"Stemming is aimed at reducing vocabulary and aid understanding of morphological processes. This helps people understand the morphology of words and reduce size of corpus."

After stemming using Porter's algorithm, this sentence will be reduced to the following:

"Stem is aim at reduce vocabulari and aid understand of morpholog process . Thi help peopl understand the morpholog of word and reduc size of corpu ."

Note how different forms of *morphology*, *understand*, and *reduce* are all tokenized to the same form.

Lemmatization approaches this task in a more sophisticated manner, using vocabularies and morphological analysis of words. In the study of linguistics, a morpheme is a unit smaller than or equal to a word. When a morpheme is a word in itself, it is called a root or a free morpheme. Conversely, every word can be decomposed into one or more morphemes. The study of morphemes is called morphology. Using this morphological information, a word's root form can be returned post-tokenization. This base or dictionary form of the word is called a *lemma*, hence the process is called lemmatization. StanfordNLP includes lemmatization as part of processing.

 The *Lemmatization* section of the notebook has the code shown here.

Here is a simple piece of code to take the preceding sentences and parse them:

```
text = "Stemming is aimed at reducing vocabulary and aid understanding
of morphological processes. This helps people understand the morphology
of words and reduce size of corpus."

lemma = en(text)
```

After processing, we can iterate through the tokens to get the lemma of each word. This is shown in the following code fragment. The lemma of a word is exposed as the .lemma property of each word inside a token. For the sake of brevity of code, a simplifying assumption is made here that each token has only one word.

The POS for each word is also printed out to help us understand how the process was performed. Some key words in the following output are highlighted:

```
lemmas = ""
for sentence in lemma.sentences:
        for token in sentence.tokens:
            lemmas += token.words[0].lemma +"/" + \
                    token.words[0].upos + " "
        lemmas += "\n"


print(lemmas)
```

```
stem/NOUN be/AUX aim/VERB at/SCONJ reduce/VERB vocabulary/NOUN and/
CCONJ aid/NOUN understanding/NOUN of/ADP morphological/ADJ process/NOUN
./PUNCT
this/PRON help/VERB people/NOUN understand/VERB the/DET morphology/NOUN
of/ADP word/NOUN and/CCONJ reduce/VERB size/NOUN of/ADP corpus/ADJ ./
PUNCT
```

Compare this output to the output of the Porter stemmer earlier. One immediate thing to notice is that lemmas are actual words as opposed to fragments, as was the case with the Porter stemmer. In the case of *reduce*, the usage in both sentences is in the form of a verb, so the choice of lemma is consistent. Focus on the words *understand* and *understanding* in the preceding output. As the POS tag shows, it is used in two different forms. Consequently, it is not reduced to the same lemma. This is different from the Porter stemmer. The same behavior can be observed for *morphology* and *morphological*. This is a quite sophisticated behavior.

Now that text normalization is completed, we can begin the vectorization of text.

Vectorizing text

While building models for the SMS message spam detection thus far, only aggregate features based on counts or distributions of lexical or grammatical features have been considered. The actual words in the messages have not been used thus far. There are a couple of challenges in using the text content of messages. The first is that text can be of arbitrary lengths. Comparing this to image data, we know that each image has a fixed width and height. Even if the corpus of images has a mixture of sizes, images can be resized to a common size with minimal loss of information by using a variety of compression mechanisms. In NLP, this is a bigger problem compared to computer vision. A common approach to handle this is to truncate the text. We will see various ways to handle variable-length texts in various examples throughout the book.

The second issue is that of the representation of words with a numerical quantity or feature. In computer vision, the smallest unit is a pixel. Each pixel has a set of numerical values indicating color or intensity. In a text, the smallest unit could be a word. Aggregating the Unicode values of the characters does not convey or embody the meaning of the word. In fact, these character codes embody no information at all about the character, such as its prevalence, whether it is a consonant or a vowel, and so on. However, averaging the pixels in a section of an image could be a reasonable approximation of that region of the image. It may represent how that region would look if seen from a large distance. A core problem then is to construct a numerical representation of words. Vectorization is the process of converting a word to a vector of numbers that embodies the information contained in the word. Depending on the vectorization technique, this vector may have additional properties that may allow comparison with other words, as will be shown in the *Word vectors* section later in this chapter.

The simplest approach for vectorizing is to use counts of words. The second approach is more sophisticated, with its origins in information retrieval, and is called TF-IDF. The third approach is relatively new, having been published in 2013, and uses RNNs to generate embeddings or word vectors. This method is called Word2Vec. The newest method in this area as of the time of writing was BERT, which came out in the last quarter of 2018. The first three methods will be discussed in this chapter. BERT will be discussed in detail in *Chapter 3*, *Named Entity Recognition (NER) with BiLSTMs, CRFs, and Viterbi Decoding*.

Count-based vectorization

The idea behind count-based vectorization is really simple. Each unique word appearing in the corpus is assigned a column in the vocabulary. Each document, which would correspond to individual messages in the spam example, is assigned a row. The counts of the words appearing in that document are entered in the relevant cell corresponding to the document and the word. With n unique documents containing m unique words, this results in a matrix of n rows by m columns. Consider a corpus like so:

```
corpus = [
        "I like fruits. Fruits like bananas",
        "I love bananas but eat an apple",
        "An apple a day keeps the doctor away"
]
```

There are three documents in this corpus of text. The scikit-learn (sklearn) library provides methods for undertaking count-based vectorization.

Modeling after count-based vectorization

In Google Colab, this library should already be installed. If it is not installed in your Python environment, it can be installed via the notebook like so:

```
!pip install sklearn
```

The CountVectorizer class provides a built-in tokenizer that separates the tokens of two or more characters in length. This class takes a variety of options including a custom tokenizer, a stop word list, the option to convert characters to lowercase prior to tokenization, and a binary mode that converts every positive count to 1. The defaults provide a reasonable choice for an English language corpus:

```
from sklearn.feature_extraction.text import CountVectorizer

vectorizer = CountVectorizer()
X = vectorizer.fit_transform(corpus)

vectorizer.get_feature_names()
```

```
['an',
 'apple',
 'away',
 'bananas',
 'but',
 'day',
 'doctor',
 'eat',
 'fruits',
 'keeps',
 'like',
 'love',
 'the']
```

In the preceding code, a model is fit to the corpus. The last line prints out the tokens that are used as columns. The full matrix can be seen as follows:

```
X.toarray()
```

```
array([[0, 0, 0, 1, 0, 0, 0, 0, 2, 0, 2, 0, 0],
       [1, 1, 0, 1, 1, 0, 0, 1, 0, 0, 0, 1, 0],
       [1, 1, 1, 0, 0, 1, 1, 0, 0, 1, 0, 0, 1]])
```

This process has now converted a sentence such as "I like fruits. Fruits like bananas" into a vector (0, 0, 0, 1, 0, 0, 0, 2, 0, 2, 0, 0). This is an example of **context-free** vectorization. Context-free refers to the fact that the order of the words in the document did not make any difference in the generation of the vector. This is merely counting the instances of the words in a document. Consequently, words with multiple meanings may be grouped into one, for example, *bank*. This may refer to a place near the river or a place to keep money. However, it does provide a method to compare documents and derive similarity. The cosine similarity or distance can be computed between two documents, to see which documents are similar to which other documents:

```
from sklearn.metrics.pairwise import cosine_similarity

cosine_similarity(X.toarray())

array([[1.        , 0.13608276, 0.        ],
       [0.13608276, 1.        , 0.3086067 ],
       [0.        , 0.3086067 , 1.        ]])
```

This shows that the first sentence and the second sentence have a 0.136 similarity score (on a scale of 0 to 1). The first and third sentence have nothing in common. The second and third sentence have a similarity score of 0.308 – the highest in this set. Another use case of this technique is to check the similarity of the documents with given keywords. Let's say that the query is *apple and bananas*. This first step is to compute the vector of this query, and then compute the cosine similarity scores against the documents in the corpus:

```
query = vectorizer.transform(["apple and bananas"])

cosine_similarity(X, query)

array([[0.23570226],
       [0.57735027],
       [0.26726124]])
```

This shows that this query matches the second sentence in the corpus the best. The third sentence would rank second, and the first sentence would rank lowest. In a few lines, a basic search engine has been implemented, along with logic to serve queries! At scale, this is a very difficult problem, as the number of words or columns in a web crawler would top 3 billion. Every web page would be represented as a row, so that would also require billions of rows. Computing a cosine similarity in milliseconds to serve an online query and keeping the content of this matrix updated is a massive undertaking.

The next step from this rather simple vectorization scheme is to consider the information content of each word in constructing this matrix.

Term Frequency-Inverse Document Frequency (TF-IDF)

In creating a vector representation of the document, only the presence of words was included – it does not factor in the importance of a word. If the corpus of documents being processed is about a set of recipes with fruits, then one may expect words like *apples, raspberries,* and *washing* to appear frequently. **Term Frequency** (TF) represents how often a word or token occurs in a given document. This is exactly what we did in the previous section. In a set of documents about fruits and cooking, a word like *apple* may not be terribly specific to help identify a recipe. However, a word like *tuile* may be uncommon in that context. Therefore, it may help to narrow the search for recipes much faster than a word like *raspberry*. On a side note, feel free to search the web for raspberry tuile recipes. If a word is rare, we want to give it a higher weight, as it may contain more information than a common word. A term can be upweighted by the inverse of the number of documents it appears in. Consequently, words that occur in a lot of documents will get a smaller score compared to terms that appear in fewer documents. This is called the **Inverse Document Frequency (IDF)**.

Mathematically, the score of each term in a document can be computed as follows:

$$TF - IDF(t, d) = TF(t, d) \times IDF(t)$$

Here, t represents the word or term, and d represents a specific document.

It is common to normalize the TF of a term in a document by the total number of tokens in that document.

The IDF is defined as follows:

$$IDF(t) = \log \frac{N}{1 + n_t}$$

Here, N represents the total number of documents in the corpus, and n_t represents the number of documents where the term is present. The addition of 1 in the denominator avoids the divide-by-zero error. Fortunately, `sklearn` provides methods to compute TF-IDF.

The *TF-IDF Vectorization* section of the notebook contains the code for this section.

Let's convert the counts from the previous section into their TF-IDF equivalents:

```
import pandas as pd
from sklearn.feature_extraction.text import TfidfTransformer

transformer = TfidfTransformer(smooth_idf=False)
tfidf = transformer.fit_transform(X.toarray())

pd.DataFrame(tfidf.toarray(),
             columns=vectorizer.get_feature_names())
```

This produces the following output:

	an	apple	away	bananas	but	day	doctor	eat	fruits	keeps	like	love	the
0	0.000000	0.000000	0.000000	0.230408	0.000000	0.000000	0.000000	0.000000	0.688081	0.000000	0.688081	0.000000	0.000000
1	0.321267	0.321267	0.000000	0.321267	0.479709	0.000000	0.000000	0.479709	0.000000	0.000000	0.000000	0.479709	0.000000
2	0.275785	0.275785	0.411797	0.000000	0.000000	0.411797	0.411797	0.000000	0.000000	0.411797	0.000000	0.000000	0.411797

This should give some intuition on how TF-IDF is computed. Even with three toy sentences and a very limited vocabulary, many of the columns in each row are 0. This vectorization produces **sparse representations**.

Now, this can be applied to the problem of detecting spam messages. Thus far, the features for each message have been computed based on some aggregate statistics and added to the pandas DataFrame. Now, the content of the message will be tokenized and converted into a set of columns. The TF-IDF score for each word or token will be computed for each message in the array. This is surprisingly easy to do with sklearn, as follows:

```
from sklearn.feature_extraction.text import TfidfVectorizer
from sklearn. pre-processing import LabelEncoder

tfidf = TfidfVectorizer(binary=True)

X = tfidf.fit_transform(train['Message']).astype('float32')

X_test = tfidf.transform(test['Message']).astype('float32')

X.shape
```

```
(4459, 7741)
```

The second parameter shows that 7,741 tokens were uniquely identified. These are the columns of features that will be used in the model later. Note that the vectorizer was created with the binary flag. This implies that even if a token appears multiple times in a message, it is counted as one. The next line trains the TF-IDF model on the training dataset. Then, it converts the words in the test set according to the TF-IDF scores learned from the training set. Let's train a model on just these TF-IDF features.

Modeling using TF-IDF features

With these TF-IDF features, let's train a model and see how it does:

```
_, cols = X.shape
model2 = make_model(cols)  # to match tf-idf dimensions

y_train = train[['Spam']]
y_test = test[['Spam']]

model2.fit(X.toarray(), y_train, epochs=10, batch_size=10)
```

```
Train on 4459 samples
Epoch 1/10
4459/4459 [==============================] - 2s 380us/sample - loss:
0.3505 - accuracy: 0.8903
...
Epoch 10/10
4459/4459 [==============================] - 1s 323us/sample - loss:
0.0027 - accuracy: 1.0000
```

Whoa – we are able to classify every one correctly! In all honesty, the model is probably overfitting, so some regularization should be applied. The test set gives this result:

```
model2.evaluate(X_test.toarray(), y_test)
```

```
1115/1115 [==============================] - 0s 134us/sample - loss:
0.0581 - accuracy: 0.9839
[0.05813191874545786, 0.9838565]
```

An accuracy rate of 98.39% is by far the best we have gotten in any model so far. Checking the confusion matrix, it is evident that this model is indeed doing very well:

```
y_test_pred = model2.predict_classes(X_test.toarray())
tf.math.confusion_matrix(tf.constant(y_test.Spam),
                         y_test_pred)

<tf.Tensor: shape=(2, 2), dtype=int32, numpy=
array([[958,    2],
       [ 16, 139]], dtype=int32)>
```

Only 2 regular messages were classified as spam, while only 16 spam messages were classified as being not spam. This is indeed a very good model. Note that this dataset has Indonesian (or Bahasa) words as well as English words in it. Bahasa uses the Latin alphabet. This model, without using a lot of pretraining and knowledge of language, vocabulary, and grammar, was able to do a very reasonable job with the task at hand.

However, this model ignores the relationships between words completely. It treats the words in a document as unordered items in a set. There are better models that vectorize the tokens in a way that preserves some of the relationships between the tokens. This is explored in the next section.

Word vectors

In the previous example, a row vector was used to represent a document. This was used as a feature for the classification model to predict spam labels. However, no information can be gleaned reliably from the relationships between words. In NLP, a lot of research has been focused on learning the words or representations in an unsupervised way. This is called representation learning. The output of this approach is a representation of a word in some vector space, and the word can be considered **embedded** in that space. Consequently, these word vectors are also called embeddings.

The core hypothesis behind word vector algorithms is that words that occur near each other are related to each other. To see the intuition behind this, consider two words, *bake* and *oven*. Given a sentence fragment of five words, where one of these words is present, what would be the probability of the other being present as well? You would be right in guessing that the probability is likely quite high. Suppose now that words are being mapped into some two-dimensional space. In that space, these two words should be closer to each other, and probably further away from words like *astronomy* and *tractor*.

The task of learning these embeddings for the words can be then thought of as adjusting words in a giant multidimensional space where similar words are closer to each other and dissimilar words are further apart from each other.

A revolutionary approach to do this is called Word2Vec. This algorithm was published by Tomas Mikolov and collaborators from Google in 2013. This approach produces dense vectors of the order of 50-300 dimensions generally (though larger are known), where most of the values are non-zero. In contrast, in our previous trivial spam example, the TF-IDF model had 7,741 dimensions. The original paper had two algorithms proposed in it: **continuous bag-of-words** and **continuous skip-gram**. On semantic tasks and overall, the performance of skip-gram was state of the art at the time of its publication. Consequently, the continuous skip-gram model with negative sampling has become synonymous with Word2Vec. The intuition behind this model is fairly straightforward.

Consider this sentence fragment from a recipe: "Bake until the cookie is golden brown all over." Under the assumption that a word is related to the words that appear near it, a word from this fragment can be picked and a classifier can be trained to predict the words around it:

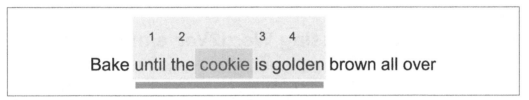

Figure 1.14: A window of 5 centered on cookie

Taking an example of a window of five words, the word in the center is used to predict two words before and two words after it. In the preceding figure, the fragment is *until the cookie is golden,* with the focus on the word *cookie.* Assuming that there are 10,000 words in the vocabulary, a network can be trained to predict binary decisions given a pair of words. The training objective is that the network predicts `true` for pairs like (*cookie, golden*) while predicting `false` for (*cookie, kangaroo*). This particular approach is called **Skip-Gram Negative Sampling (SGNS)** and it considerably reduces the training time required for large vocabularies. Very similar to the single-layer neural model in the previous section, a model can be trained with a one-to-many as the output layer. The sigmoid activation would be changed to a `softmax` function. If the hidden layer has 300 units, then its dimensions would be 10,000 x 300, that is, for each of the words, there will be a set of weights. The objective of the training is to learn these weights. In fact, these weights become the embedding for that word once training is complete.

The choice of units in the hidden layer is a hyperparameter that can be adapted for specific applications. 300 is commonly found as it is available through pretrained embeddings on the Google News dataset. Finally, the error is computed as the sum of the categorical cross-entropy of all the word pairs in negative and positive examples.

The beauty of this model is that it does not require any supervised training data. Running sentences can be used to provide positive examples. For the model to learn effectively, it is important to provide negative samples as well. Words are randomly sampled using their probability of occurrence in the training corpus and fed as negative examples.

To understand how the Word2Vec embeddings work, let's download a set of pretrained embeddings.

 The code shown in the following section can be found in the *Word Vectors* section of the notebook.

Pretrained models using Word2Vec embeddings

Since we are only interested in experimenting with a pretrained model, we can use the Gensim library and its pretrained embeddings. Gensim should already be installed in Google Colab. It can be installed like so:

```
!pip install gensim
```

After the requisite imports, pretrained embeddings can be downloaded and loaded. Note that these particular embeddings are approximately 1.6 GB in size, so may take a very long time to load (you may encounter some memory issues as well):

```
from gensim.models.word2vec import Word2Vec
import gensim.downloader as api
model_w2v = api.load("word2vec-google-news-300")
```

Another issue that you may run into is the Colab session expiring if left alone for too long while waiting for the download to finish. This may be a good time to switch to a local notebook, which will also be helpful in future chapters. Now, we are ready to inspect the similar words:

```
model_w2v.most_similar("cookies",topn=10)
```

```
[('cookie', 0.745154082775116),
 ('oatmeal_raisin_cookies', 0.6887780427932739),
 ('oatmeal_cookies', 0.662139892578125),
 ('cookie_dough_ice_cream', 0.6520504951477051),
 ('brownies', 0.6479344964027405),
 ('homemade_cookies', 0.6476464867591858),
 ('gingerbread_cookies', 0.6461867690086365),
 ('Cookies', 0.6341644525527954),
 ('cookies_cupcakes', 0.6275068521499634),
 ('cupcakes', 0.6258294582366943)]
```

This is pretty good. Let's see how this model does at a word analogy task:

```
model_w2v.doesnt_match(["USA","Canada","India","Tokyo"])
```

```
'Tokyo'
```

The model is able to guess that compared to the other words, which are all countries, Tokyo is the odd one out, as it is a city. Now, let's try a very famous example of mathematics on these word vectors:

```
king = model_w2v['king']
man = model_w2v['man']
woman = model_w2v['woman']

queen = king - man + woman
model_w2v.similar_by_vector(queen)
```

```
[('king', 0.8449392318725586),
 ('queen', 0.7300517559051514),
 ('monarch', 0.6454660892486572),
 ('princess', 0.6156251430511475),
 ('crown_prince', 0.5818676948547363),
 ('prince', 0.5777117609977722),
 ('kings', 0.5613663792610168),
 ('sultan', 0.5376776456832886),
 ('Queen_Consort', 0.5344247817993164),
 ('queens', 0.5289887189865112)]
```

Given that *King* was provided as an input to the equation, it is simple to filter the inputs from the outputs and *Queen* would be the top result. SMS spam classification could be attempted using these embeddings. However, future chapters will cover the use of GloVe embeddings and BERT embeddings for sentiment analysis.

A pretrained model like the preceding can be used to vectorize a document. Using these embeddings, models can be trained for specific purposes. In later chapters, newer methods of generating contextual embeddings, such as BERT, will be discussed in detail.

Summary

In this chapter, we worked through the basics of NLP, including collecting and labeling training data, tokenization, stop word removal, case normalization, POS tagging, stemming, and lemmatization. Some vagaries of these in languages such as Japanese and Russian were also covered. Using a variety of features derived from these approaches, we trained a model to classify spam messages, where the messages had a combination of English and Bahasa Indonesian words. This got us to a model with 94% accuracy.

However, the major challenge in using the content of the messages was in defining a way to represent words as vectors such that computations could be performed on them. We started with a simple count-based vectorization scheme and then graduated to a more sophisticated TF-IDF approach, both of which produced sparse vectors. This TF-IDF approach gave a model with 98%+ accuracy in the spam detection task.

Finally, we saw a contemporary method of generating dense word embeddings, called Word2Vec. This method, though a few years old, is still very relevant in many production applications. Once the word embeddings are generated, they can be cached for inference and that makes an ML model using these embeddings run with relatively low latency.

We used a very basic deep learning model for solving the SMS spam classification task. Like how **Convolutional Neural Networks (CNNs)** are the predominant architecture in computer vision, **Recurrent Neural Networks (RNNs)**, especially those based on **Long Short-Term Memory (LSTM)** and **Bi-directional LSTMs (BiLSTMs)**, are most commonly used to build NLP models. In the next chapter, we cover the structure of LSTMs and build a sentiment analysis model using BiLSTMs. These models will be used extensively in creative ways to solve different NLP problems in future chapters.

2
Understanding Sentiment in Natural Language with BiLSTMs

Natural Language Understanding (NLU) is a significant subfield of **Natural Language Processing (NLP)**. In the last decade, there has been a resurgence of interest in this field with the dramatic success of chatbots such as Amazon's Alexa and Apple's Siri. This chapter will introduce the broad area of NLU and its main applications.

Specific model architectures called **Recurrent Neural Networks (RNNs)**, with special units called **Long Short-Term Memory (LSTM)** units, have been developed to make the task of understanding natural language easier. LSTMs in NLP are analogous to convolution blocks in computer vision. We will take two examples to build models that can understand natural language. Our first example is understanding the sentiment of movie reviews. This will be the focus of this chapter. The other example is one of the fundamental building blocks of NLU, **Named Entity Recognition (NER)**. That will be the main focus of the next chapter.

Building models capable of understanding sentiments requires the use of **Bi-Directional LSTMs (BiLSTMs)** in addition to the use of techniques from *Chapter 1, Essentials of NLP*. Specifically, the following will be covered in this chapter:

- Overview of NLU and its applications
- Overview of RNNs and BiRNNS using LSTMs and BiLSTMS

- Analyzing the sentiment of movie reviews with LSTMs and BiLSTMs
- Using `tf.data` and the TensorFlow Datasets package to manage the loading of data
- Optimizing the performance of data loading for effective utilization of the CPU and GPU

We will start with a quick overview of NLU and then get right into BiLSTMs.

Natural language understanding

NLU enables the processing of unstructured text and extracts meaning and critical pieces of information that are actionable. Enabling a computer to understand sentences of text is a very hard challenge. One aspect of NLU is understanding the meaning of sentences. Sentiment analysis of a sentence becomes possible after understanding the sentence. Another useful application is the classification of sentences to a topic. This topic classification can also help in the disambiguation of entities. Consider the following sentence: "A CNN helps improve the accuracy of object recognition." Without understanding that this sentence is about machine learning, an incorrect inference may be made about the entity CNN. It may be interpreted as the news organization as opposed to a deep learning architecture used in computer vision. An example of a sentiment analysis model is built using a specific RNN architecture called BiLSTMs later in this chapter.

Another aspect of NLU is to extract information or commands from free-form text. This text can be sourced from converting speech, as spoken to Amazon's Echo device, for example, into text. Rapid advances in speech recognition now allow considering speech as equivalent to text. Extracting commands from the text, like an object and an action to perform, allows control of devices through voice commands. Consider the example sentence "Lower the volume." Here, the object is "volume" and the action is "lower." After extraction from text, these actions can be matched to a list of available actions and executed. This capability enables advanced **human-computer interaction (HCI)**, allowing control of home appliances through voice commands. NER is used for detecting key tokens in sentences.

This technique is incredibly useful in building form filling or slot filling chatbots. NER also forms the basis of other NLU techniques that perform tasks such as relation extraction. Consider the sentence "Sundar Pichai is the CEO of Google." In this sentence, what is the relationship between the entities "Sundar Pichai" and "Google"? The right answer is CEO. This is an example of relation extraction, and NER was used to identify the entities in the sentence. The focus of the next chapter is on NER using a specific architecture that has been quite effective in this space.

A common building block of both sentiment analysis and NER models is Bi-directional RNN models. The next section describes BiLSTMs, which is Bi-directional RNN using LSTM units, prior to building a sentiment analysis model with it.

Bi-directional LSTMs – BiLSTMs

LSTMs are one of the styles of recurrent neural networks, or RNNs. RNNs are built to handle sequences and learn the structure of them. An RNN does that by using the output generated after processing the previous item in the sequence along with the current item to generate the next output.

Mathematically, this can be expressed like so:

$$f_t(x_t) = f\big(f_{\{t-1\}}(x_{t-1}, x_t; \theta)\big)$$

This equation says that to compute the output at time *t*, the output at *t-1* is used as an input along with the input data x_t at the same time step. Along with this, a set of parameters or learned weights, represented by θ, are also used in computing the output. The objective of training an RNN is to learn these weights θ. This particular formulation of an RNN is unique. In previous examples, we have not used the output of a batch to determine the output of a future batch. While we focus on applications of RNNs on language where a sentence is modeled as a sequence of words appearing one after the other, RNNs can be applied to build general time-series models.

RNN building blocks

The previous section outlined the basic mathematical intuition of a recursive function that is a simplification of the RNN building block. *Figure 2.1* represents a few time steps and also adds details to show different weights used for computation for a basic RNN building block or cell.

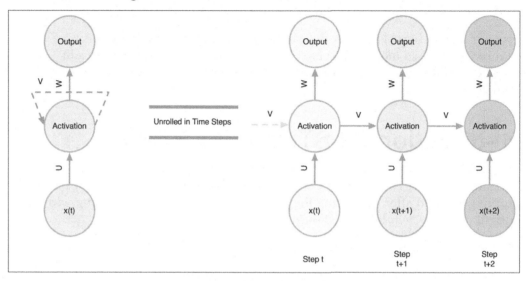

Figure 2.1: RNN unraveled

The basic cell is shown on the left. The input vector at a specific time or sequence step *t* is multiplied by a weight vector, represented in the diagram as *U*, to generate an activation in the middle part. The key part of this architecture is the loop in this activation part. The output of a previous step is multiplied by a weight vector, denoted by *V* in the figure, and added to the activation. This activation can be multiplied by another weight vector, represented by *W*, to produce the output of that step shown at the top. In terms of sequence or time steps, this network can be unrolled. This unrolling is virtual. However, it is represented on the right side of the figure. Mathematically, activation at time step *t* can be represented by:

$$a_t = U.x_t + V.a_{t-1}$$

Output at the same step can be computed like so:

$$o_t = W.a_t$$

 The mathematics of RNNs has been simplified to provide intuition about RNNs.

Structurally, the network is very simple as it is a single unit. To exploit and learn the structure of inputs passing through, weight vectors U, V, and W are shared across time steps. The network does not have layers as seen in fully connected or convolutional networks. However, as it is unrolled over time steps, it can be thought of as having as many layers as steps in the input sequences. There are additional criteria that would need to be satisfied to make a Deep RNN. More on that later in this section. These networks are trained using backpropagation and stochastic gradient descent techniques. The key thing to note here is that backpropagation is happening through the sequence or time steps before backpropogating through layers.

Having this structure enables processing sequences of arbitrary lengths. However, as the length of sequences increases, there are a couple of challenges that emerge:

- **Vanishing and exploding gradients**: As the lengths of these sequences increase, the gradients going back will become smaller and smaller. This will cause the network to train slowly or not learn at all. This effect will be more pronounced as sequence lengths increase. In the previous chapter, we built a network of a handful of layers. Here, a sentence of 10 words would equate to a network of 10 layers. A 1-minute audio sample of 10 ms would generate 6,000 steps! Conversely, gradients can also explode if the output is increasing. The simplest way to manage vanishing gradients is through the use of ReLUs. For managing exploding gradients, a technique called **gradient clipping** is used. This technique artificially clips gradients if their magnitude exceeds a threshold. This prevents gradients from becoming too large or exploding.

- **Inability to manage long-term dependencies**: Let's say that the third word in an eleven-word sentence is highly informative. Here is a toy example: "I think soccer is the most popular game across the world." As the processing reaches the end of the sentence, the contribution of the words prior earlier in the sequence will become smaller and smaller due to repeated multiplication with the vector V as shown above.

- **Two specific RNN cell designs mitigate these problems**: **Long-Short Term Memory (LSTM)** and **Gated Recurrent Unit (GRU)**. These are described next. However, note that TensorFlow provides implementations of both types of cells out of the box. So, building RNNs with these cell types is almost trivial.

Long short-term memory (LSTM) networks

LSTM networks were proposed in 1997 and improved upon and popularized by many researchers. They are widely used today for a variety of tasks and produce amazing results.

LSTM has four main parts:

- **Cell value** or memory of the network, also referred to as the cell, which stores accumulated knowledge
- **Input gate**, which controls how much of the input is used in computing the new cell value
- **Output gate**, which determines how much of the cell value is used in the output
- **Forget gate**, which determines how much of the current cell value is used for updating the cell value

These are shown in the figure below:

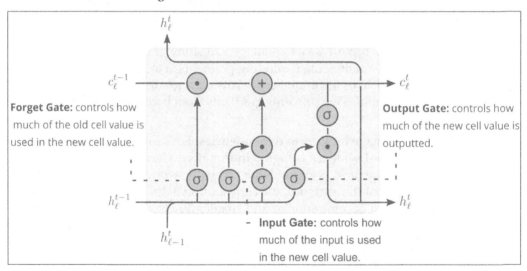

Figure 2.2: LSTM cell
(Source: Madsen, "Visualizing memorization in RNNs," Distill, 2019)

 Training RNNs is a very complicated process fraught with many frustrations. Modern tools such as TensorFlow do a great job of managing the complexity and reducing the pain to a great extent. However, training RNNs still is a challenging task, especially without GPU support. But the rewards of getting it right are well worth it, especially in the field of NLP.

After a quick introduction to GRUs, we will pick up on LSTMs, talk about BiLSTMs, and build a sentiment classification model.

Gated recurrent units (GRUs)

GRUs are another popular, and more recent, type of RNN unit. They were invented in 2014. They are simpler than LSTMs:

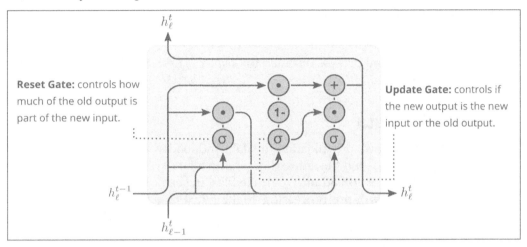

Figure 2.3: Gated recurrent unit (GRU) architecture

Compared to the LSTM, it has fewer gates. Input and forget gates are combined into a single update gate. Some of the internal cell state and hidden state is merged together as well. This reduction in complexity makes it easier to train. It has shown great results in the speech and sound domains. However, in neural machine translation tasks, LSTMs have shown superior performance. In this chapter, we will focus on using LSTMs. Before we discuss BiLSTMs, let's take a sentiment classification problem and solve it with LSTMs. Then, we will try and improve the model with BiLSTMs.

Sentiment classification with LSTMs

Sentiment classification is an oft-cited use case of NLP. Models that predict the movement of stock prices by using sentiment analysis features from tweets have shown promising results. Tweet sentiment is also used to determine customers' perceptions of brands. Another use case is processing user reviews for movies, or products on e-commerce or other websites. To see LSTMs in action, let's use a dataset of movie reviews from IMDb. This dataset was published at the ACL 2011 conference in a paper titled *Learning Word Vectors for Sentiment Analysis*. This dataset has 25,000 review samples in the training set and another 25,000 in the test set.

A local notebook will be used for the code for this example. *Chapter 10, Installation and Setup Instructions for Code*, provides detailed instructions on how to set up the development environment. In short, you will need Python 3.7.5 and the following libraries to start:

- pandas 1.0.1
- NumPy 1.18.1
- TensorFlow 2.4 and the `tensorflow_datasets` 3.2.1 package
- Jupyter notebook

We will follow the overall process outlined in *Chapter 1, Essentials of NLP*. We start by loading the data we need.

Loading the data

In the previous chapter, we downloaded the data and loaded it with the pandas library. This approach loaded the entire dataset into memory. However, sometimes data can be quite large, or spread into multiple files. In such cases, it may be too large for loading and need lots of pre-processing. Making text data ready to be used in a model requires normalization and vectorization at the very least. Often, this needs to be done outside of the TensorFlow graph using Python functions. This may cause issues in the reproducibility of code. Further, it creates issues for data pipelines in production where there is a higher chance of breakage as different dependent stages are being executed separately.

TensorFlow provides a solution for the loading, transformation, and batching of data through the use of the `tf.data` package. In addition, a number of datasets are provided for download through the `tensorflow_datasets` package. We will use a combination of these to download the IMDb data, and perform the tokenization, encoding, and vectorization steps before training an LSTM model.

 All the code for the sentiment review example can be found in the GitHub repo under the `chapter2-nlu-sentiment-analysis-bilstm` folder. The code is in an IPython notebook called `IMDB Sentiment analysis.ipynb`.

The first step is to install the appropriate packages and download the datasets:

```
!pip install tensorflow_datasets
import tensorflow as tf
import tensorflow_datasets as tfds
import numpy as np
```

The `tfds` package comes with a number of datasets in different domains such as images, audio, video, text, summarization, and so on. To see the datasets available:

```
", ".join(tfds.list_builders())
```

```
'abstract_reasoning, aeslc, aflw2k3d, amazon_us_reviews, arc,
bair_robot_pushing_small, beans, big_patent, bigearthnet, billsum,
binarized_mnist, binary_alpha_digits, c4, caltech101, caltech_
birds2010, caltech_birds2011, cars196, cassava, cats_vs_dogs, celeb_a,
celeb_a_hq, cfq, chexpert, cifar10, cifar100, cifar10_1, cifar10_
corrupted, citrus_leaves, cityscapes, civil_comments, clevr, cmaterdb,
cnn_dailymail, coco, coil100, colorectal_histology, colorectal_
histology_large, cos_e, curated_breast_imaging_ddsm, cycle_gan, deep_
weeds, definite_pronoun_resolution, diabetic_retinopathy_detection,
div2k, dmlab, downsampled_imagenet, dsprites, dtd, duke_ultrasound,
dummy_dataset_shared_generator, dummy_mnist, emnist, eraser_multi_
rc, esnli, eurosat, fashion_mnist, flic, flores, food101, gap,
gigaword, glue, groove, higgs, horses_or_humans, i_naturalist2017,
image_label_folder, imagenet2012, imagenet2012_corrupted, imagenet_
resized, imagenette, imagewang, imdb_reviews, iris, kitti, kmnist,
lfw, librispeech, librispeech_lm, libritts, lm1b, lost_and_found,
lsun, malaria, math_dataset, mnist, mnist_corrupted, movie_rationales,
moving_mnist, multi_news, multi_nli, multi_nli_mismatch, natural_
questions, newsroom, nsynth, omniglot, open_images_v4, opinosis,
oxford_flowers102, oxford_iiit_pet, para_crawl, patch_camelyon,
pet_finder, places365_small, plant_leaves, plant_village, plantae_k,
qa4mre, quickdraw_bitmap, reddit_tifu, resisc45, rock_paper_scissors,
rock_you, scan, scene_parse150, scicite, scientific_papers, shapes3d,
smallnorb, snli, so2sat, speech_commands, squad, stanford_dogs,
stanford_online_products, starcraft_video, sun397, super_glue, svhn_
cropped, ted_hrlr_translate, ted_multi_translate, tf_flowers, the300w_
lp, tiny_shakespeare, titanic, trivia_qa, uc_merced, ucf101, vgg_face2,
visual_domain_decathlon, voc, wider_face, wikihow, wikipedia, wmt14_
translate, wmt15_translate, wmt16_translate, wmt17_translate, wmt18_
translate, wmt19_translate, wmt_t2t_translate, wmt_translate, xnli,
xsum, yelp_polarity_reviews'
```

That is a list of 155 datasets. Details of the datasets can be obtained on the catalog page at https://www.tensorflow.org/datasets/catalog/overview.

IMDb data is provided in three splits – training, test, and unsupervised. The training and testing splits have 25,000 rows each, with two columns. The first column is the text of the review, and the second is the label. "0" represents a review with negative sentiment while "1" represents a review with positive sentiment. The following code loads the training and testing data splits:

```
imdb_train, ds_info = tfds.load(name="imdb_reviews", split="train",
```

```
                              with_info=True, as_supervised=True)
  imdb_test = tfds.load(name="imdb_reviews", split="test",
                            as_supervised=True)
```

Note that this command may take a little bit of time to execute as data is
downloaded. `ds_info` contains information about the dataset. This is returned when
the `with_info` parameter is supplied. Let's see the information contained in `ds_info`:

```
print(ds_info)
```

```
tfds.core.DatasetInfo(
    name='imdb_reviews',
    version=1.0.0,
    description='Large Movie Review Dataset.
This is a dataset for binary sentiment classification containing
substantially more data than previous benchmark datasets. We provide a
set of 25,000 highly polar movie reviews for training, and 25,000 for
testing. There is additional unlabeled data for use as well.',
    homepage='http://ai.stanford.edu/~amaas/data/sentiment/',
    features=FeaturesDict({
        'label': ClassLabel(shape=(), dtype=tf.int64, num_classes=2),
        'text': Text(shape=(), dtype=tf.string),
    }),
    total_num_examples=100000,
    splits={
        'test': 25000,
        'train': 25000,
        'unsupervised': 50000,
    },
    supervised_keys=('text', 'label'),
    citation="""@InProceedings{maas-EtAl:2011:ACL-HLT2011,
      author    = {Maas, Andrew L.  and  Daly, Raymond E.  and
Pham, Peter T.  and  Huang, Dan  and  Ng, Andrew Y.  and  Potts,
Christopher},
      title     = {Learning Word Vectors for Sentiment Analysis},
      booktitle = {Proceedings of the 49th Annual Meeting of
the Association for Computational Linguistics: Human Language
Technologies},
      month     = {June},
      year      = {2011},
      address   = {Portland, Oregon, USA},
      publisher = {Association for Computational Linguistics},
      pages     = {142--150},
```

```
    url          = {http://www.aclweb.org/anthology/P11-1015}
    }""",
    redistribution_info=,
)
```

We can see that two keys, `text` and `label`, are available in the supervised mode. Using the `as_supervised` parameter is key to loading the dataset as a tuple of values. If this parameter is not specified, data is loaded and made available as dictionary keys. In cases where the data has multiple inputs, that may be preferable. To get a sense of the data that has been loaded:

```
for example, label in imdb_train.take(1):
    print(example, '\n', label)
```

```
tf.Tensor(b"This was an absolutely terrible movie. Don't be lured in by
Christopher Walken or Michael Ironside. Both are great actors, but this
must simply be their worst role in history. Even their great acting
could not redeem this movie's ridiculous storyline. This movie is an
early nineties US propaganda piece. The most pathetic scenes were those
when the Columbian rebels were making their cases for revolutions.
Maria Conchita Alonso appeared phony, and her pseudo-love affair with
Walken was nothing but a pathetic emotional plug in a movie that was
devoid of any real meaning. I am disappointed that there are movies
like this, ruining actor's like Christopher Walken's good name. I could
barely sit through it.", shape=(), dtype=string)
tf.Tensor(0, shape=(), dtype=int64)
```

The above review is an example of a negative review. The next step is tokenization and vectorization of the reviews.

Normalization and vectorization

In *Chapter 1, Essentials of NLP*, we discussed a number of different normalization methods. Here, we are only going to tokenize the text into words and construct a vocabulary, and then encode the words using this vocabulary. This is a simplified approach. There can be a number of different approaches that can be used for building additional features. Using techniques discussed in the first chapter, such as POS tagging, a number of features can be built, but that is left as an exercise for the reader. In this example, our aim is to use the same set of features on an RNN with LSTMs followed by using the same set of features on an improved model with BiLSTMs.

A vocabulary of the tokens occurring in the data needs to be constructed prior to vectorization. Tokenization breaks up the words in the text into individual tokens. The set of all the tokens forms the vocabulary.

Normalization of the text, such as converting to lowercase, etc., is performed along with this tokenization step. `tfds` comes with a set of feature builders for text in the `tfds.features.text` package. First, a set of all the words in the training data needs to be created:

```
tokenizer = tfds.features.text.Tokenizer()

vocabulary_set = set()
MAX_TOKENS = 0

for example, label in imdb_train:
    some_tokens = tokenizer.tokenize(example.numpy())
    if MAX_TOKENS < len(some_tokens):
        MAX_TOKENS = len(some_tokens)
    vocabulary_set.update(some_tokens)
```

By iterating through the training examples, each review is tokenized and the words in the review are added to a set. These are added to a set to get unique words. Note that tokens or words have not been converted to lowercase. This means that the size of the vocabulary is going to be slightly larger. Using this vocabulary, an encoder can be created. `TokenTextEncoder` is one of three out-of-the-box encoders that are provided in `tfds`. Note how the list of tokens is converted into a set to ensure only unique tokens are retained in the vocabulary. The tokenizer used for generating the vocabulary is passed in, so that every successive call to encode a string can use the same tokenization scheme. This encoder expects that the tokenizer object provides a `tokenize()` and a `join()` method. If you want to use StanfordNLP or some other tokenizer as discussed in the previous chapter, all you need to do is to wrap the StanfordNLP interface in a custom object and implement methods to split the text into tokens and join the tokens back into a string:

```
imdb_encoder = tfds.features.text.TokenTextEncoder(vocabulary_set,
                                                   tokenizer=tokenizer)
vocab_size = imdb_encoder.vocab_size

print(vocab_size, MAX_TOKENS)
```

```
93931 2525
```

The vocabulary has 93,931 tokens. The longest review has 2,525 tokens. That is one wordy review! Reviews are going to have different lengths. LSTMs expect sequences of equal length. Padding and truncating operations make reviews of equal length. Before we do that, let's test whether the encoder works correctly:

```
for example, label in imdb_train.take(1):
    print(example)
    encoded = imdb_encoder.encode(example.numpy())
    print(imdb_encoder.decode(encoded))
```

```
tf.Tensor(b"This was an absolutely terrible movie. Don't be lured in by
Christopher Walken or Michael Ironside. Both are great actors, but this
must simply be their worst role in history. Even their great acting
could not redeem this movie's ridiculous storyline. This movie is an
early nineties US propaganda piece. The most pathetic scenes were those
when the Columbian rebels were making their cases for revolutions.
Maria Conchita Alonso appeared phony, and her pseudo-love affair with
Walken was nothing but a pathetic emotional plug in a movie that was
devoid of any real meaning. I am disappointed that there are movies
like this, ruining actor's like Christopher Walken's good name. I could
barely sit through it.", shape=(), dtype=string)
This was an absolutely terrible movie Don t be lured in by Christopher
Walken or Michael Ironside Both are great actors but this must simply
be their worst role in history Even their great acting could not redeem
this movie s ridiculous storyline This movie is an early nineties US
propaganda piece The most pathetic scenes were those when the Columbian
rebels were making their cases for revolutions Maria Conchita Alonso
appeared phony and her pseudo love affair with Walken was nothing but a
pathetic emotional plug in a movie that was devoid of any real meaning
I am disappointed that there are movies like this ruining actor s like
Christopher Walken s good name I could barely sit through it
```

Note that punctuation is removed from these reviews when they are reconstructed from the encoded representations.

> One convenience feature provided by the encoder is persisting the vocabulary to disk. This enables a one-time computation of the vocabulary and distribution for production use cases. Even during development, computation of the vocabulary can be a resource intensive task prior to each run or restart of the notebook. Saving the vocabulary and the encoder to disk enables picking up coding and model building from anywhere after the vocabulary building step is complete. To save the encoder, use the following:
>
> ```
> imdb_encoder.save_to_file("reviews_vocab")
> ```

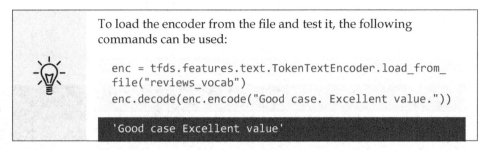

To load the encoder from the file and test it, the following commands can be used:

```
enc = tfds.features.text.TokenTextEncoder.load_from_
file("reviews_vocab")
enc.decode(enc.encode("Good case. Excellent value."))
```

```
'Good case Excellent value'
```

Tokenization and encoding were done for a small set of rows at a time. TensorFlow provides mechanisms to perform these actions in bulk over large datasets, which can be shuffled and loaded in batches. This allows very large datasets to be loaded without running out of memory during training. To enable this, a function needs to be defined that performs a transformation on a row of data. Note that multiple transformations can be chained one after the other. It is also possible to use a Python function in defining these transformations. For processing the review above, the following steps need to be performed:

- **Tokenization**: Reviews need to be tokenized into words.
- **Encoding**: These words need to be mapped to integers using the vocabulary.
- **Padding**: Reviews can have variable lengths, but LSTMs expect vectors of the same length. So, a constant length is chosen. Reviews shorter than this length are padded with a specific vocabulary index, usually 0 in TensorFlow. Reviews longer than this length are truncated. Fortunately, TensorFlow provides such a function out of the box.

The following functions perform this:

```
from tensorflow.keras.preprocessing import sequence

def encode_pad_transform(sample):
    encoded = imdb_encoder.encode(sample.numpy())
    pad = sequence.pad_sequences([encoded], padding='post',
                                 maxlen=150)
    return np.array(pad[0], dtype=np.int64)


def encode_tf_fn(sample, label):
    encoded = tf.py_function(encode_pad_transform,
                                inp=[sample],
                                Tout=(tf.int64))
    encoded.set_shape([None])
```

```
label.set_shape([])
return encoded, label
```

encode_tf_fn is called by the dataset API with one example at a time. This means a tuple of the review and its label. This function in turn calls another function, encode_pad_transform, which is wrapped in the tf.py_function call that performs the actual transformation. In this function, tokenization is performed first, followed by encoding, and finally padding and truncating. A maximum length of 150 tokens or words is chosen for padding/truncating sequences. Any Python logic can be used in this second function. For example, the StanfordNLP package could be used to perform POS tagging of the words, or stopwords could be removed as shown in the previous chapter. Here, we try to keep things simple for this example.

 Padding is an important step as different layers in TensorFlow cannot handle tensors of different widths. Tensors of different widths are called **ragged tensors**. There is ongoing work to incorporate support for ragged tensors and the support is improving. However, the support for ragged tensors is not universal in TensorFlow. Consequently, ragged tensors are avoided in this text.

Transforming the data is quite trivial. Let's try the code on a small sample of the data:

```
subset = imdb_train.take(10)
tst = subset.map(encode_tf_fn)
for review, label in tst.take(1):
    print(review, label)
    print(imdb_encoder.decode(review))
```

```
tf.Tensor(
[40205  9679 51728 91747 21013  7623  6550 40338 18966 36012 64846
80722
 81643 29176 14002 73549 52960 40359 49248 62585 75017 67425 18181
2673
 44509 18966 87701 56336 29928 64846 41917 49779 87701 62585 58974
82970
  1902  2754 18181  7623  2615  7927 67321 40205  7623 43621 51728
91375
 41135 71762 29392 58948 76770 15030 74878 86231 49390 69836 18353
84093
 76562 47559 49390 48352 87701 62200 13462 80285 76037 75121  1766
59655
  6569 13077 40768 86201 28257 76220 87157 29176  9679 65053 67425
```

```
 93397
  74878 67053 61304 64846 93397   7623 18560   9679 50741 44024 79648
 7470
  28203 13192 47453   6386 18560 79892 49248   7158 91321 18181 88633
 13929
   2615 91321 81643 29176   2615 65285 63778 13192 82970 28143 14618
 44449
  39028      0      0      0      0      0      0      0      0      0      0
 0
      0      0      0      0      0      0      0      0      0      0      0
 0
      0      0      0      0      0      0], shape=(150,), dtype=int64)
tf.Tensor(0, shape=(), dtype=int64)
This was an absolutely terrible movie Don t be lured in by Christopher
Walken or Michael Ironside Both are great actors but this must simply
be their worst role in history Even their great acting could not redeem
this movie s ridiculous storyline This movie is an early nineties US
propaganda piece The most pathetic scenes were those when the Columbian
rebels were making their cases for revolutions Maria Conchita Alonso
appeared phony and her pseudo love affair with Walken was nothing but a
pathetic emotional plug in a movie that was devoid of any real meaning
I am disappointed that there are movies like this ruining actor s like
Christopher Walken s good name I could barely sit through it
```

Note the "0" at the end of the encoded tensor in the first part of the output. That is a consequence of padding to 150 words.

Running this map over the entire dataset can be done like so:

```
encoded_train = imdb_train.map(encode_tf_fn)
encoded_test = imdb_test.map(encode_tf_fn)
```

This should execute really fast. When the training loop executes, the mapping will be executed at that time. Other commands that are available and useful in the `tf.data.DataSet` class, of which `imdb_train` and `imdb_test` are instances, are `filter()`, `shuffle()`, and `batch()`. `filter()` can remove certain types of data from the dataset. It can be used to filter out reviews above or below a certain length, or separate out positive and negative examples to construct a more balanced dataset. The second method shuffles the data between training epochs. The last one batches data for training. Note that different datasets will result if these methods are applied in a different sequence.

Performance optimization with `tf.data`:

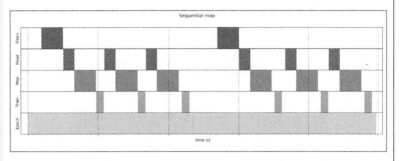

Figure 2.4: Illustrative example of the time taken by sequential execution of the map function
(Source: Better Performance with the tf.data API at tensorflow.org/guide/data_performance)

As can be seen in the figure above, a number of operations contribute to the overall training time in an epoch. This example chart above shows the case where files need to be opened, as shown in the topmost row, data needs to be read in the row below, a map transformation needs to be executed on the data being read, and then training can happen. Since these steps are happening in sequence, it can make the overall training time longer. Instead, the mapping step can happen in parallel. This will result in shorter execution times overall. CPU power is used to prefetch, batch, and transform the data, while the GPU is used for training computation and operations such as gradient calculation and updating weights. This can be enabled by making a small change in the call to the `map` function above:

```
encoded_train = imdb_train.map(encode_tf_fn,
        num_parallel_calls=tf.data.experimental.
AUTOTUNE)
encoded_test = imdb_test.map(encode_tf_fn,
        num_parallel_calls=tf.data.experimental.
AUTOTUNE)
```

Passing the additional parameter enables TensorFlow to use multiple subprocesses to execute the transformation on.

This can result in a speedup as shown below:

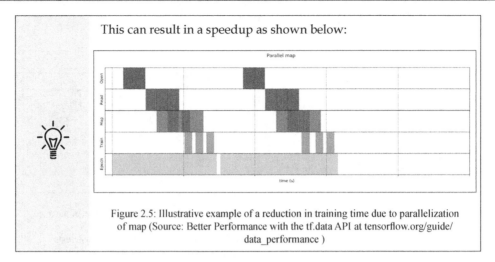

Figure 2.5: Illustrative example of a reduction in training time due to parallelization of map (Source: Better Performance with the tf.data API at tensorflow.org/guide/data_performance)

While we have normalized and encoded the text of the reviews, we have not converted it into word vectors or embeddings. This step is performed along with the model training in the next step. So, we are ready to start building a basic RNN model using LSTM now.

LSTM model with embeddings

TensorFlow and Keras make it trivial to instantiate an LSTM-based model. In fact, adding a layer of LSTMs is one line of code. The simplest form is shown below:

```
tf.keras.layers.LSTM(rnn_units)
```

Here, the `rnn_units` parameter determines how many LSTMs are strung together in one layer. There are a number of other parameters that can be configured, but the defaults are fairly reasonable on them. The TensorFlow documentation details these options and possible values with examples quite well. However, the review text tokens cannot be fed as is into the LSTM layer. They need to be vectorized using an embedding scheme. There are a couple of different approaches that can be used. The first approach is to learn these embeddings as the model trains. This is the approach we're going to use, as it is the simplest approach. In cases where the text data you may have is unique to a domain, like medical transcriptions, this is also probably the best approach. This approach, however, requires significant amounts of data for training for the embeddings to learn the right relationships with the words. The second approach is to use pre-trained embeddings, like Word2vec or GloVe, as shown in the previous chapter, and use them to vectorize the text. This approach has really worked well in general-purpose text models and can even be adapted to work very well in specific domains. Working with transfer learning is the focus of *Chapter 4, Transfer Learning with BERT,* though.

Coming back to learning embeddings, TensorFlow provides an embedding layer that can be added before the LSTM layer. Again, this layer has several options that are well documented. To complete the binary classification model, all that remains is a final dense layer with one unit for classification. A utility function that can build models with some configurable parameters can be configured like so:

```
def build_model_lstm(vocab_size, embedding_dim, rnn_units, batch_size):
  model = tf.keras.Sequential([
    tf.keras.layers.Embedding(vocab_size, embedding_dim,
                              mask_zero=True,
                              batch_input_shape=[batch_size, None]),
    tf.keras.layers.LSTM(rnn_units),
    tf.keras.layers.Dense(1, activation='sigmoid')
  ])
  return model
```

This function exposes a number of configurable parameters to allow trying out different architectures. In addition to these parameters, batch size is another important parameter. These can be configured as follows:

```
vocab_size = imdb_encoder.vocab_size

# The embedding dimension
embedding_dim = 64

# Number of RNN units
rnn_units = 64

# batch size
BATCH_SIZE=100
```

With the exception of the vocabulary size, all other parameters can be changed around to see the impact on model performance. With these configurations set, the model can be constructed:

```
model = build_model_lstm(
  vocab_size = vocab_size,
  embedding_dim=embedding_dim,
  rnn_units=rnn_units,
  batch_size=BATCH_SIZE)

model.summary()
```

```
Model: "sequential_3"

Layer (type)                 Output Shape              Param #
=================================================================
embedding_3 (Embedding)      (100, None, 64)           6011584

lstm_3 (LSTM)                (100, 64)                 33024

dense_5 (Dense)              (100, 1)                  65
=================================================================
Total params: 6,044,673
Trainable params: 6,044,673
Non-trainable params: 0
```

Such a small model has over 6 million trainable parameters. It is easy to check the size of the embedding layer. The total number of tokens in the vocabulary was 93,931. Each token is represented by a 64-dimensional embedding, which provides 93,931 X 64 = 6,011,584 million parameters.

This model is now ready to be compiled with the specification of the loss function, optimizer, and evaluation metrics. In this case, since there are only two labels, binary cross-entropy is used as the loss. The Adam optimizer is a very good choice with great defaults. Since we are doing binary classification, accuracy, precision, and recall are the metrics we would like to track during training. Then, the dataset needs to be batched and training can be started:

```
model.compile(loss='binary_crossentropy',
              optimizer='adam',
              metrics=['accuracy', 'Precision', 'Recall'])

encoded_train_batched = encoded_train.batch(BATCH_SIZE)
model.fit(encoded_train_batched, epochs=10)
```

```
Epoch 1/10
250/250 [==============================] - 23s 93ms/step - loss: 0.4311
- accuracy: 0.7920 - Precision: 0.7677 - Recall: 0.8376
Epoch 2/10
250/250 [==============================] - 21s 83ms/step - loss: 0.1768
- accuracy: 0.9353 - Precision: 0.9355 - Recall: 0.9351
...
Epoch 10/10
250/250 [==============================] - 21s 85ms/step - loss: 0.0066
- accuracy: 0.9986 - Precision: 0.9986 - Recall: 0.9985
```

That is a very good result! Let's compare it to the test set:

```
model.evaluate(encoded_test.batch(BATCH_SIZE))
```

```
    250/Unknown - 20s 80ms/step - loss: 0.8682 - accuracy: 0.8063 -
Precision: 0.7488 - Recall: 0.9219
```

The difference between the performance on the training and test set implies there is overfitting happening in the model. One way to manage overfitting is to introduce a dropout layer after the LSTM layer. This is left as an exercise to you.

 The model above was trained using an NVIDIA RTX 2070 GPU. You may see longer times per epoch when training using a CPU only.

Now, let's see how BiLSTMs would perform on this task.

BiLSTM model

Building BiLSTMs is easy in TensorFlow. All that is required is a one-line change in the model definition. In the build_model_lstm() function, the line that adds the LSTM layer needs to be modified. The new function would look like this, with the modified line highlighted:

```
def build_model_bilstm(vocab_size, embedding_dim, rnn_units, batch_
size):
  model = tf.keras.Sequential([
    tf.keras.layers.Embedding(vocab_size, embedding_dim,
                              mask_zero=True,
                              batch_input_shape=[batch_size, None]),
    tf.keras.layers.Bidirectional(tf.keras.layers.LSTM(rnn_units)),
    tf.keras.layers.Dense(1, activation='sigmoid')
  ])
  return model
```

But first, let's understand what a BiLSTM is:

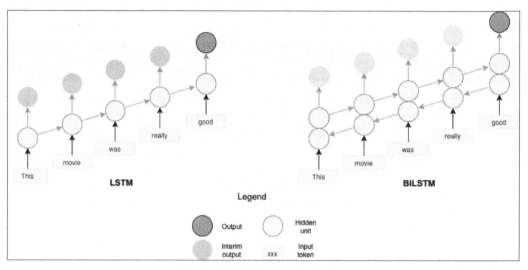

Figure 2.6: LSTMs versus BiLSTMs

In a regular LSTM network, tokens or words are fed in one direction. As an example, take the review "This movie was really good." Each token starting from the left is fed into the LSTM unit, marked as a hidden unit, one at a time. The diagram above shows a version unrolled in time. What this means is that each successive word is considered as occurring at a time increment from the previous word. Each step produces an output that may or may not be useful. That is dependent on the problem at hand. In the IMDb sentiment prediction case, only the final output is important as it is fed to the dense layer to make a decision on whether the review was positive or negative.

If you are working with right-to-left languages such as Arabic and Hebrew, please feed the tokens right to left. It is important to understand the direction the next word or token comes from. If you are using a BiLSTM, then the direction may not matter as much.

Due to this time unrolling, it may appear as if there are multiple hidden units. However, it is the same LSTM unit, as shown in *Figure 2.2* earlier in the chapter. The output of the unit is fed back into the same unit at the next time step. In the case of BiLSTM, there is a pair of hidden units. One set operates on the tokens from left to right, while the other set operates on the tokens from right to left. In other words, a forward LSTM model can only learn from tokens from the past time steps. A BiLSTM model can learn from tokens from **the past and the future**.

This method allows the capturing of more dependencies between words and the structure of the sentence and improves the accuracy of the model. Suppose the task is to predict the next word in this sentence fragment:

I jumped into the …

There are many possible completions to this sentence. Further, suppose that you had access to the words after the sentence. Think about these three possibilities:

1. *I jumped into the …. with only a small blade*
2. *I jumped into the … and swam to the other shore*
3. *I jumped into the … from the 10m diving board*

Battle or *fight* would be likely words in the first example, *river* for the second, and *swimming pool* for the last one. In each case, the beginning of the sentence was exactly the same but the words from the end helped disambiguate which word should fill in the blank. This illustrates the difference between LSTMs and BiLSTMs. An LSTM can only learn from the past tokens, while the BiLSTM can learn from both past and future tokens.

This new BiLSTM model has a little over 12M parameters.

```
bilstm = build_model_bilstm(
  vocab_size = vocab_size,
  embedding_dim=embedding_dim,
  rnn_units=rnn_units,
  batch_size=BATCH_SIZE)
```

```
bilstm.summary()
```

```
Model: "sequential_1"

Layer (type)                 Output Shape              Param #
=================================================================
embedding_1 (Embedding)      (50, None, 128)           12023168

dropout (Dropout)            (50, None, 128)           0

bidirectional (Bidirectional (50, None, 128)           98816

dropout_1 (Dropout)          (50, None, 128)           0

bidirectional_1 (Bidirection (50, 128)                 98816
```

```
dropout_2 (Dropout)          (50, 128)              0

dense_1 (Dense)              (50, 1)               129
=================================================================
Total params: 12,220,929
Trainable params: 12,220,929
Non-trainable params: 0
```

If you run the model shown above with no other changes, you will see a boost in the accuracy and precision of the model:

```
bilstm.fit(encoded_train_batched, epochs=5)
```

```
Epoch 1/5
500/500 [==============================] - 80s 160ms/step - loss:
0.3731 - accuracy: 0.8270 - Precision: 0.8186 - Recall: 0.8401
...
Epoch 5/5
500/500 [==============================] - 70s 139ms/step - loss:
0.0316 - accuracy: 0.9888 - Precision: 0.9886 - Recall: 0.9889


bilstm.evaluate(encoded_test.batch(BATCH_SIZE))


500/Unknown - 20s 40ms/step - loss: 0.7280 - accuracy: 0.8389 -
Precision: 0.8650 - Recall: 0.8032
```

Note that the model is severely overfitting. It is important to add some form of regularization to the model. Out of the box, with no feature engineering or use of the unsupervised data for learning better embeddings, the accuracy of the model is above 83.5%. The current state-of-the-art results on this data, published in August 2019, have an accuracy of 97.42%. Some ideas that can be tried to improve this model include stacking layers of LSTMs or BiLSTMs, with some dropout for regularization, using the unsupervised split of the dataset along with training and testing review text data to learn better embeddings and using those in the final network, adding more features such as word shapes, and POS tags, among others. We will pick up this example again in *Chapter 4, Transfer Learning with BERT*, when we discuss language models such as BERT. Maybe this example will be an inspiration for you to try your own model and publish a paper with your state-of-the-art results!

Note that BiLSTMs, while powerful, may not be suitable for all applications. Using a BiLSTM architecture assumes that the entire text or sequence is available at the same time. This assumption may not be true in some cases.

In the case of the speech recognition of commands in a chatbot, only the sounds spoken so far by the users are available. It is not known what words a user is going to utter in the future. In real-time time-series analytics, only data from the past is available. In such applications, BiLSTMs cannot be used. Also, note that RNNs really shine with very large amounts of data training over several epochs. The IMDb dataset with 25,000 training examples is on the smaller side for RNNs to show their power. You may find you achieve similar or better results using TF-IDF and logistic regression with some feature engineering.

Summary

This is a foundational chapter in our journey through advanced NLP problems. Many advanced models use building blocks such as BiRNNs. First, we used the TensorFlow Datasets package to load data. Our work of building a vocabulary, tokenizer, and encoder for vectorization was simplified through the use of this library. After understanding LSTMs and BiLSTMs, we built models to do sentiment analysis. Our work showed promise but was far away from the state-of-the-art results, which will be addressed in future chapters. However, we are now armed with the fundamental building blocks that will enable us to tackle more challenging problems.

Armed with this knowledge of LSTMs, we are ready to build our first NER model using BiLSTMs in the next chapter. Once this model is built, we will try to improve it using CRFs and Viterbi decoding.

3
Named Entity Recognition (NER) with BiLSTMs, CRFs, and Viterbi Decoding

One of the fundamental building blocks of NLU is **Named Entity Recognition (NER)**. The names of people, companies, products, and quantities can be tagged in a piece of text with NER, which is very useful in chatbot applications and many other use cases in information retrieval and extraction. NER will be the main focus of this chapter. Building and training a model capable of doing NER requires several techniques, such as **Conditional Random Fields (CRFs)** and **Bi-directional LSTMs (BiLSTMs)**. Advanced TensorFlow techniques like custom layers, losses, and training loops are also used. We will build on the knowledge of BiLSTMs gained from the previous chapter. Specifically, the following will be covered:

- Overview of NER
- Building an NER tagging model with BiLSTM
- CRFs and Viterbi algorithms
- Building a custom Keras layer for CRFs
- Building a custom loss function in Keras and TensorFlow
- Training a model with a custom training loop

It all starts with understanding NER, which is the focus of the next section.

Named Entity Recognition

Given a sentence or a piece of text, the objective of an NER model is to locate and classify text tokens as named entities in categories such as people's names, organizations and companies, physical locations, quantities, monetary quantities, times, dates, and even protein or DNA sequences. NER should tag the following sentence:

Ashish paid Uber $80 to go to the Twitter offices in San Francisco.

as follows:

[Ashish]$_{PER}$ paid [Uber]$_{ORG}$ [$80]$_{MONEY}$ to go the [Twitter]$_{ORG}$ offices in [San Francisco]$_{LOC}$.

Here is an example from the Google Cloud Natural Language API, with several additional classes:

Figure 3.1: An NER example from the Google Cloud Natural Language API

The most common tags are listed in the table below:

Type	Example Tag	Example
Person	PER	*Gregory* went to the castle.
Organization	ORG	*WHO* just issued an epidemic advisory.
Location	LOC	She lives in *Seattle*.
Money	MONEY	You owe me *twenty dollars*.
Percentage	PERCENT	Stocks have risen *10%* today.
Date	DATE	Let's meet on *Wednesday*.
Time	TIME	Is it *5 pm* already?

There are different data sets and tagging schemes that can be used to train NER models. Different data sets will have different subsets of the tags listed above. In other domains, there may be additional tags specific to the domain. The Defence Science Technology Laboratory in the UK created a data set called **re3d** (`https://github.com/dstl/re3d`), which has entity types such as vehicle (Boeing 777), weapon (rifle), and military platform (tank). The availability of adequately sized labeled data sets in various languages is a significant challenge. Here is a link to a good collection of NER data sets: `https://github.com/juand-r/entity-recognition-datasets`. In many use cases, you will need to spend a lot of time collecting and annotating data. For example, if you are building a chatbot for ordering pizza, the entities could be bases, sauces, sizes, and toppings.

There are a few different ways to build an NER model. If the sentence is considered a sequence, then this task can be modeled as a word-by-word labeling task. Hence, models similar to the models used for **Part of Speech** (**POS**) tagging are applicable. Features can be added to a model to improve labeling. The POS of a word and its neighboring words are the most straightforward features to add. Word shape features that model lowercase letters can add a lot of information, principally because a lot of the entity types deal with proper nouns, such as those for people and organizations. Organization names can be abbreviated. For example, the World Health Organization can be represented as WHO. Note that this feature will only work in languages that distinguish between lowercase and uppercase letters.

Another vital feature involves checking a word in a **gazetteer**. A gazetteer is like a database of important geographical entities. See `geonames.org` for an example of a data set licensed under Creative Commons. A set of people's names in the USA can be sourced from the US Social Security Administration at `https://www.ssa.gov/oact/babynames/state/namesbystate.zip`. The linked ZIP file has the names of people born in the United States since 1910, grouped by state. Similarly, Dunn and Bradstreet, popularly known as D&B, offers a data set of companies with over 200 million businesses across the world that can be licensed. The biggest challenge with this approach is the complexity of maintaining these lists over time.

In this chapter, we will focus on a model that does not rely on additional external data on top of labelled data for training, like a gazetteer, and also has no dependence on hand-crafted features. We will try to get to as high a level of accuracy as possible using deep neural networks and some additional techniques. The model we will use will be a combination of BiLSTM and a CRF on top. This model is based on the paper titled *Neural Architectures for Named Entity Recognition*, written by Guillaume Lample et al. and presented at the NAACL-HTL conference in 2016. This paper was state of the art in 2016 with an F1 score of 90.94. Currently, the SOTA has an F1-score of 93.5, where the model uses extra training data. These numbers are measured on the CoNLL 2003 English data set. The GMB data set will be used in this chapter. The next section describes this data set.

The GMB data set

With all the basics in the bag, we are ready to build a model that classifies NERs. For this task, the **Groningen Meaning Bank (GMB)** data set will be used. This dataset is not considered a gold standard. This means that this data set is built using automatic tagging software, followed by human raters updating subsets of the data. However, this is a very large and rich data set. This data has a lot of useful annotations that make it quite suitable for training models. It is also constructed from public domain text, making it easy to use for training. The following named entities are tagged in this corpus:

- geo = Geographical entity
- org = Organization
- per = Person
- gpe = Geopolitical entity
- tim = Time indicator
- art = Artifact
- eve = Event
- nat = Natural phenomenon

In each of these categories, there can be subcategories. For example, *tim* may be further sub-divided and represented as *tim-dow* representing a time entity corresponding to a day of the week, or *tim-dat*, which represents a date. For this exercise, these sub-entities are going to be aggregated into the eight top-level entities listed above. The number of examples varies widely between the sub-entities. Consequently, the accuracy varies widely due to the lack of enough training data for some of these subcategories.

The data set also provides the NER entity for each word. In many cases, an entity may comprise multiple words. If *Hyde Park* is a geographical entity, both words will be tagged as a *geo* entity. In terms of training models for NER, there is another way to represent this data that can have a significant impact on the accuracy of the model. This requires the usage of the BIO tagging scheme. In this scheme, the first word of an entity, single word or multi-word, is tagged with *B-{entity tag}*. If the entity is multi-word, each successive word would be tagged as *I-{entity tag}*. In the example above, *Hyde Park* would be tagged as *B-geo I-geo*. All these are steps of pre-processing that are required for a data set. All the code for this example can be found in the NER with BiLSTM and CRF.ipynb notebook in the chapter3-ner-with-lstm-crf folder of the GitHub repository.

Let's get started by loading and processing the data.

Loading the data

Data can be downloaded from the University of Groningen website as follows:

```
# alternate: download the file from the browser and put
# in the same directory as this notebook
!wget https://gmb.let.rug.nl/releases/gmb-2.2.0.zip
!unzip gmb-2.2.0.zip
```

Please note that the data is quite large – over 800MB. If wget is not available on your system, you may use any other tool such as, curl or a browser to download the data set. This step may take some time to complete. If you have a challenge accessing the data set from the University server, you may download a copy from Kaggle: https://www.kaggle.com/bradbolliger/gmb-v220. Also note that since we are going to be working on large data sets, some of the following steps may take some time to execute. In the world of **Natural Language Processing (NLP)**, more training data and training time is key to great results.

 All the code for this example can be found in the NER with BiLSTM and CRF.ipynb notebook in the chapter3-ner-with-lstm-crf folder of the GitHub repository.

The data unzips into the gmb-2.2.0 folder. The data subfolder has a number of subfolders with different files. README supplied with the data set provides details about the various files and their contents. For this example, we will be using only files named en.tags in various subdirectories. These files are tab-separated files with each word of a sentence in a row.

There are ten columns of information:

- The token itself

- A POS tag as used in the Penn Treebank (`ftp://ftp.cis.upenn.edu/pub/treebank/doc/tagguide.ps.gz`)

- A lemma

- A named-entity tag, or 0 if none

- A WordNet word sense number for the respective lemma-POS combinations, or 0 if not applicable (`http://wordnet.princeton.edu`)

- For verbs and prepositions, a list of the VerbNet roles of the arguments in order of combination in the **Combinatory Categorial Grammar** (CCG) derivation, or [ ] if not applicable (`http://verbs.colorado.edu/~mpalmer/projects/verbnet.html`)

- Semantic relation in noun-noun compounds, possessive apostrophes, temporal modifiers, and so on. Indicated using a preposition, or 0 if not applicable

- An animacy tag as proposed by Zaenen et al. (2004), or 0 if not applicable (`http://dl.acm.org/citation.cfm?id=1608954`)

- A supertag (lexical category of CCG)

- The lambda-DRS representing the semantics of the token in Boxer's Prolog format

Out of these fields, we are going to use only the token and the named entity tag. However, we will work through loading the POS tag for a future exercise. The following code gets all the paths for these tags files:

```python
import os
data_root = './gmb-2.2.0/data/'

fnames = []
for root, dirs, files in os.walk(data_root):
    for filename in files:
        if filename.endswith(".tags"):
            fnames.append(os.path.join(root, filename))

fnames[:2]

['./gmb-2.2.0/data/p57/d0014/en.tags', './gmb-2.2.0/data/p57/d0382/en.tags']
```

A few processing steps need to happen. Each file has a number of sentences, with each words in a row. The entire sentence as a sequence and the corresponding sequence of NER tags need to be fed in as inputs while training the model. As mentioned above, the NER tags also need to be simplified to the top-level entities only. Secondly, the NER tags need to be converted to the IOB format. **IOB** stands for **In-Other-Begin**. These letters are used as a prefix to the NER tag. The sentence fragment in the table below shows how this scheme works:

Reverend	Terry	Jones	arrived	in	New	York
B-per	I-per	I-per	O	O	B-geo	I-geo

The table above shows this tagging scheme after processing. Note that New York is one location. As soon as *New* is encountered, it marks the start of the geo NER tag, hence it is assigned B-geo. The next word is *York*, which is a continuation of the same geographical entity. For any network, classifying the word *New* as the start of the geographical entity is going to be very challenging. However, a BiLSTM network would be able to see the succeeding words, which helps quite a bit with disambiguation. Furthermore, the advantage of IOB tags is that the accuracy of the model improves considerably in terms of detection. This happens because once the beginning of an NER tag is detected, the choices for the next tag become quite limited.

Let's get to the code. First, create a directory to store all the processed files:

```
!mkdir ner
```

We want to process the tags so that we strip the subcategories of the NER tags out. It would also be nice to collect some stats on the types of tags in the documents:

```
import csv
import collections

ner_tags = collections.Counter()
iob_tags = collections.Counter()

def strip_ner_subcat(tag):
    # NER tags are of form {cat}-{subcat}
    # eg tim-dow. We only want first part
    return tag.split("-")[0]
```

The NER tag and IOB tag counters are set up above. A method for stripping the subcategory out of the NER tags is defined. The next method takes a sequence of tags and converts them into IOB format:

```python
def iob_format(ners):
    # converts IO tags into IOB format
    # input is a sequence of IO NER tokens
    # convert this: O, PERSON, PERSON, O, O, LOCATION, O
    # into: O, B-PERSON, I-PERSON, O, O, B-LOCATION, O
    iob_tokens = []
    for idx, token in enumerate(ners):
        if token != 'O':  # !other
            if idx == 0:
                token = "B-" + token #start of sentence
            elif ners[idx-1] == token:
                token = "I-" + token  # continues
            else:
                token = "B-" + token
        iob_tokens.append(token)
        iob_tags[token] += 1
    return iob_tokens
```

Once these two convenience functions are ready, all the tags files need to be read and processed:

```python
total_sentences = 0
outfiles = []
for idx, file in enumerate(fnames):
    with open(file, 'rb') as content:
        data = content.read().decode('utf-8').strip()
        sentences = data.split("\n\n")
        print(idx, file, len(sentences))
        total_sentences += len(sentences)

        with open("./ner/"+str(idx)+"-"+os.path.basename(file),
  'w') as outfile:
            outfiles.append("./ner/"+str(idx)+"-"+
os.path.basename(file))
            writer = csv.writer(outfile)

            for sentence in sentences:
                toks = sentence.split('\n')
                words, pos, ner = [], [], []
```

```
for tok in toks:
    t = tok.split("\t")
    words.append(t[0])
    pos.append(t[1])
    ner_tags[t[3]] += 1
    ner.append(strip_ner_subcat(t[3]))
writer.writerow([" ".join(words),
                " ".join(iob_format(ner)),
                " ".join(pos)])
```

First, a counter is set for the number of sentences. A list of files written with paths are also initialized. As processed files are written out, their paths are added to the outfiles variable. This list will be used later to load all the data and to train the model. Files are read and split into two empty newline characters. That is the marker for the end of a sentence in the file. Only the actual words, POS tokens, and NER tokens are used from the file. Once these are collected, a new CSV file is written with three columns: the sentence, a sequence of POS tags, and a sequence of NER tags. This step may take a little while to execute:

```
print("total number of sentences: ", total_sentences)
```

```
total number of sentences:  62010
```

To confirm the distribution of the NER tags before and after processing, we can use the following code:

```
print(ner_tags)
print(iob_tags)
```

```
Counter({'O': 1146068, 'geo-nam': 58388, 'org-nam': 48034, 'per-nam':
23790, 'gpe-nam': 20680, 'tim-dat': 12786, 'tim-dow': 11404, 'per-tit':
9800, 'per-fam': 8152, 'tim-yoc': 5290, 'tim-moy': 4262, 'per-giv':
2413, 'tim-clo': 891, 'art-nam': 866, 'eve-nam': 602, 'nat-nam': 300,
'tim-nam': 146, 'eve-ord': 107, 'org-leg': 60, 'per-ini': 60, 'per-
ord': 38, 'tim-dom': 10, 'art-add': 1, 'per-mid': 1})
Counter({'O': 1146068, 'B-geo': 48876, 'B-tim': 26296, 'B-org': 26195,
'I-per': 22270, 'B-per': 21984, 'I-org': 21899, 'B-gpe': 20436,
'I-geo': 9512, 'I-tim': 8493, 'B-art': 503, 'B-eve': 391, 'I-art': 364,
'I-eve': 318, 'I-gpe': 244, 'B-nat': 238, 'I-nat': 62})
```

As is evident, some tags were very infrequent, like *tim-dom*. It would be next to impossible for a network to learn them. Aggregating up one level helps increase the signal for these tags. To check if the entire process completed properly, check that the ner folder has 10,000 files. Now, let us load the processed data to normalize, tokenize, and vectorize it.

Normalizing and vectorizing data

For this section, pandas and numpy methods will be used. The first step is to load the contents of the processed files into one `DataFrame`:

```
import glob
import pandas as pd

# could use `outfiles` param as well
files = glob.glob("./ner/*.tags")

data_pd = pd.concat([pd.read_csv(f, header=None,
                                names=["text", "label", "pos"])
            for f in files], ignore_index = True)
```

This step may take a while given that it is processing 10,000 files. Once the content is loaded, we can check the structure of the `DataFrame`:

```
data_pd.info()
```

```
<class 'pandas.core.frame.DataFrame'>
RangeIndex: 62010 entries, 0 to 62009
Data columns (total 3 columns):
 #   Column  Non-Null Count  Dtype
---  ------  --------------  -----
 0   text    62010 non-null  object
 1   label   62010 non-null  object
 2   pos     62010 non-null  object
dtypes: object(3)
memory usage: 1.4+ MB
```

Both the text and NER tags need to be tokenized and encoded into numbers for use in training. We are going to be using core methods provided by the `keras.preprocessing` package. First, the tokenizer will be used to tokenize the text. In this example, the text only needs to be tokenized by white spaces, as it has been broken up already:

```
### Keras tokenizer
from tensorflow.keras.preprocessing.text import Tokenizer
text_tok = Tokenizer(filters='[\\]^\t\n', lower=False,
                    split=' ', oov_token='<OOV>')

pos_tok = Tokenizer(filters='\t\n', lower=False,
                    split=' ', oov_token='<OOV>')
```

```
ner_tok = Tokenizer(filters='\t\n', lower=False,
                    split=' ', oov_token='<OOV>')
```

The default values for the tokenizer are quite reasonable. However, in this particular case, it is important to only tokenize on spaces and not clean the special characters out. Otherwise the data will become mis-formatted:

```
text_tok.fit_on_texts(data_pd['text'])
pos_tok.fit_on_texts(data_pd['pos'])
ner_tok.fit_on_texts(data_pd['label'])
```

 Even though we do not use the POS tags, the processing for them is included. Use of the POS tags can have an impact on the accuracy of an NER model. Many NER entities are nouns, for example. However, we will see how to process POS tags but not use them in the model as features. This is left as an exercise to the reader.

This tokenizer has some useful features. It provides a way to restrict the size of the vocabulary by word counts, TF-IDF, and so on. If the num_words parameter is passed with a numeric value, the tokenizer will limit the number of tokens by word frequencies to that number. The fit_on_texts method takes in all the texts, tokenizes them, and constructs dictionaries with tokens that will be used later to tokenize and encode in one go. A convenience function, get_config(), can be called after the tokenizer has been fit on texts to provide information about the tokens:

```
ner_config = ner_tok.get_config()
text_config = text_tok.get_config()
print(ner_config)
```

```
{'num_words': None, 'filters': '\t\n', 'lower': False, 'split': ' ',
'char_level': False, 'oov_token': '<OOV>', 'document_count': 62010,
'word_counts': '{"B-geo": 48876, "O": 1146068, "I-geo": 9512, "B-per":
21984, "I-per": 22270, "B-org": 26195, "I-org": 21899, "B-tim": 26296,
"I-tim": 8493, "B-gpe": 20436, "B-art": 503, "B-nat": 238, "B-eve":
391, "I-eve": 318, "I-art": 364, "I-gpe": 244, "I-nat": 62}', 'word_
docs': '{"I-geo": 7738, "O": 61999, "B-geo": 31660, "B-per": 17499,
"I-per": 13805, "B-org": 20478, "I-org": 11011, "B-tim": 22345,
"I-tim": 5526, "B-gpe": 16565, "B-art": 425, "B-nat": 211, "I-eve":
201, "B-eve": 361, "I-art": 207, "I-gpe": 224, "I-nat": 50}', 'index_
docs': '{"10": 7738, "2": 61999, "3": 31660, "7": 17499, "6": 13805,
"5": 20478, "8": 11011, "4": 22345, "11": 5526, "9": 16565, "12": 425,
"17": 211, "15": 201, "13": 361, "14": 207, "16": 224, "18": 50}',
```

```
'index_word': '{"1": "<OOV>", "2": "O", "3": "B-geo", "4": "B-tim",
"5": "B-org", "6": "I-per", "7": "B-per", "8": "I-org", "9": "B-gpe",
"10": "I-geo", "11": "I-tim", "12": "B-art", "13": "B-eve", "14":
"I-art", "15": "I-eve", "16": "I-gpe", "17": "B-nat", "18": "I-nat"}',
'word_index': '{"<OOV>": 1, "O": 2, "B-geo": 3, "B-tim": 4, "B-org": 5,
"I-per": 6, "B-per": 7, "I-org": 8, "B-gpe": 9, "I-geo": 10, "I-tim":
11, "B-art": 12, "B-eve": 13, "I-art": 14, "I-eve": 15, "I-gpe": 16,
"B-nat": 17, "I-nat": 18}'}
```

The `index_word` dictionary property in the config provides a mapping between IDs and tokens. There is a considerable amount of information in the config. The vocabularies can be obtained from the config:

```
text_vocab = eval(text_config['index_word'])
ner_vocab = eval(ner_config['index_word'])

print("Unique words in vocab:", len(text_vocab))
print("Unique NER tags in vocab:", len(ner_vocab))
```

```
Unique words in vocab: 39422
Unique NER tags in vocab: 18
```

Tokenizing and encoding text and named entity labels is quite easy:

```
x_tok = text_tok.texts_to_sequences(data_pd['text'])
y_tok = ner_tok.texts_to_sequences(data_pd['label'])
```

Since sequences are of different sizes, they will all be padded or truncated to a size of 50 tokens. A helper function is used for this task:

```
# now, pad sequences to a maximum length
from tensorflow.keras.preprocessing import sequence

max_len = 50

x_pad = sequence.pad_sequences(x_tok, padding='post',
                              maxlen=max_len)
y_pad = sequence.pad_sequences(y_tok, padding='post',
                              maxlen=max_len)
print(x_pad.shape, y_pad.shape)
```

```
(62010, 50) (62010, 50)
```

The last step above is to ensure that shapes are correct before moving to the next step. Verifying shapes is a very important part of developing code in TensorFlow.

There is an additional step that needs to be performed on the labels. Since there are multiple labels, each label token needs to be one-hot encoded like so:

```
num_classes = len(ner_vocab) + 1

Y = tf.keras.utils.to_categorical(y_pad, num_classes=num_classes)
Y.shape
```

```
(62010, 50, 19)
```

Now, we are ready to build and train a model.

A BiLSTM model

The first model we will try is a BiLSTM model. First, the basic constants need to be set up:

```
# Length of the vocabulary
vocab_size = len(text_vocab) + 1

# The embedding dimension
embedding_dim = 64

# Number of RNN units
rnn_units = 100

#batch size
BATCH_SIZE=90

# num of NER classes
num_classes = len(ner_vocab)+1
```

Next, a convenience function for instantiating models is defined:

```
from tensorflow.keras.layers import Embedding, Bidirectional, LSTM,
TimeDistributed, Dense

dropout=0.2
def build_model_bilstm(vocab_size, embedding_dim, rnn_units, batch_
size, classes):
```

```
model = tf.keras.Sequential([
    Embedding(vocab_size, embedding_dim, mask_zero=True,
                        batch_input_shape=[batch_size,
None]),
    Bidirectional(LSTM(units=rnn_units,
                        return_sequences=True,
                        dropout=dropout,
                        kernel_initializer=\
                        tf.keras.initializers.he_normal())),
    TimeDistributed(Dense(rnn_units, activation='relu')),
    Dense(num_classes, activation="softmax")
])
```

We are going to train our own embeddings. The next chapter will talk about using pre-trained embeddings and using them in models. After the embedding layer, there is a BiLSTM layer, followed by a `TimeDistributed` dense layer. This last layer is different from the sentiment analysis model, where there was only a single unit for binary output. In this problem, for each word in the input sequence, an NER token needs to be predicted. So, the output has as many tokens as the input sequence. Consequently, output tokens correspond 1-to-1 with input tokens and are classified as one of the NER classes. The `TimeDistributed` layer provides this capability. The other thing to note in this model is the use of regularization. It is important that the model does not overfit the training data. Since LSTMs have high model capacity, using regularization is very important. Feel free to play with some of these hyperparameters to get a feel for how the model will react.

Now the model can be compiled:

```
model = build_model_bilstm(
                        vocab_size = vocab_size,
                        embedding_dim=embedding_dim,
                        rnn_units=rnn_units,
                        batch_size=BATCH_SIZE,
                        classes=num_classes)
model.summary()
model.compile(optimizer="adam", loss="categorical_crossentropy",
    metrics=["accuracy"])
```

```
Model: "sequential_1"
Layer (type)                Output Shape              Param #
=================================================================
embedding_9 (Embedding)     (90, None, 64)            2523072
```

```
bidirectional_9 (Bidirection (90, None, 200)          132000

time_distributed_6 (TimeDist (None, None, 100)        20100

dense_16 (Dense)              (None, None, 19)         1919
=================================================================
Total params: 2,677,091
Trainable params: 2,677,091
Non-trainable params: 0
```

This simplistic model has over 2.6 million parameters!

 If you notice, the bulk of the parameters are coming from the size of the vocabulary. The vocabulary has 39,422 words. This increases the model training time and computational capacity required. One way to reduce this is to make the vocabulary size smaller. The easiest way to do this would be to only consider words that have more than a certain frequency of occurrence or to remove words smaller than a certain number of characters. The vocabulary can also be reduced by converting all characters to lower case. However, in NER, case is a very important feature.

This model is ready for training. The last thing that is needed is to split the data into train and test sets:

```
# to enable TensorFlow to process sentences properly
X = x_pad
# create training and testing splits
total_sentences = 62010
test_size = round(total_sentences / BATCH_SIZE * 0.2)
X_train = X[BATCH_SIZE*test_size:]
Y_train = Y[BATCH_SIZE*test_size:]

X_test = X[0:BATCH_SIZE*test_size]
Y_test = Y[0:BATCH_SIZE*test_size]
```

Now, the model is ready for training:

```
model.fit(X_train, Y_train, batch_size=BATCH_SIZE, epochs=15)
```

```
Train on 49590 samples
Epoch 1/15
```

```
49590/49590 [==============================] - 20s 409us/sample - loss:
0.1736 - accuracy: 0.9113
...
Epoch 8/15
49590/49590 [==============================] - 15s 312us/sample - loss:
0.0153 - accuracy: 0.9884
...
Epoch 15/15
49590/49590 [==============================] - 15s 312us/sample - loss:
0.0065 - accuracy: 0.9950
```

Over 15 epochs of training, the model is doing quite well with over 99% accuracy. Let's see how the model performs on the test set and whether the regularization helped:

```
model.evaluate(X_test, Y_test, batch_size=BATCH_SIZE)
```

```
12420/12420 [==============================] - 3s 211us/sample - loss:
0.0926 - accuracy: 0.9624
```

The model performs well on the test data set, with over 96.5% accuracy. The difference between the train and test accuracies is still there, implying that the model could use some additional regularization. You can play with the dropout variable or add additional dropout layers between the embedding and BiLSTM layers, and between the `TimeDistributed` layer and the final Dense layer.

Here is an example of a sentence fragment tagged by this model:

	Faure	Gnassingbe	said	in	a	speech	carried	by	state	media	Friday
Actual	B-per	I-per	O	O	O	O	O	O	O	O	B-tim
Model	B-per	I-per	O	O	O	O	O	O	O	O	B-tim

This model is not doing poorly at all. It was able to identify the person and time entities in the sentence.

As good as this model is, it does not use an important characteristic of named entity tags – a given tag is highly correlated with the tag coming after it. CRFs can take advantage of this information and further improve the accuracy of NER tasks. Let's understand how CRFs work and add them to the network above next.

Conditional random fields (CRFs)

BiLSTM models look at a sequence of input words and predict the label for the current word. In making this determination, only the information of previous inputs is considered. Previous predictions play no role in making this decision. However, there is information encoded in the sequence of labels that is being discounted. To illustrate this point, consider a subset of NER tags: **O**, **B-Per**, **I-Per**, **B-Geo**, and **I-Geo**. This represents two domains of person and geographical entities and an *Other* category for everything else. Based on the structure of IOB tags, we know that any **I-** tag must be preceded by a **B-I** from the same domain. This also implies that an **I-** tag cannot be preceded by an **O** tag. The following diagram shows the possible state transitions between these tags:

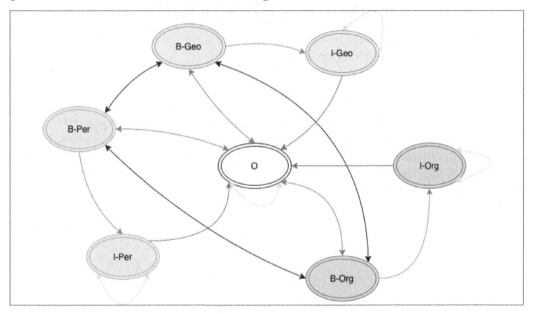

Figure 3.2: Possible NER tag transitions

Figure 3.2 color codes similar types of transitions with the same color. An **O** tag can transition only to a **B** tag. A **B** tag can go to its corresponding **I** tag or back to the **O** tag. An **I** tag can transition back to itself, an **O** tag, or a **B** tag of a different domain (not represented in the diagram for simplicity). For a set of **N** tags, these transitions can be represented by a matrix of dimension $N \times N$. $P_{i,j}$ denotes the possibility of tag j coming after tag i. Note that these transition weights can be learned based on the data. Such a learned transition weights matrix could be used during prediction to consider the entire sequence of predicted labels and make updates to the probabilities.

Here is an illustrative matrix with indicative transition weights:

From > To	O	B-Geo	I-Geo	B-Org	I-Org
O	3.28	2.20	0.00	3.66	0.00
B-Geo	-0.25	-0.10	4.06	0.00	0.00
I-Geo	-0.17	-0.61	3.51	0.00	0.00
B-Org	-0.10	-0.23	0.00	-1.02	4.81
I-Org	-0.33	-1.75	0.00	-1.38	5.10

As per the table above, the weight of the edge connecting I-Org to B-Org has a weight of -1.38, implying that this transition is extremely unlikely to happen. Practically, implementing a CRF has three main steps. The first step is modifying the score generated by the BiLSTM layer and accounting for the transition weights, as shown above. A sequence of predictions

$$\boldsymbol{y} = (y_1, y_2, \ldots, y_n)$$

generated by the BiLSTM layer above for a sequence of n tags in the space of k unique tags is available, which operates on an input sequence X. P represents a matrix of dimensions $n \times k$, where the element $P_{i,j}$ represents the probability of jth tag for output at the position y_i. Let A be a square matrix of transition probabilities as shown above, with a dimension of $(k + 2) \times (k + 2)$ where two additional tokens are added for start- and end-of-sentence markers. Element $A_{i,j}$ represents the transition probability from i to tag j. Using these values, a new score can be calculated like so:

$$s(\boldsymbol{X}, \boldsymbol{y}) = \sum_{i=0}^{n} A_{y_i, y_{i+1}} + \sum_{i=1}^{n} P_{i, y_i}$$

A softmax can be calculated over all possible tag sequences to get the probability for a given sequence y:

$$p(y|X) = \frac{e^{s(X,y)}}{\sum \tilde{y} \in Y_X e^{s(X,\tilde{y})}}$$

Y_x represents all possible tag sequences, including those that may not conform to the IOB tag format. To train using this softmax, a log-likelihood can be calculated over this. Through clever use of dynamic programming, a combinatorial explosion can be avoided, and the denominator can be computed quite efficiently.

> Only simplistic math is shown to help build an intuition of how this method works. The actual computations will become clear in the custom layer implementation below.

While decoding, the output sequence is the one that has the maximum score among these possible sequences, calculated conceptually using an `argmax` style function. The Viterbi algorithm is commonly used to implement a dynamic programming solution for decoding. First, let us code the model and the training for it before getting into decoding.

NER with BiLSTM and CRFs

Implementing a BiLSTM network with CRFs requires adding a CRF layer on top of the BiLSTM network developed above. However, a CRF is not a core part of the TensorFlow or Keras layers. It is available through the `tensorflow_addons` or `tfa` package. The first step is to install this package:

```
!pip install tensorflow_addons==0.11.2
```

There are many sub-packages, but the convenience functions for the CRF are in the `tfa.text` subpackage:

Figure 3.3: tfa.text methods

While low-level methods for implementing the CRF layer are provided, a high-level layer-like construct is not provided. The implementation of a CRF requires a custom layer, a loss function, and a training loop. Post training, we will look at how to implement a customized inference function that will use Viterbi decoding.

Implementing the custom CRF layer, loss, and model

Similar to the flow above, there will be an embedding layer and a BiLSTM layer. The output of the BiLSTM needs to be evaluated with the CRF log-likelihood loss described above. This is the loss that needs to be used to train the model. The first step in implementation is creating a custom layer. Implementing a custom layer in Keras requires subclassing `keras.layers.Layer`. The main method to be implemented is `call()`, which takes inputs to the layer, transforms them, and returns the result. Additionally, the constructor to the layer can also set up any parameters that are needed. Let's start with the constructor:

```python
from tensorflow.keras.layers import Layer
from tensorflow.keras import backend as K

class CRFLayer(Layer):
    """
    Computes the log likelihood during training
    Performs Viterbi decoding during prediction
    """
    def __init__(self,
                 label_size, mask_id=0,
                 trans_params=None, name='crf',
                 **kwargs):
        super(CRFLayer, self).__init__(name=name, **kwargs)
        self.label_size = label_size
        self.mask_id = mask_id
        self.transition_params = None

        if trans_params is None:  # not reloading pretrained params
            self.transition_params = tf.Variable(
tf.random.uniform(shape=(label_size, label_size)),
                trainable=False)
        else:
            self.transition_params = trans_params
```

The main parameters that are needed are:

- **The number of labels and the transition matrix**: As described in the section above, a transition matrix needs to be learned. The dimension of that square matrix is the number of labels. The transition matrix is initialized using the parameters. This transition parameters matrix is not trainable through gradient descent. It is calculated as a consequence of computing the log-likelihoods. The transition parameters matrix can also be passed into this layer if it has been learned in the past.

- **The mask id**: Since the sequences are padded, it is important to recover the original sequence lengths for computing transition scores. By convention, a value of 0 is used for the mask, and that is the default. This parameter is set up for future configurability.

The second method is to compute the result of applying this layer. Note that as a layer, the CRF layer merely regurgitates the outputs during training time. The CRF layer is useful only during inference. At inference time, it uses the transition matrix and logic to correct the sequences' output by the BiLSTM layers before returning them. For now, this method is quite simple:

```
def call(self, inputs, seq_lengths, training=None):

    if training is None:
        training = K.learning_phase()

    # during training, this layer just returns the logits
    if training:
        return inputs
    return inputs    # to be replaced later
```

This method takes the inputs as well as a parameter that helps specify if this method is called during training or during inference. If this variable is not passed, it is pulled from the Keras backend. When models are trained with the `fit()` method, `learning_phase()` returns `True`. When the `.predict()` method is called on a model, this flag is set to `false`.

As sequences being passed are masked, this layer needs to know the real sequence lengths during inference time for decoding. A variable is passed for it but is unused at this time. Now that the basic CRF layer is ready, let's build the model.

A custom CRF model

Since the model builds on a number of preexisting layers in addition to the custom CRF layer above, explicit imports help the readability of the code:

```
from tensorflow.keras import Model, Input, Sequential
from tensorflow.keras.layers import LSTM, Embedding, Dense,
TimeDistributed
from tensorflow.keras.layers import Dropout, Bidirectional
from tensorflow.keras import backend as K
```

The first step is to define a constructor that will create the various layers and store the appropriate dimensions:

```
class NerModel(tf.keras.Model):
    def __init__(self, hidden_num, vocab_size, label_size,
                 embedding_size,
                 name='BilstmCrfModel', **kwargs):
        super(NerModel, self).__init__(name=name, **kwargs)
        self.num_hidden = hidden_num
        self.vocab_size = vocab_size
        self.label_size = label_size

        self.embedding = Embedding(vocab_size, embedding_size,
                                   mask_zero=True,
                                   name="embedding")
        self.biLSTM =Bidirectional(LSTM(hidden_num,
                                   return_sequences=True),
                                   name="bilstm")
        self.dense = TimeDistributed(tf.keras.layers.Dense(
                                   label_size), name="dense")
        self.crf = CRFLayer(self.label_size, name="crf")
```

This constructor takes in the number of hidden units for the BiLSTM later, the size of words in the vocabulary, the number of NER labels, and the size of the embeddings. Additionally, a default name is set by the constructor, which can be overridden at the time of instantiation. Any additional parameters supplied are passed along as keyword arguments.

During training and prediction, the following method will be called:

```python
def call(self, text, labels=None, training=None):
        seq_lengths = tf.math.reduce_sum(
tf.cast(tf.math.not_equal(text, 0), dtype=tf.int32), axis=-1)

        if training is None:
            training = K.learning_phase()

        inputs = self.embedding(text)
        bilstm = self.biLSTM(inputs)
        logits = self.dense(bilstm)
        outputs = self.crf(logits, seq_lengths, training)

        return outputs
```

So, in a few lines of code, we have implemented a customer model using the custom CRF layer developed above. The only thing that we need now to train this model is a loss function.

A custom loss function for NER using a CRF

Let's implement the loss function as part of the CRF layer, encapsulated in a function of the same name. Note that when this function is called, it is usually passed the labels and predicted values. We will model our loss function on the custom loss functions in TensorFlow. Add this code to the CRF layer class:

```python
def loss(self, y_true, y_pred):
    y_pred = tf.convert_to_tensor(y_pred)
    y_true = tf.cast(self.get_proper_labels(y_true), y_pred.dtype)

    seq_lengths = self.get_seq_lengths(y_true)
    log_likelihoods, self.transition_params =\
tfa.text.crf_log_likelihood(y_pred,
            y_true, seq_lengths)

    # save transition params
    self.transition_params = tf.Variable(self.transition_params,
      trainable=False)
    # calc loss
    loss = - tf.reduce_mean(log_likelihoods)
    return loss
```

This function takes the true labels and predicted labels. Both of these tensors are usually of the shape (batch size, max sequence length, number of NER labels). However, the log-likelihood function in the `tfa` package expects the labels to be in a (batch size, max sequence length)-shaped tensor. So a convenience function, implemented as part of the CRF layer and shown below, is used to perform the conversion of label shapes:

```
def get_proper_labels(self, y_true):
    shape = y_true.shape
    if len(shape) > 2:
        return tf.argmax(y_true, -1, output_type=tf.int32)
    return y_true
```

The log-likelihood function also requires the actual sequence lengths for each example. These sequence lengths can be computed from the labels and the mask identifier that was set up in the constructor of this layer (see above). This process is encapsulated in another convenience function, also part of the CRF layer:

```
def get_seq_lengths(self, matrix):
    # matrix is of shape (batch_size, max_seq_Len)
    mask = tf.not_equal(matrix, self.mask_id)
    seq_lengths = tf.math.reduce_sum(
                            tf.cast(mask, dtype=tf.int32),
                            axis=-1)

    return seq_lengths
```

First, a Boolean mask is generated from the labels by comparing the value of the label to the mask ID. Then, through casting the Boolean as an integer and summing across the row, the length of the sequence is regenerated. Now, the `tfa.text.crf_log_likelihood()` function is called to calculate and return the log-likelihoods and the transition matrix. The CRF layer's transition matrix is updated with the transition matrix returned from the function call. Finally, the loss is computed by summing up all the log-likelihoods returned.

At this point, our coded custom model is ready to start training. We will need to set up the data and create a custom training loop.

Implementing custom training

The model needs to be instantiated and initialized for training:

```
# Length of the vocabulary
vocab_size = len(text_vocab) + 1
```

```
# The embedding dimension
embedding_dim = 64

# Number of RNN units
rnn_units = 100

#batch size
BATCH_SIZE=90

# num of NER classes
num_classes = len(ner_vocab) + 1

blc_model = NerModel(rnn_units, vocab_size, num_classes,
embedding_dim, dynamic=True)
optimizer = tf.keras.optimizers.Adam(learning_rate=1e-3)
```

As in past examples, an Adam optimizer will be used. Next, we will construct `tf.data.DataSet` from the DataFrames loaded in the BiLSTM section above:

```
# create training and testing splits
total_sentences = 62010
test_size = round(total_sentences / BATCH_SIZE * 0.2)
X_train = x_pad[BATCH_SIZE*test_size:]
Y_train = Y[BATCH_SIZE*test_size:]

X_test = x_pad[0:BATCH_SIZE*test_size]
Y_test = Y[0:BATCH_SIZE*test_size]
Y_train_int = tf.cast(Y_train, dtype=tf.int32)

train_dataset = tf.data.Dataset.from_tensor_slices((X_train,
Y_train_int))
train_dataset = train_dataset.batch(BATCH_SIZE,
drop_remainder=True)
```

Roughly 20% of the data is reserved for testing. The rest is used for training.

To implement a custom training loop, TensorFlow 2.0 exposes a gradient tape. This allows low-level management of the main steps required for training any model with gradient descent. These steps are:

1. Computing the forward pass predictions
2. Computing the loss when these predictions are compared with the labels

3. Computing the gradients for the trainable parameters based on the loss and then using the optimizer to adjust the weights

Let us train this model for 5 epochs and watch the loss as training progresses. Compare this to the 15 epochs of training for the previous model. The custom training loop is shown below:

```python
loss_metric = tf.keras.metrics.Mean()

epochs = 5

# Iterate over epochs.
for epoch in range(epochs):
    print('Start of epoch %d' % (epoch,))

    # Iterate over the batches of the dataset.
    for step, (text_batch, labels_batch) in enumerate(
train_dataset):
        labels_max = tf.argmax(labels_batch, -1,
output_type=tf.int32)
        with tf.GradientTape() as tape:
            logits = blc_model(text_batch, training=True)
            loss = blc_model.crf.loss(labels_max, logits)

            grads = tape.gradient(loss,
blc_model.trainable_weights)
            optimizer.apply_gradients(zip(grads,
blc_model.trainable_weights))

            loss_metric(loss)
        if step % 50 == 0:
            print('step %s: mean loss = %s' %
(step, loss_metric.result()))
```

A metric is created to keep track of the average loss over time. For 5 epochs, inputs and labels are pulled from the training data set, one batch at a time. Using tf.GradientTape() to keep track of the operations, the steps outlined in the bullets above are implemented. Note that we pass the trainable variable manually as this is a custom training loop. Finally, the loss metric is printed every 50th step to show training progress. This yields the results below, which have been abbreviated:

```
Start of epoch 0
step 0: mean loss = tf.Tensor(71.14853, shape=(), dtype=float32)
```

```
step 50: mean loss = tf.Tensor(31.064453, shape=(), dtype=float32)
...
Start of epoch 4
step 0: mean loss = tf.Tensor(4.4125915, shape=(), dtype=float32)
step 550: mean loss = tf.Tensor(3.8311224, shape=(), dtype=float32)
```

Given we implemented a custom training loop, without requiring a compilation of the model, we could not obtain a summary of the model parameters before. To get an idea of the size of the model, a summary can be obtained now:

```
blc_model.summary()
```

```
Model: "BilstmCrfModel"

_____
Layer (type)                Output Shape              Param #
====================================================================
embedding (Embedding)       multiple                  2523072

_____
bilstm (Bidirectional)      multiple                  132000

_____
dense (TimeDistributed)     multiple                  3819

_____
crf (CRFLayer)              multiple                  361
====================================================================
Total params: 2,659,252
Trainable params: 2,658,891
Non-trainable params: 361

_____
```

It is comparable in size to the previous model but has some untrainable parameters. These are coming from the transition matrix. The transition matrix is not learned through gradient descent. Thus, they are classified as non-trainable parameters.

However, training loss is hard to interpret. To compute accuracy, we need to implement decoding, which is the focus of the next section. For the moment, let's assume that decoding is available and examine the results of training for 5 epochs. For illustration purposes, here is a sentence from the test set with the results pulled at the end of the first epoch and at the end of five epochs.

The example sentence is:

```
Writing in The Washington Post newspaper , Mr. Ushakov also
said it is inadmissible to move in the direction of demonizing Russia .
```

The corresponding true label is:

```
O O B-org I-org I-org O O B-per B-org O O O O O O O O O O O B-geo O
```

This is a difficult example for NER with *The Washington Post* as a three-word organization, where the first word is very common and used in multiple contexts, and the second word is also the name of a geographical location. Also note the imperfect labels of the GMB data set, where the second tag of the name *Ushakov* is tagged as an organization. At the end of the first epoch of training, the model predicts:

```
O O O B-geo I-org O O B-per I-per O O O O O O O O O O O B-geo O
```

It gets confused by the organization not being where it expects it to be. It also shows that it hasn't learned the transition probabilities by putting an I-org tag after a B-geo tag. However, it does not make a mistake in the person portion. Unfortunately for the model, it will not get credit for this great prediction of the person tag, and due to imperfect labels, it will still count as a miss. The result after five epochs of training is better than the original:

```
O O B-org I-org I-org O O B-per I-per O O O O O O O O O O O B-geo O
```

This is a great result, given the limited amount of training we have done. Now, let's see how we can decode the sentence in the CRF layer to get these sequences. The algorithm used for decoding is called the Viterbi decoder.

Viterbi decoding

A straightforward way to predict the sequence of labels is to output the label that has the highest activation from the previous layers of the network. However, this could be sub-optimal as it assumes that each label prediction is independent of the previous or successive predictions. The Viterbi algorithm is used to take the predictions for each word in the sequence and apply a maximization algorithm so that the output sequence has the highest likelihood. In future chapters, we will see another way of accomplishing the same objective through beam search. Viterbi decoding involves maximizing over the entire sequence as opposed to optimizing at each word of the sequence. To illustrate this algorithm and way of thinking, let's take an example of a sentence of 5 words, and a set of 3 labels. These labels could be O, B-geo, and I-geo as an example.

This algorithm needs the transition matrix values between labels. Recall that this was generated and stored in the custom CRF layer above. Let's say that the matrix looks like so:

From > To	Mask	O	B-geo	I-geo
Mask	0.6	0.3	0.2	0.01
O	0.8	0.5	0.6	0.01
B-geo	0.2	0.4	0.01	0.7
I-geo	0.3	0.4	0.01	0.5

To explain how the algorithm works, the figure shown below will be used:

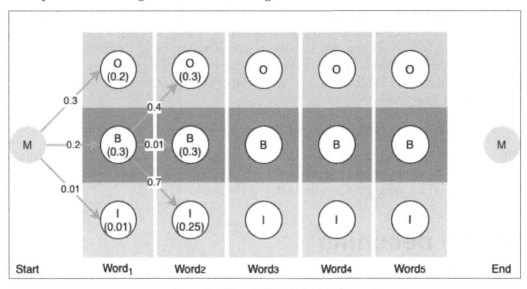

Figure 3.4: Steps in the Viterbi decoder

The sentence starts from the left. Arrows from the start of the word to the first token represent the probability of the transition between the two tokens. The numbers on the arrows should match the values in the transition matrix above. Within the circles denoting labels, scores generated by the neural network, the BiLSTM model, in our case, are shown for the first word. These scores need to be added together to give the final score of the words. Note that we switched the terminology from probabilities to scores as normalization is not being performed for this particular example.

The probability of the first word label

Score of *O*: 0.3 (transition score) + 0.2 (activation score) = 0.5

Score of *B-geo*: 0.2 (transition score) + 0.3 (activation score) = 0.5

Score of *I-geo*: 0.01 (transition score) + 0.01 (activation score) = 0.02

At this point, it is equally likely that an *O* or *B-geo* tag will be the starting tag. Let's consider the next tag and calculate the scores using the same approach for the following sequences:

(*O, B-geo*) = 0.6 + 0.3 = 0.9	(*B-geo, O*) = 0.4 + 0.3 = 0.7
(*O, I-geo*) = 0.01 + 0.25 = 0.26	(*B-geo, B-geo*) = 0.01 + 0.3 = 0.31
(*O, O*) = 0.5 + 0.3 = 0.8	(*B-geo, I-geo*) = 0.7 + 0.25 = 0.95

This process is called the forward pass. It should also be noted, even though this is a contrived example, that activations at a given input may not be the best predictor of the right label for that word once the previous labels have been considered. If the sentence was only two words, then the scores for various sequences could be calculated by summing by each step:

(*Start, O, B-Geo*) = 0.5 + 0.9 = 1.4	(*Start, B-Geo, O*) = 0.5 + 0.7 = 1.2
(*Start, O, O*) = 0.5 + 0.8 = 1.3	(*Start, B-geo, B-geo*) = 0.5 + 0.31 = 0.81
(*Start, O, I-Geo*) = 0.5 + 0.26 = 0.76	(*Start, B-geo, I-geo*) = 0.5 + 0.95) = 1.45

If only the activation scores were considered, the most probable sequences would be either (*Start, B-geo, O*) or (*Start, B-geo, B-geo*). However, using the transition scores along with the activations means that the sequence with the highest probability is (*Start, B-geo, I-geo*) in this example. While the forward pass gives the highest score of the entire sequence given the last token, the backward pass process would reconstruct the sequence that resulted in this highest score. This is essentially the Viterbi algorithm, which uses dynamic programming to perform these steps in an efficient manner.

Implementing this algorithm is aided by the fact the core computation is provided as a method in the `tfa` package. This decoding step will be implemented in the `call()` method of the CRF layer implemented above. Modify this method to look like so:

```
def call(self, inputs, seq_lengths, training=None):
  if training is None:
      training = K.learning_phase()

  # during training, this layer just returns the logits
```

```
if training:
    return inputs

# viterbi decode logic to return proper
# results at inference
_, max_seq_len, _ = inputs.shape
seqlens = seq_lengths
paths = []
for logit, text_len in zip(inputs, seqlens):
    viterbi_path, _ = tfa.text.viterbi_decode(logit[:text_len],
                                    self.transition_params)
    paths.append(self.pad_viterbi(viterbi_path, max_seq_len))

return tf.convert_to_tensor(paths)
```

The new lines added have been highlighted. The `viterbi_decode()` method takes the activations from the previous layers and the transition matrix along with the maximum sequence length to compute the path with the highest score. This score is also returned, but we ignore it for our purposes of inference. This process needs to be performed for each sequence in the batch. Note that this method returns sequences on different lengths. This makes it harder to convert into tensors, so a utility function is used to pad the returned sequences:

```
def pad_viterbi(self, viterbi, max_seq_len):
    if len(viterbi) < max_seq_len:
        viterbi = viterbi + [self.mask_id] * \
                            (max_seq_len - len(viterbi))
    return viterbi
```

A dropout layer works completely opposite to the way this CRF layer works. A dropout layer modifies the inputs only during training time. During inference, it merely passes all the inputs through.

Our CRF layer works in the exact opposite fashion. It passes the inputs through during training, but it transforms inputs using the Viterbi decoder during inference time. Note the use of the `training` parameter to control the behavior.

Now that the layer is modified and ready, the model needs to be re-instantiated and trained. Post-training, inference can be performed like so:

```
Y_test_int = tf.cast(Y_test, dtype=tf.int32)

test_dataset = tf.data.Dataset.from_tensor_slices((X_test,
                                                    Y_test_int))
test_dataset = test_dataset.batch(BATCH_SIZE, drop_remainder=True)

out = blc_model.predict(test_dataset.take(1))
```

This will run inference on a small batch of testing data. Let's check the result for the example sentence:

```
text_tok.sequences_to_texts([X_test[2]])
```

```
['Writing in The Washington Post newspaper , Mr. Ushakov also said it
is inadmissible to move in the direction of demonizing Russia . <OOV>
<OOV> <OOV> <OOV> <OOV> <OOV> <OOV> <OOV> <OOV> <OOV> <OOV> <OOV> <OOV>
<OOV> <OOV> <OOV> <OOV> <OOV> <OOV> <OOV> <OOV> <OOV> <OOV> <OOV> <OOV>
<OOV> <OOV>']
```

As we can see in the highlighted output, the results are better than the actual data!

```
print("Ground Truth: ",
ner_tok.sequences_to_texts([tf.argmax(Y_test[2],
                                      -1).numpy()]))
print("Prediction: ", ner_tok.sequences_to_texts([out[2]]))
```

```
Ground Truth:   ['O O B-org I-org I-org O O B-per B-org O O O O O O O
O O O O B-geo O <OOV> <SNIP> <OOV>']
Prediction:   ['O O B-org I-org I-org O O B-per I-per O O O O O O O O
O O O B-geo O <OOV> <SNIP> <OOV>']
```

To get a sense of the accuracy of the training, a custom method needs to be implemented. This is shown below:

```
def np_precision(pred, true):
    # expect numpy arrays
    assert pred.shape == true.shape
    assert len(pred.shape) == 2
    mask_pred = np.ma.masked_equal(pred, 0)
    mask_true = np.ma.masked_equal(true, 0)
    acc = np.equal(mask_pred, mask_true)
    return np.mean(acc.compressed().astype(int))
```

Using numpy's MaskedArray feature, the predictions and labels are compared and converted to an integer array, and the mean is calculated to compute the accuracy:

```
np_precision(out, tf.argmax(Y_test[:BATCH_SIZE], -1).numpy())
```

```
0.9664461247637051
```

This is a pretty accurate model, just after 5 epochs of training and with very simple architecture, all while using embeddings that are trained from scratch. A recall metric can also be implemented in a similar fashion. A BiLSTM-only model, shown earlier, took 15 epochs of training to get to a similar accuracy!

This completes the implementation of an NER model using BiLSTMs and CRFs. If this is interesting and you would like to continue working on this, look for the CoNLL 2003 data set for NER. Even today, papers are being published that aim to improve the accuracy of the models based on that data set.

Summary

We have covered quite a lot of ground in this chapter. NER and its importance in the industry were explained. To build NER models, BiLSTMs and CRFs are needed. Using BiLSTMs, which we learned about in the previous chapter while building a sentiment classification model, we built a first version of a model that can label named entities. This model was further improved using CRFs. In the process of building these models, we covered the use of the TensorFlow DataSet API. We also built advanced models for CRF mode by building a custom Keras layer, a custom model, custom loss function, and a custom training loop.

Thus far, we have trained embeddings for tokens in the models. A considerable amount of lift can be achieved by using pre-trained embeddings. In the next chapter, we'll focus on the concept of transfer learning and the use of pre-trained embeddings like BERT.

4

Transfer Learning with BERT

Deep learning models really shine with large amounts of training data. Having enough labeled data is a constant challenge in the field, especially in NLP. A successful approach that has yielded great results in the last couple of years is that of transfer learning. A model is trained in an unsupervised or semi-supervised way on a large corpus and then fine-tuned for a specific application. Such models have shown excellent results. In this chapter, we will build on the IMDb movie review sentiment analysis and use transfer learning to build models using **GloVe (Global Vectors for Word Representation)** pre-trained embeddings and **BERT (Bi-Directional Encoder Representations from Transformers)** contextual models. In this chapter, we will cover the following topics:

- Overview of transfer learning and use in NLP
- Loading pre-trained GloVe embeddings in a model
- Building a sentiment analysis model using pre-trained GloVe embeddings and fine-tuning
- Overview of contextual embeddings using Attention – BERT
- Loading pre-trained BERT models using the Hugging Face library
- Using pre-trained and custom BERT-based fine-tuned models for sentiment analysis

Transfer learning is a core concept that has made rapid advances in NLP possible. We will discuss transfer learning first.

Transfer learning overview

Traditionally, a machine learning model is trained for performance on a specific task. It is only expected to work for that task and is not likely to have high performance beyond that task. Let's take the example of the problem of classifying the sentiment of IMDb movie reviews *Chapter 2, Understanding Sentiment in Natural Language with BiLSTMs*. The model that was trained for this particular task was optimized for performance on this task alone. A separate set of labeled data specific to a different task is required if we wish to train another model. Building another model might not be effective if there isn't enough labeled data for that task.

Transfer learning is the concept of learning a fundamental representation of the data that can be adapted to different tasks. In the case of transfer learning, a more abundantly available dataset may be used to distill knowledge and in building a new ML model for a specific task. Through the use of this knowledge, this new ML model can have decent performance even when there is not enough labeled data available for a traditional ML approach to return good results. For this scheme to be effective, there are a few important considerations:

- The knowledge distillation step, called **pre-training**, should have an abundant amount of data available relatively cheaply

- Adaptation, often called fine-tuning, should be done with data that shares similarities with the data used for pre-training

The figure below illustrates this concept:

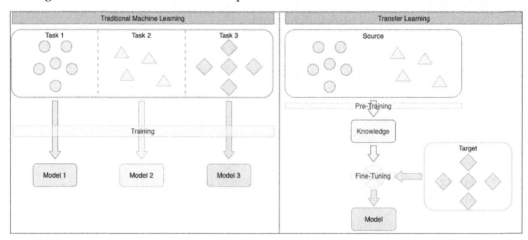

Figure 4.1: Comparing traditional machine learning with transfer learning

This technique has been very effective in computer vision. ImageNet is often used as the dataset for pre-training. Specific models are then fine-tuned for a variety of tasks such as image classification, object detection, image segmentation, and pose detection, among others.

Types of transfer learning

The concepts of **domains** and **tasks** underpin the concept of transfer learning. A domain represents a specific area of knowledge or data. News articles, social media posts, medical records, Wikipedia entries, and court judgments could be considered examples of different domains. A task is a specific objective or action within a domain. Sentiment analysis and stance detection of tweets are specific tasks in the social media posts domain. Detection of cancer and fractures could be different tasks in the domain of medical records. Different types of transfer learning have different combinations of source and target domains and tasks. Three main types of transfer learning, namely domain adaptation, multi-task learning, and sequential learning, are described below.

Domain adaptation

In this setting, the domains of source and target tasks are usually the same. However, the differences are related to the distribution of training and testing data. This case of transfer learning is related to a fundamental assumption in any machine learning task – the assumption that training and testing data are *i.i.d.* The first *i* stands for *independent*, which implies that each sample is independent of the others. In practice, this assumption can be violated when there are feedback loops, like in recommendation systems. The second section is *i.d.*, which stands for *identically distributed* and implies that the distribution of labels and other characteristics between training and test samples is the same.

Suppose the domain was animal photos, and the task was identifying cats in the photos. This task can be modeled as a binary classification problem. The identically distributed assumption implies that the distribution of cats in the photos between training and test samples is similar. This also implies that characteristics of photos, such as resolutions, lighting conditions, and orientations, are very similar. In practice, this assumption is also frequently violated.

There is a case about a very early perceptron model built to identify tanks in the woods. The model was performing quite well on the training set. When the test set was expanded, it was discovered that all the pictures of tanks in woods were taken on sunny days, whereas the pictures of woods without tanks were taken on a cloudy day.

In this case, the network learned to differentiate sunny and cloudy conditions more than the presence or absence of tanks. During testing, the pictures supplied were from a different distribution, but the same domain, which led to the model failing.

Dealing with similar situations is called domain adaptation. There are many techniques for domain adaptation, one of which is data augmentation. In computer vision, images in the training set can be cropped, warped, or rotated, and varying amounts of exposure or contrast or saturation can be applied to them. These transformations would increase the training data and could mitigate the gap between training and potential testing data. Similar techniques are used in speech and audio by adding random noises, including street sounds or background chatter, to an audio sample. Domain adaptation techniques are well known in traditional machine learning with several resources already available on it.

However, what makes transfer learning exciting is using data from a different source domain or task for pre-training results in improvements in model performance on a different task or domain. There are two types of transfer learning in this area. The first one is multi-task learning, and the second one is sequential learning.

Multi-task learning

In multi-task learning, data from different but related tasks are passed through a set of common layers. Then, there may be task-specific layers on the top that learn about a particular task objective. *Figure 4.2* shows the multi-task learning setting:

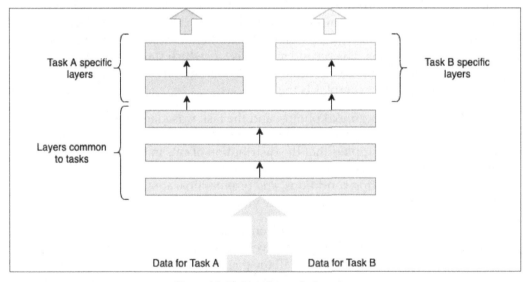

Figure 4.2: Multi-task transfer learning

The output of these task-specific layers would be evaluated on different loss functions. All the training examples for all the tasks are passed through all the layers of the model. The task-specific layers are not expected to do well for all the tasks. The expectation is that the common layers learn some of the underlying structure that is shared by the different tasks. This information about structure provides useful signals and improves the performance of all the models. The data for each task has many features. However, these features may be used to construct representations that can be useful in other related tasks.

Intuitively, people learn some elementary skills before mastering more complex skills. Learning to write requires first becoming skilled in holding a pen or pencil. Writing, drawing, and painting can be considered different tasks that share a standard "layer" of holding a pen or pencil. The same concept applies while learning a new language where the structure and grammar of one language may help with learning a related language. Learning Latin-based languages like French, Italian, and Spanish becomes more comfortable if one of the other Latin languages is known, as these languages share word roots.

Multi-task learning increases the amount of data available for training by pooling data from different tasks together. Further, it forces the network to generalize better by trying to learn representations that are common across tasks in shared layers.

Multi-task learning is a crucial reason behind the recent success of models such as GPT-2 and BERT. It is the most common technique used for pre-training models that are then used for specific tasks.

Sequential learning

Sequential learning is the most common form of transfer learning. It is named so because it involves two simple steps executed in sequence. The first step is pre-training and the second step is fine-tuning. These steps are shown in *Figure 4.3*:

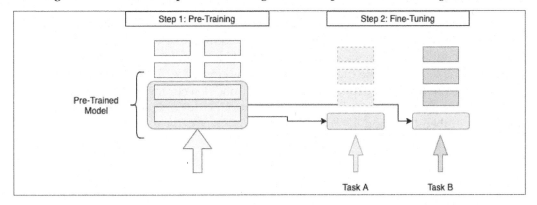

Figure 4.3: Sequential learning

The first step is to pre-train a model. The most successful pre-trained models use some form of multi-task learning objectives, as depicted on the left side of the figure. A portion of the model used for pre-training is then used for different tasks shown on the right in the figure. This reusable part of the pre-trained model depends on the specific architecture and may have a different set of layers. The reusable partition shown in *Figure 4.3* is just illustrative. In the second step, the pre-trained model is loaded and added as the starting layer of a task-specific model. The weights learned by the pre-trained model can be frozen during the training of the task-specific model, or those weights can be updated or fine-tuned. When the weights are frozen, then this pattern of using the pre-trained model is called *feature extraction*.

Generally, fine-tuning gives better performance than a feature extraction approach. However, there are some pros and cons to both approaches. In fine-tuning, not all weights get updated as the task-specific training data may be much smaller in size. If the pre-trained model is an embedding for words, then other embeddings can become stale. If the task is such that it has a small vocabulary or has many out-of-vocabulary words, then this can hurt the performance of the model. Generally, if the source and target tasks are similar, then fine-tuning would produce better results.

An example of such a pre-trained model is Word2vec, which we saw in *Chapter 1, Essentials of NLP*. There is another model of generating word-level embeddings called **GloVe** or **Global Vectors for Word Representation**, introduced in 2014 by researchers from Stanford. Let's take a practical tour of transfer learning by re-building the IMDb movie sentiment analysis using GloVe embeddings in the next section. After that, we shall take a tour of BERT and apply BERT in the same sequential learning setting.

IMDb sentiment analysis with GloVe embeddings

In *Chapter 2, Understanding Sentiment in Natural Language with BiLSTMs*, a BiLSTM model was built to predict the sentiment of IMDb movie reviews. That model learned embeddings of the words from scratch. This model had an accuracy of 83.55% on the test set, while the SOTA result was closer to 97.4%. If pre-trained embeddings are used, we expect an increase in model accuracy. Let's try this out and see the impact of transfer learning on this model. But first, let's understand the GloVe embedding model.

GloVe embeddings

In *Chapter 1, Essentials of NLP*, we discussed the Word2Vec algorithm, which is based on skip-grams with negative sampling. The GloVe model came out in 2014, a year after the Word2Vec paper came out. The GloVe and Word2Vec models are similar as the embeddings generated for a word are determined by the words that occur around it. However, these context words occur with different frequencies. Some of these context words appear more frequently in the text compared to other words. Due to this difference in frequencies of occurrence, training data for some words may be more common than other words.

Beyond this part, Word2Vec does not use these statistics of co-occurrence in any way. GloVe takes these frequencies into account and posits that the co-occurrences provide vital information. The *Global* part of the name refers to the fact that the model considers these co-occurrences over the entire corpus. Rather than focus on the probabilities of co-occurrence, GloVe focuses on the ratios of co-occurrence considering probe words.

In the paper, the authors take the example of the words *ice* and *steam* to illustrate the concept. Let's say that *solid* is another word that is going to be used to probe the relationship between ice and steam. A probability of occurrence of solid given steam is $p_{solid \mid steam}$. Intuitively, we expect this probability to be small. Conversely, the probability of occurrence of solid with ice is represented by $p_{solid \mid ice}$ and is expected to be large. If $\dfrac{P_{solid \mid ice}}{P_{solid \mid steam}}$ is computed, we expect this value to be significant. If the same ratio is computed with the probe word being gas, the opposite behavior would be expected. In cases where both are equally probable, either due to the probe word being unrelated, or equally probable to occur with the two words, then the ratio should be closer to 1. An example of a probe word close to both ice and steam is *water*. An example of a word unrelated to ice or steam is *fashion*. GloVe ensures that this relationship is factored into the embeddings generated for the words. It also has optimizations for rare co-occurrences, numerical stability issues computation, and others.

Now let us see how to use these pre-trained embeddings for predicting sentiment. The first step is to load the data. The code here is identical to the code used in *Chapter 2, Understanding Sentiment in Natural Language with BiLSTMs*; it's provided here for the sake of completeness.

All the code for this exercise is in the file `imdb-transfer-learning.ipynb` located in the `chapter4-Xfer-learning-BERT` directory in GitHub.

Loading IMDb training data

TensorFlow Datasets or the `tfds` package will be used to load the data:

```
import tensorflow as tf
import tensorflow_datasets as tfds
import numpy as np
import pandas as pd


imdb_train, ds_info = tfds.load(name="imdb_reviews",
                        split="train",
                        with_info=True, as_supervised=True)

imdb_test = tfds.load(name="imdb_reviews", split="test",
                        as_supervised=True)
```

Note that the additional 50,000 reviews that are unlabeled are ignored for the purpose of this exercise. After the training and test sets are loaded as shown above, the content of the reviews needs to be tokenized and encoded:

```
# Use the default tokenizer settings
tokenizer = tfds.features.text.Tokenizer()

vocabulary_set = set()
MAX_TOKENS = 0

for example, label in imdb_train:
  some_tokens = tokenizer.tokenize(example.numpy())
  if MAX_TOKENS < len(some_tokens):
            MAX_TOKENS = len(some_tokens)
  vocabulary_set.update(some_tokens)
```

The code shown above tokenizes the review text and constructs a vocabulary. This vocabulary is used to construct a tokenizer:

```
imdb_encoder = tfds.features.text.TokenTextEncoder(vocabulary_set,
                                        lowercase=True,
                                        tokenizer=tokenizer)

vocab_size = imdb_encoder.vocab_size

print(vocab_size, MAX_TOKENS)
```

```
93931 2525
```

Note that text was converted to lowercase before encoding. Converting to lowercase helps reduce the vocabulary size and may benefit the lookup of corresponding GloVe vectors later on. Note that capitalization may contain important information, which may help in tasks such as NER, which we covered in previous chapters. Also note that all languages do not distinguish between capital and small letters. Hence, this particular transformation should be applied after due consideration.

Now that the tokenizer is ready, the data needs to be tokenized, and sequences padded to a maximum length. Since we are interested in comparing performance with the model trained in *Chapter 2, Understanding Sentiment in Natural Language with BiLSTMs*, we can use the same setting of sampling a maximum of 150 words of the review. The following convenience methods help in performing this task:

```python
# transformation functions to be used with the dataset
from tensorflow.keras.preprocessing import sequence

def encode_pad_transform(sample):
    encoded = imdb_encoder.encode(sample.numpy())
    pad = sequence.pad_sequences([encoded], padding='post',
                                 maxlen=150)
    return np.array(pad[0], dtype=np.int64)


def encode_tf_fn(sample, label):
    encoded = tf.py_function(encode_pad_transform,
                             inp=[sample],
                             Tout=(tf.int64))
    encoded.set_shape([None])
    label.set_shape([])
    return encoded, label
```

Finally, the data is encoded using the convenience functions above like so:

```python
encoded_train = imdb_train.map(encode_tf_fn,
                  num_parallel_calls=tf.data.experimental.AUTOTUNE)
encoded_test = imdb_test.map(encode_tf_fn,
                  num_parallel_calls=tf.data.experimental.AUTOTUNE)
```

At this point, all the training and test data is ready for training.

 Note that in limiting the size of the reviews, only the first 150 tokens will be counted for a long review. Typically, the first few sentences of the review have the context or description, and the latter part of the review has the conclusion. By limiting to the first part of the review, valuable information could be lost. The reader is encouraged to try a different padding scheme where tokens from the first part of the review are dropped instead of the second part and observe the difference in the accuracy.

The next step is the foremost step in transfer learning – loading the pre-trained GloVe embeddings and using these as the weights of the embedding layer.

Loading pre-trained GloVe embeddings

First, the pre-trained embeddings need to be downloaded and unzipped:

```
# Download the GloVe embeddings
!wget http://nlp.stanford.edu/data/glove.6B.zip
!unzip glove.6B.zip

Archive:  glove.6B.zip
  inflating: glove.6B.50d.txt
  inflating: glove.6B.100d.txt
  inflating: glove.6B.200d.txt
  inflating: glove.6B.300d.txt
```

Note that this is a huge download of over 800 MB, so this step may take some time to execute. Upon unzipping, there will be four different files, as shown in the output above. Each file has a vocabulary of 400,000 words. The main difference is the dimensions of embeddings generated.

In the previous chapter, an embedding dimension of 64 was used for the model. The nearest GloVe dimension is 50, so let's use that. The file format is quite simple. Each line of the text has multiple values separated by spaces. The first item of each row is the word, and the rest of the items are the values of the vector for each dimension. So, in the 50-dimensional file, each row will have 51 columns. These vectors need to be loaded up in memory:

```
dict_w2v = {}
with open('glove.6B.50d.txt', "r") as file:
    for line in file:
```

```
        tokens = line.split()
        word = tokens[0]
        vector = np.array(tokens[1:], dtype=np.float32)

        if vector.shape[0] == 50:
            dict_w2v[word] = vector
        else:
            print("There was an issue with " + word)

# let's check the vocabulary size
print("Dictionary Size: ", len(dict_w2v))
```

```
Dictionary Size:  400000
```

If the code processed the file correctly, you shouldn't see any errors and you should see a dictionary size of 400,000 words. Once these vectors are loaded, an embedding matrix needs to be created.

Creating a pre-trained embedding matrix using GloVe

So far, we have a dataset, its vocabulary, and a dictionary of GloVe words and their corresponding vectors. However, there is no correlation between these two vocabularies. The way to connect them is through the creation of an embedding matrix. First, let's initialize an embedding matrix of zeros:

```
embedding_dim = 50
embedding_matrix = np.zeros((imdb_encoder.vocab_size, embedding_dim))
```

Note that this is a crucial step. When a pre-trained word list is used, finding a vector for each word in the training/test is not guaranteed. Recall the discussion on transfer learning earlier, where the source and target domains are different. One way this difference manifests itself is through having a mismatch in tokens between the training data and the pre-trained model. As we go through the next steps, this will become more apparent.

After this embedding matrix of zeros is initialized, it needs to be populated. For each word in the vocabulary of reviews, the corresponding vector is retrieved from the GloVe dictionary.

The ID of the word is retrieved using the encoder, and then the embedding matrix entry corresponding to that entry is set to the retrieved vector:

```
unk_cnt = 0
unk_set = set()
for word in imdb_encoder.tokens:
    embedding_vector = dict_w2v.get(word)

    if embedding_vector is not None:
        tkn_id = imdb_encoder.encode(word)[0]
        embedding_matrix[tkn_id] = embedding_vector
    else:
        unk_cnt += 1
        unk_set.add(word)

# Print how many weren't found
print("Total unknown words: ", unk_cnt)
```

```
Total unknown words:  14553
```

During the data loading step, we saw that the total number of tokens was 93,931. Out of these, 14,553 words could not be found, which is approximately 15% of the tokens. For these words, the embedding matrix will have zeros. This is the first step in transfer learning. Now that the setup is completed, we will need to use TensorFlow to use these pre-trained embeddings. There will be two different models that will be tried – the first will be based on feature extraction and the second one on fine-tuning.

Feature extraction model

As discussed earlier, the feature extraction model freezes the pre-trained weights and does not update them. An important issue with this approach in the current setup is that there are a large number of tokens, over 14,000, that have zero embedding vectors. These words could not be matched to an entry in the GloVe word list.

To minimize the chances of not finding matches between the pre-trained vocabulary and task-specific vocabulary, ensure that similar tokenization schemes are used. GloVe uses a word-based tokenization scheme like the one provided by the Stanford tokenizer. As seen in *Chapter 1, Essentials of NLP*, this works better than a whitespace tokenizer, which is used for the training data above. We see 15% unmatched tokens due to different tokenizers. As an exercise, the reader can implement the Stanford tokenizer and see the reduction in unknown tokens.

Newer methods like BERT use parts of subword tokenizers. Subword tokenization schemes can break up words into parts, which minimizes this chance of mismatch in tokens. Some examples of subword tokenization schemes are **Byte Pair Encoding (BPE)** or WordPiece tokenization. The BERT section of this chapter explains subword tokenization schemes in more detail.

If pre-trained vectors were not used, then the vectors for all the words would start with nearly zero and get trained through gradient descent. In this case, the vectors are already trained, so we expect the training to go along much faster. For a baseline, one epoch of training of the BiLSTM model while training embeddings takes between 65 seconds and 100 seconds, with most values around 63 seconds on an Ubuntu machine with an i5 processor and an Nvidia RTX-2070 GPU.

Now, let's build the model and plug in the embedding matrix generated above into the model. Some basic parameters need to be set up:

```
# Length of the vocabulary in chars
vocab_size = imdb_encoder.vocab_size # Len(chars)

# Number of RNN units
rnn_units = 64

#batch size
BATCH_SIZE=100
```

A convenience function being set up will enable fast switching. This method enables building models with the same architecture but different hyperparameters:

```
from tensorflow.keras.layers import Embedding, LSTM, \
                                     Bidirectional, Dense


def build_model_bilstm(vocab_size, embedding_dim,
                       rnn_units, batch_size, train_emb=False):
    model = tf.keras.Sequential([
      Embedding(vocab_size, embedding_dim, mask_zero=True,
                weights=[embedding_matrix], trainable=train_emb),
      Bidirectional(LSTM(rnn_units, return_sequences=True,
                                    dropout=0.5)),
      Bidirectional(LSTM(rnn_units, dropout=0.25)),
      Dense(1, activation='sigmoid')
    ])
    return model
```

The model is identical to what was used in the previous chapter with the exception of the highlighted code pieces above. First, a flag can now be passed to this method that specifies whether the embeddings should be trained further or frozen. This parameter is set to false as it's the default value. The second change is in the definition of the Embedding layer. A new parameter, weights, loads the embedding matrix as the weights for the layer. Just after this parameter, a Boolean parameter called trainable is passed that determines whether the weights of this layer should be updated during training time. A feature extraction-based model can now be created like so:

```
model_fe = build_model_bilstm(
    vocab_size = vocab_size,
    embedding_dim=embedding_dim,
    rnn_units=rnn_units,
    batch_size=BATCH_SIZE)

model_fe.summary()
```

```
Model: "sequential_5"

Layer (type)                  Output Shape             Param #
=================================================================
embedding_5 (Embedding)       (None, None, 50)         4696550

bidirectional_6 (Bidirection  (None, None, 128)        58880
```

```
bidirectional_7 (Bidirection (None, 128)           98816

dense_5 (Dense)              (None, 1)              129
=================================================================
Total params: 4,854,375
Trainable params: 157,825
Non-trainable params: 4,696,550
```

This model has about 4.8 million trainable parameters. It should be noted that this model is considerably smaller than the previous BiLSTM model, which had over 12 million parameters. A simpler or smaller model will train faster and possibly be less likely to overfit as the model capacity is lower.

This model needs to be compiled with the loss function, optimizer, and metrics for observation progress of the model. Binary cross-entropy is the right loss function for this problem of binary classification. The Adam optimizer is a decent choice in most cases.

Adaptive Moment Estimation or Adam Optimizer

The simplest optimization algorithm used in backpropagation for the training of deep neural networks is mini-batch **Stochastic Gradient Descent (SGD)**. Any error in the prediction is propagated back and weights, called parameters, of the various units are adjusted according to the error. Adam is a method that eliminates some of the issues of SGD such as getting trapped in sub-optimal local optima, and having the same learning rate for each parameter. Adam computes adaptive learning rates for each parameter and adjusts them based on not only the error but also previous adjustments. Consequently, Adam converges much faster than other optimization methods and is recommended as the default choice.

The metrics that will be observed are the same as before, accuracy, precision, and recall:

```
model_fe.compile(loss='binary_crossentropy',
            optimizer='adam',
            metrics=['accuracy', 'Precision', 'Recall'])
```

After setting up batches for preloading, the model is ready for training. Similar to previously, the model will be trained for 10 epochs:

```
# Prefetch for performance
encoded_train_batched = encoded_train.batch(BATCH_SIZE).prefetch(100)

model_fe.fit(encoded_train_batched, epochs=10)
```

```
Epoch 1/10
250/250 [==============================] - 28s 113ms/step - loss:
0.5896 - accuracy: 0.6841 - Precision: 0.6831 - Recall: 0.6870
Epoch 2/10
250/250 [==============================] - 17s 70ms/step - loss: 0.5160
- accuracy: 0.7448 - Precision: 0.7496 - Recall: 0.7354
...
Epoch 9/10
250/250 [==============================] - 17s 70ms/step - loss: 0.4108
- accuracy: 0.8121 - Precision: 0.8126 - Recall: 0.8112
Epoch 10/10
250/250 [==============================] - 17s 70ms/step - loss: 0.4061
- accuracy: 0.8136 - Precision: 0.8147 - Recall: 0.8118
```

A few things can be seen immediately. The model trained significantly faster. Each epoch took approximately 17 seconds with a maximum of 28 seconds for the first epoch. Secondly, the model has not overfit. The final accuracy is just over 81% on the training set. In the previous setup, the accuracy on the training set was 99.56%.

It should also be noted that the accuracy was still increasing at the end of the tenth epoch, with lots of room to go. This indicates that training this model for longer would probably increase accuracy further. Quickly changing the number of epochs to 20 and training the model yields an accuracy of just over 85% on the testing set, with precision at 80% and recall at 92.8%.

For now, let's understand the utility of this model. To make an assessment of the quality of this model, performance on the test set should be evaluated:

```
model_fe.evaluate(encoded_test.batch(BATCH_SIZE))
```

```
250/Unknown - 21s 85ms/step - loss: 0.3999 - accuracy: 0.8282 -
Precision: 0.7845 - Recall: 0.9050
```

Compared to the previous model's accuracy of 83.6% on the test set, this model produces an accuracy of 82.82%. This performance is quite impressive because this model is just 40% of the size of the previous model and represents a 70% reduction in training time for a less than 1% drop in accuracy. This model has a slightly better recall for slightly worse accuracy. This result should not be entirely unexpected. There are over 14,000 word vectors that are zeros in this model! To fix this issue, and also to try the fine-tuning sequential transfer learning approach, let's build a fine-tuning-based model.

Fine-tuning model

Creating the fine-tuning model is trivial when using the convenience function. All that is needed is to pass the train_emb parameter as true:

```
model_ft = build_model_bilstm(
    vocab_size=vocab_size,
    embedding_dim=embedding_dim,
    rnn_units=rnn_units,
    batch_size=BATCH_SIZE,
    train_emb=True)


model_ft.summary()
```

This model is identical to the feature extraction model in size. However, since the embeddings will be fine-tuned, training is expected to take a little longer. There are several thousand zero embeddings, which can now be updated. The resulting accuracy is expected to be much better than the previous model. The model is compiled with the same loss function, optimizer, and metrics, and trained for 10 epochs:

```
model_ft.compile(loss='binary_crossentropy',
            optimizer='adam',
            metrics=['accuracy', 'Precision', 'Recall'])


model_ft.fit(encoded_train_batched, epochs=10)
```

```
Epoch 1/10
250/250 [==============================] - 35s 139ms/step - loss:
0.5432 - accuracy: 0.7140 - Precision: 0.7153 - Recall: 0.7111
Epoch 2/10
250/250 [==============================] - 24s 96ms/step - loss: 0.3942
- accuracy: 0.8234 - Precision: 0.8274 - Recall: 0.8171
...
```

```
Epoch 9/10
250/250 [==============================] - 24s 97ms/step - loss: 0.1303
- accuracy: 0.9521 - Precision: 0.9530 - Recall: 0.9511
Epoch 10/10
250/250 [==============================] - 24s 96ms/step - loss: 0.1132
- accuracy: 0.9580 - Precision: 0.9583 - Recall: 0.9576
```

This accuracy is very impressive but needs to be checked against the test set:

```
model_ft.evaluate(encoded_test.batch(BATCH_SIZE))
```

```
250/Unknown - 22s 87ms/step - loss: 0.4624 - accuracy: 0.8710 -
Precision: 0.8789 - Recall: 0.8605
```

That is the best result we have obtained so far at an accuracy of 87.1%. Data about state-of-the-art results on datasets are maintained by the paperswithcode. com website. Research papers that have reproducible code are featured on the leaderboards for datasets. This result would be about seventeenth on the SOTA result on the paperswithcode.com website at the time of writing!

It can also be seen that the network is overfitting a little bit. A Dropout layer can be added between the Embedding layer and the first LSTM layer to help reduce this overfitting. It should also be noted that this network is still much faster than training embeddings from scratch. Most epochs took 24 seconds for training. Overall, this model is smaller in size, takes much less time to train, and has much higher accuracy! This is why transfer learning is so important in machine learning in general and NLP more specifically.

So far, we have seen the use of context-free word embeddings. The major challenge with this approach is that a word could have multiple meanings depending on the context. The word *bank* could refer to a place for storing money and valuables and also the side of a river. A more recent innovation in this area is BERT, published in May 2019. The next step in improving the accuracy of movie review sentiment analysis is to use a pre-trained BERT model. The next section explains the BERT model, its vital innovations, and the impact of using this model for the task at hand. Please note that the BERT model is enormous! If you do not have adequate local computing resources, using Google Colab with a GPU accelerator would be an excellent choice for the next section.

BERT-based transfer learning

Embeddings like GloVe are context-free embeddings. Lack of context can be limiting in NLP contexts. As discussed before, the word bank can mean different things depending on the context. **Bi-directional Encoder Representations from Transformers**, or **BERT**, came out of Google Research in May 2019 and demonstrated significant improvements on baselines. The BERT model builds on several innovations that came before it. The BERT paper also introduces several innovations of ERT works.

Two foundational advancements that enabled BERT are the **encoder-decoder network** architecture and the **Attention mechanism**. The Attention mechanism further evolved to produce the **Transformer architecture**. The Transformer architecture is the fundamental building block of BERT. These concepts are covered next and detailed further in later chapters. After these two sections, we will discuss specific innovations and structures of the BERT model.

Encoder-decoder networks

We have seen the use of LSTMs and BiLSTMs on sentences modeled as sequences of words. These sequences can be of varying lengths as sentences are composed of a different number of words. Recall that in *Chapter 2, Understanding Sentiment in Natural Language with BiLSTMs*, we discussed the core concept of an LSTM being a unit unrolled in time. For each input token, the LSTM unit generated an output. Consequently, the number of outputs produced by the LSTM depends on the number of input tokens. All of these input tokens are combined through a `TimeDistributed()` layer for use by later `Dense()` layers in the network. The main issue is that the input and output sequence lengths are linked. This model cannot handle variable-length sequences effectively. Translation-type tasks where the input and the output may have different lengths, consequently, won't do well with this architecture.

The solution to these challenges was posed in a paper titled *Sequence to Sequence Learning with Neural Networks* written by Ilya Sutskever et al. in 2014. This model is also referred to as the **seq2seq** model.

The basic idea is shown in the figure below:

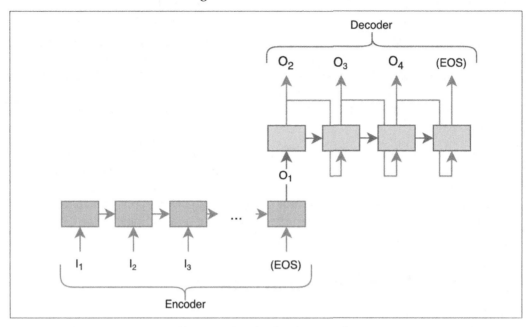

Figure 4.4: Encoder-decoder network

The model is divided into two parts – an encoder and a decoder. A special token that denotes the end of the input sequence is appended to the input sequence. Note that now the input sequence can have any length as this end of sentence token, **(EOS)** in the figure above, denotes the end. In the figure above, the input sequence is denoted by tokens $(I_1, I_2, I_3, \ldots)$. Each input token, after vectorization, is passed to an LSTM model. The output is only collected from the last **(EOS)** token. The vector generated by the encoder LSTM network for the **(EOS)** token is a representation of the entire input sequence. It can be thought of as a summary of the entire input. A variable-length sequence has not been transformed into a fixed-length or dimensional vector.

This vector becomes the input to the decoder layer. The model is auto-regressive in the sense that the output generated by the previous step of the decoder is fed into the next step as input. Output generation continues until the special **(EOS)** token is generated. This scheme allows the model to determine the length of the output sequence. It breaks apart the dependency between the length of the input and output sequences. Conceptually, this is a straightforward model to understand. However, this is a potent model. Many tasks can be cast as a sequence-to-sequence problem.

Some examples include translating a sentence from one language to another, summarizing an article where the input sequence is the text of the article and the output sequence is the summary, or question-answering where the question is the input sequence and the output is the answer. Speech recognition is a sequence-to-sequence problem with input sequences of 10 ms samples of voice, and the output is text. At the time of its release, it garnered much attention because it had a massive impact on the quality of Google Translate. In nine months of work using this model, the team behind the seq2seq model was able to provide much higher performance than that after over 10 years of improvements in Google Translate.

The Great A.I. Awakening

The New York Times published a fantastic article with the above title in 2016 that documents the journey of deep learning and especially the authors of the seq2seq paper and its dramatic effect on the quality of Google Translate. This article is highly recommended to see how transformational this architecture was for NLP. This article is available at `https://www.nytimes.com/2016/12/14/magazine/the-great-ai-awakening.html`.

With these techniques at hand, the next innovation was the use of the Attention mechanism, which allows the modeling of dependencies between tokens irrespective of their distance. The Attention model became the cornerstone of the **Transformer model**, described in the next section.

Attention model

In the encoder-decoder model, the encoder part of the network creates a fixed dimensional representation of the input sequence. As the input sequence length grows, more and more of the input is compressed into this vector. The encodings or hidden states generated by processing the input tokens are not available to the decoder layer. The encoder states are hidden from the decoder. The Attention mechanism allows the decoder part of the network to see the encoder hidden states. These hidden states are depicted in *Figure 4.4* as the output of each of the input tokens, (I_1, I_2, I_3,...), but shown only as feeding in to the next input token.

In the Attention mechanism, these input token encodings will also be made available to the decoder layer. This is called **General Attention**, and it refers to the ability of output tokens to directly have a dependence on the encodings or hidden states of input tokens. The main innovation here is the decoder operates on a sequence of vectors generating by encoding the input rather than one fixed vector generated at the end of the input. The Attention mechanism allows the decoder to focus its attention on a subset of the encoded input vectors while decoding, hence the name.

There is another form of attention, called **self-attention**. Self-attention enables connections between different encodings of input tokens in different positions. As depicted in the model in *Figure 4.4*, an input token only sees the encoding of the previous token. Self-attention will allow it to look at the encodings of previous tokens. Both forms are an improvement to the encoder-decoder architecture.

While there are many Attention architectures, a prevalent form is called **Bahdanau Attention**. It is named after the first author of the paper, published in 2016, where this Attention mechanism was proposed. Building on the encoder-decoder network, this form enables each output state to look at the encoded inputs and learn some weights for each of these inputs. Consequently, each output could focus on different input tokens. An illustration of this model is shown in *Figure 4.5*, which is a modified version of *Figure 4.4*:

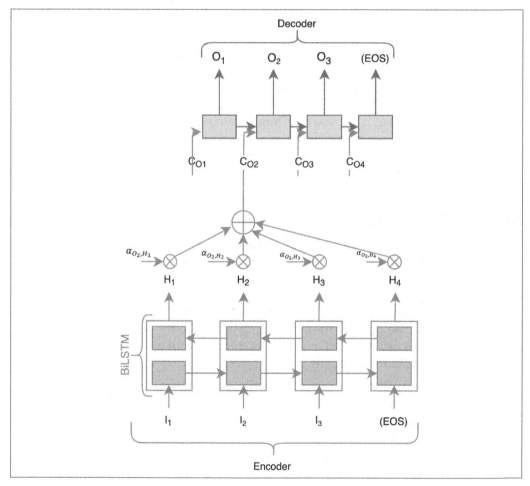

Figure 4.5: Bahdanau Attention architecture

Two specific changes have been made in the Attention mechanism when compared to the encoder-decoder architecture. The first change is in the encoder. The encoder layer here uses BiLSTMs. The use of BiLSTMs allows each word to learn from the words preceding and succeeding them both. In the standard encoder-decoder architecture, LSTMs were used, which meant each input word could only learn from the words before it.

The second change is related to how the decoder uses the output of the encoders. In the previous architecture, only the output of the last token, the end-of-sentence token, used the summary of the entire input sequence. In the Bahdanau Attention architecture, the hidden state output of each input token is multiplied by an *alignment weight* that represents the degree of match between the input token at a specific position with the output token in question. A context vector is computed by multiplying each input hidden state output with the corresponding alignment weight and concatenating all the results. This context vector is fed to the output token along with the previous output token.

Figure 4.5 shows this computation, for only the second output token. This alignment model with the weights for each output token can help point to the most helpful input tokens in generating that output token. Note that some of the details have been simplified for brevity and can be found in the paper. We will implement Attention from scratch in later chapters.

Attention is not an explanation

It can be tempting to interpret the alignment scores or attention weights as an explanation of the model predicting a particular output token. A paper with the title of this information box was published that tests this hypothesis that Attention is an explanation. The conclusion from the research is that Attention should not be interpreted as an explanation. Different attention weights on the same set of inputs may result in the same outputs.

The next advancement to the Attention model came in the form of the Transformer architecture in 2017. The Transformer model is the key to the BERT architecture, so let's understand that next.

Transformer model

Vaswani et al. published a ground-breaking paper in 2017 titled *Attention Is All You Need*. This paper laid the foundation of the Transformer model, which has been behind most of the recent advanced models such as ELMo, GPT, GPT-2, and BERT. The transformer model is built on the Attention model by taking the critical innovation from it – enabling the decoder to see all of the input hidden states while getting rid of the recurrence in it, which makes the model slow to train due to the sequential nature of processing the input sequences.

The Transformer model has an encoder and a decoder part. This encoder-decoder structure enables it to perform best on machine translation-type tasks. However, not all tasks need full encoder and decoder layers. BERT only uses the encoder part, while generative models like GPT-2 use the decoder part. In this section, only the encoder part of the architecture is covered. The next chapter deals with the generation of text and the best models that use the Transformer decoder. Hence, the decoder will be covered in that chapter.

What is a Language Model?

A **Language Model (LM)** task is traditionally defined as predicting the next word in a sequence of words. LMs are particularly useful for text generation, but less for classification. GPT-2 is an example of a model that fits this definition of an LM. Such a model only has context from the words or tokens that have occurred on its left (reverse for a right-to-left language). This is a trade-off that is appropriate in the generation of text. However, in other tasks such as question-answering or translation, the full sentence should be available. In such a case, using a bi-directional model that can use the context from both sides is useful. BERT is such a model. It loses the auto-regression property in favor of gaining context from both sides of a word of the token.

An encoder block of the Transformer has sub-layers parts – the multi-head self-attention sub-layer and a feed-forward sub-layer. The self-attention sub-layer looks at all the words of the input sequence and generates an encoding for these words in the context of each other. The feed-forward sublayer is composed of two layers using linear transformations and a ReLU activation in between. Each encoder block is composed of these two sub-layers, while the entire encoder is composed of six such blocks, as shown in *Figure 4.6*:

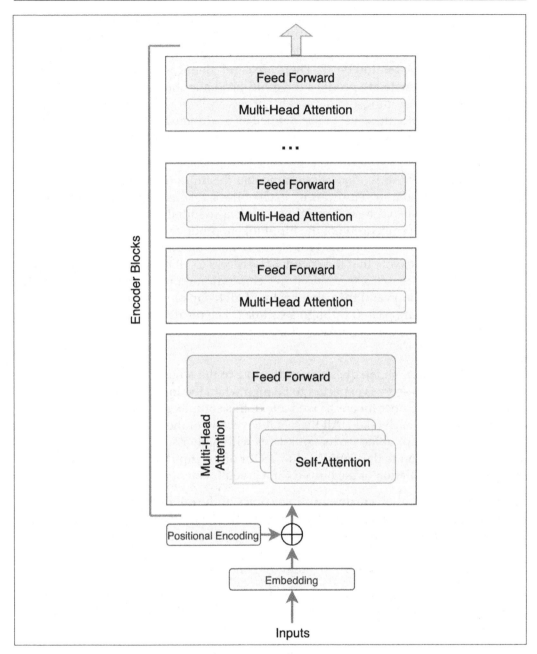

Figure 4.6: Transformer encoder architecture

A residual connection around the multi-head attention block and the feed-forward block is made in each encoder block. While adding the output of the sublayer with the input it received, layer normalization is performed. The main innovation here is the **Multi-Head Attention** block. There are eight identical attention blocks whose outputs are concatenated to produce the multi-head attention output. Each attention block takes in the encoding and defines three new vectors called the query, key, and value vectors. Each of these vectors is defined as 64-dimensional, though this size is a hyperparameter that can be tuned. The query, key, and value vectors are learned through training.

To understand how this works, let's assume that the input has three tokens. Each token has a corresponding embedding. Each of these tokens is initialized with its query, key, and value vectors. A weight vector is also initialized, which, when multiplied with the embedding of the input token, produces the key for that token. After the query vector is computed for a token, it is multiplied by the key vectors of all the input tokens. Note that the encoder has access to all the inputs, on both sides of each token. As a result, a score has now been computed by taking the query vector of the word in question and the value vector of all the tokens in the input sequence. All of these scores are passed through a softmax. The result can be interpreted as providing a sense of which tokens of the input are important to this particular input token.

In a way, the input token in question is attentive to the other tokens with a high softmax score. This score is expected to be high when the input token attends to itself but can be high for other tokens as well. Next, this softmax score is multiplied by the value vector of each token. All these value vectors of the different input tokens are then summed up. Value vectors of tokens with higher softmax scores will have a higher contribution to the output value vector of the input token in question. This completes the calculation of the output for a given token in the Attention layer.

Multi-head self-attention creates multiple copies of the query, key, and value vectors along with the weights matrix used to compute the query from the embedding of the input token. The paper proposed eight heads, though this could be experimented with. An additional weight matrix is used to combine the multiple outputs of each of the heads and concatenate them together into one output value vector.

This output value vector is fed to the feed-forward layer, and the output of the feed-forward layer goes to the next encoder block or becomes the output of the model at the final encoder block.

While the core BERT model is essentially the core Transformer encoder model, there are a few specific enhancements it introduced that are covered next. Note that using the BERT model is much easier as all of these details are abstracted. Knowing these details may, however, help in understanding BERT inputs and outputs. The code to use BERT for the IMDb sentiment analysis follows the next section.

The bidirectional encoder representations from transformers (BERT) model

The emergence of the Transformer architecture was a seminal moment in the NLP world. This architecture has driven a lot of innovation through several derivative architectures. BERT is one such model. It was released in 2018. The BERT model only uses the encoder part of the Transformer architecture. The layout of the encoder is identical to the one described earlier with twelve encoder blocks and twelve attention heads. The size of the hidden layers is 768. These sets of parameters are referred to as *BERT Base*. These hyperparameters result in a total model size of 110 million parameters. A larger model was also published with 24 encoder blocks, 16 attention heads, and a hidden unit size of 1,024. Since the paper came out, a number of different variants of BERT like ALBERT, DistilBERT, RoBERTa, CamemBERT, and so on have also emerged. Each of these models has tried to improve the BERT performance in terms of accuracy or in terms of training/inference time.

The way BERT is pre-trained is unique. It uses the multi-task transfer learning principle explained above to pre-train on two different objectives. The first objective is the **Masked Language Model (MLM)** task. In this task, some of the input tokens are masked randomly. The model has to predict the right token given the tokens on both sides of the masked token. Specifically, a token in the input sequence is replaced with a special [MASK] token 80% of the time. In 10% of the cases, the selected token is replaced with another random token from the vocabulary. In the last 10% of the cases, the token is kept unchanged. Further, this happens for 15% of the overall tokens in a batch. The consequence of this scheme is that the model cannot rely on certain tokens being present and is forced to learn a contextual representation based on the distribution of the tokens before and after any given token. Without this masking, the bidirectional nature of the model means each word would be able to indirectly *see* itself from either direction. This would make the task of predicting the target token really easy.

The second objective the model is pre-trained on is **Next Sentence Prediction** (NSP). The intuition here is that there are many NLP tasks that deal with pairs of sentences. For example, a question-answering problem can model the question as the first sentence, and the passage to be used to answer the question becomes the second sentence. The output from the model may be a span identifier that identifies the start and end token indices in the passage provided as the answer to the question. In the case of sentence similarity or paraphrasing, both sentence pairs can be passed in to get a similarity score. The NSP model is trained by passing in sentence pairs with a binary label that indicates whether the second sentence follows the first sentence. 50% of the training examples are passed as actual next sentences from the corpus with the label **IsNext**, while in the other 50% a random sentence is passed with the output label **NotNext**.

BERT also addresses a problem we saw in the GloVe example above – out-of-vocabulary tokens. About 15% of the tokens were not in the vocabulary. To address this problem, BERT uses the **WordPiece** tokenization scheme with a vocabulary size of 30,000 tokens. Note that this is much smaller than the GloVe vocabulary size. WordPiece belongs to a class of tokenization schemes called **subword** tokenization. Other members of this class are **Byte Pair Encoding (BPE)**, SentencePiece, and the Unigram language model. Inspiration for the WordPiece model came from the Google Translate team working with Japanese and Korean texts. If you recall the discussion on tokenization in the first chapter, we showed that the Japanese language does not use spaces for delimiting words. Hence, it is hard to tokenize it into words. Methods developed for creating vocabularies for such languages are quite useful for applying to languages like English and keeping the dictionary size down to a reasonable size.

Consider the German translation of the phrase *Life Insurance Company*. This would translate to *Lebensversicherungsgesellschaft*. Similarly, *Gross Domestic Product* would translate to *Bruttoinlandsprodukt*. If words are taken as such, the size of the vocabulary would be very large. A subword approach could represent these words more efficiently.

A smaller dictionary reduces training time and memory requirements. If a smaller dictionary does not come at the cost of out-of-vocabulary tokens, then it is quite useful. To help understand the concept of subword tokenization, consider an extreme example where the tokenization breaks apart the work into individual characters and numbers. The size of this vocabulary would be 37 – with 26 alphabets, 10 numbers, and space. An example of a subword tokenization scheme is to introduce two new tokens, *-ing* and *-tion*. Every word that ends with these two tokens can be broken into two subwords – the part before the suffix and one of the two suffixes. This can be done through knowledge of the language grammar and constructs, using techniques such as stemming and lemmatization. The WordPiece tokenization approach used in BERT is based on BPE. In BPE, the first step is defining a target vocabulary size.

Next, the entire text is converted to a vocabulary of just the individual character tokens and mapped to the frequency of occurrence. Now multiple passes are made on this to combine pairs of tokens so as to maximize the frequency of the bigram created. For each subword created, a special token is added to denote the end of the word so that detokenization can be performed. Further, if the subword is not the start of the word, a ## tag is added to help in reconstructing the original words. This process is continued until the desired vocabulary is hit, or the base condition of a minimum frequency of 1 is hit for tokens. BPE maximizes the frequency, and WordPiece builds on top of this to include another objective.

The objective for WordPiece includes increasing mutual information by considering the frequencies of the tokens being merged along with the frequency of the merged bigram. This introduces a minor adjustment to the model. RoBERTa from Facebook experimented with using a BPE model and did not see a material difference in performance. The GPT-2 generative model is based on the BPE model.

To take an example from the IMDb dataset, here is an example sentence:

> This was an absolutely terrible movie. Don't be **lured** in by Christopher Walken or Michael Ironside.

After tokenization with BERT, it would look like this:

> [CLS] This was an absolutely terrible movie . Don' t be **lure ##d** in by Christopher Walk ##en or Michael Iron ##side . [SEP]

Where [CLS] and [SEP] are special tokens, which will be introduced shortly. Note how the word *lured* was broken up as a consequence. Now that we understand the underlying construct of the BERT model, let's try to use it for transfer learning on the IMDb sentiment classification problem. The first step is preparing the data.

 All the code for the BERT implementation can be found in the `imdb-transfer-learning.ipynb` notebook in this chapter's GitHub folder, in the section *BERT-based transfer learning*. Please run the code in the section titled *Loading IMDb training data* to ensure the data is loaded prior to proceeding.

Tokenization and normalization with BERT

After reading the description of the BERT model, you may be bracing yourself for a difficult implementation in code. Have no fear. Our friends at Hugging Face have provided pre-trained models as well as abstractions that make working with advanced models like BERT a breeze. The general flow for getting BERT to work will be:

1. Load a pre-trained model
2. Instantiate a tokenizer and tokenize the data
3. Set up a model and compile it
4. Fit the model on the data

These steps won't take more than a few lines of code each. So let's get started. The first step is to install the Hugging Face libraries:

```
!pip install transformers==3.0.2
```

The tokenizer is the first step – it needs to be imported before it can be used:

```
from transformers import BertTokenizer

bert_name = 'bert-base-cased'
tokenizer = BertTokenizer.from_pretrained(bert_name,
                                          add_special_tokens=True,
                                          do_lower_case=False,
                                          max_length=150,
                                          pad_to_max_length=True)
```

That is all there is to load a pre-trained tokenizer! A few things to note in the code above. First, there are a number of models published by Hugging Face that are available for download. A full list of the models and their names can be found at `https://huggingface.co/transformers/pretrained_models.html`. Some key BERT models that are available are:

Model Name	Description
bert-base-uncased / bert-base-cased	Variants of the base BERT model with 12 encoder layers, hidden size of 768 units, and 12 attention heads for a total of ~110 million parameters. The only difference is whether the inputs were cased or all lowercase.
bert-large-uncased / bert-large-cased	This model has 24 encoder layers, 1,024 hidden units, and 16 attention heads for a total of ~340 million parameters. Similar split by cased and lowercase models.
bert-base-multilingual-cased	Parameters here are the same as bert-base-cased above, trained on 104 languages with the largest Wikipedia entries. However, it is not recommended to use the uncased version for international languages, while that model is available.
bert-base-cased-finetuned-mrpc	This model has been fine-tuned on the Microsoft Research Paraphrase Corpus task for paraphrase identification in the news domain.
bert-base-japanese	Same size as the base model but trained on Japanese text. Note that both the MeCab and WordPiece tokenizers are used.
bert-base-chinese	Same size as the base model but trained on cased-simplified Chinese and traditional Chinese.

Any of the values on the left can be used in the bert_name variable above to load the appropriate tokenizer. The second line in the code above downloads the configuration and the vocabulary file from the cloud and instantiates a tokenizer. This loader takes a number of parameters. Since a cased English model is being used, we don't want the tokenizer to convert words to lowercase as specified by the do_lower_case parameter. Note that the default value of this parameter is True. The input sentences will be tokenized to a maximum of 150 tokens, as we saw in the GloVe model as well. pad_to_max_length further indicates that the tokenizer should also pad the sequences it generates.

The first argument, add_special_tokens, deserves some explanation. In the example so far, we have taken a sequence and a maximum length. If the sequence is shorter than this maximum length, then the sequence is padded with a special padding token. However, BERT has a special way to encode its sequence due to the next sentence prediction task pre-training. It needs a way to provide two sequences as the input. In the case of classification, like the IMDb sentiment prediction, the second sequence is just left empty. There are three sequences that need to be provided to the BERT model:

- input_ids: This corresponds to the tokens in the inputs converted into IDs. This is what we have been doing thus far in other examples. In the IMDb example, we only have one sequence. However, if the problem required passing in two sequences, then a special token, [SEP], would be added in between the sequences. [SEP] is an example of a special token that has been added by the tokenizer. Another special token, [CLS], is appended to the start of the inputs. [CLS] stands for classifier token. The embedding for this token can be viewed as the summary of the inputs in the case of a classification problem, and additional layers on top of the BERT model would use this token. It is also possible to use the sum of the embeddings of all the inputs as an alternative.

- token_type_ids: If the input contains two sequences, for a question-answering problem, for example, then these IDs tell the model indicates which input_ids correspond to which sequence. In some texts, this is referred to as the segment identifiers. The first sequence would be the first segment, and the second sequence would be the second segment.

- attention_mask: Given that the sequences are padded, this mask tells the model where the actual tokens end so that the attention calculation does not use the padding tokens.

Given that BERT can take two sequences as input, understanding the padding is essential as it can be confusing how padding works in the context of the maximum sequence length when a pair of sequences is provided. The maximum sequence length refers to the combined length of the pair. There are three different ways to do truncation if the combined length exceeds the maximum length. The first two could be to reduce the lengths from either the first or the second sequence. The third way is to truncate from the lengthiest sequence, a token at a time so that the lengths of the pair are only off by one at maximum. In the constructor, this behavior can be configured by passing the `truncation_strategy` parameter with the values `only_first`, `only_second`, or `longest_first`.

Figure 4.7 shows how an input sequence is converted into the three input sequences listed above:

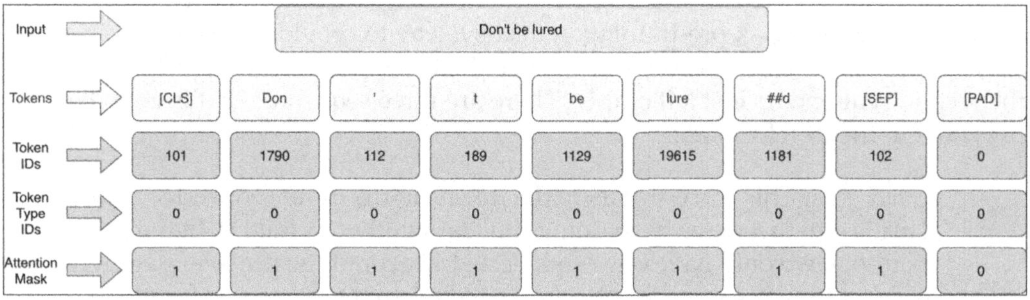

Figure 4.7: Mapping inputs to BERT sequences

If the input sequence was *Don't be lured*, then the figure above shows how it is tokenized with the WordPiece tokenizer as well as the addition of special tokens. The example above sets a maximum sequence length of nine tokens. Only one sequence is provided, hence the token type IDs or segment IDs all have the same value. The attention mask is set to 1, where the corresponding entry in the tokens is an actual token. The following code is used to generate these encodings:

```
tokenizer.encode_plus(" Don't be lured", add_special_tokens=True,
                      max_length=9,
                      pad_to_max_length=True,
                      return_attention_mask=True,
                      return_token_type_ids=True)
```

```
{'input_ids': [101, 1790, 112, 189, 1129, 19615, 1181, 102, 0], 'token_
type_ids': [0, 0, 0, 0, 0, 0, 0, 0, 0], 'attention_mask': [1, 1, 1, 1,
1, 1, 1, 1, 0]}
```

Even though we won't be using a pair of sequences in this chapter, it is useful to be aware of how the encodings look when a pair is passed. If two strings are passed to the tokenizer, then they are treated as a pair. This is shown in the code below:

```
tokenizer.encode_plus(" Don't be"," lured", add_special_tokens=True,
                      max_length=10,
                      pad_to_max_length=True,
                      return_attention_mask=True,
                      return_token_type_ids=True)
```

```
{'input_ids': [101, 1790, 112, 189, 1129, 102, 19615, 1181, 102, 0],
 'token_type_ids': [0, 0, 0, 0, 0, 0, 1, 1, 1, 0], 'attention_mask': [1,
 1, 1, 1, 1, 1, 1, 1, 1, 0]}
```

The input IDs have two separators to distinguish between the two sequences. The token type IDs help distinguish which tokens correspond to which sequence. Note that the token type ID for the padding token is set to 0. In the network, it is never used as all the values are multiplied by the attention mask.

To perform encoding of the inputs for all the IMDb reviews, a helper function is defined, as shown below:

```
def bert_encoder(review):
    txt = review.numpy().decode('utf-8')
    encoded = tokenizer.encode_plus(txt, add_special_tokens=True,
                                    max_length=150,
                                    pad_to_max_length=True,
                                    return_attention_mask=True,
                                    return_token_type_ids=True)

    return encoded['input_ids'], encoded['token_type_ids'], \
           encoded['attention_mask']
```

The method is pretty straightforward. It takes the input tensor and uses UTF-8 decoding. Using the tokenizer, this input is converted into the three sequences.

This would be a great opportunity to implement a different padding algorithm. For example, implement an algorithm that takes the last 150 tokens instead of the first 150 and compare the performance of the two methods.

Now, this needs to be applied to every review in the training data:

```
bert_train = [bert_encoder(r) for r, l in imdb_train]
bert_lbl = [l for r, l in imdb_train]
bert_train = np.array(bert_train)
bert_lbl = tf.keras.utils.to_categorical(bert_lbl, num_classes=2)
```

Labels of the reviews are also converted into categorical values. Using the `sklearn` package, the training data is split into training and validation sets:

```
# create training and validation splits
from sklearn.model_selection import train_test_split

x_train, x_val, y_train, y_val = train_test_split(bert_train,
                                                  bert_lbl,
                                                  test_size=0.2,
                                                  random_state=42)

print(x_train.shape, y_train.shape)
```

```
(20000, 3, 150) (20000, 2)
```

A little more data processing is required to wrangle the inputs into three input dictionaries in `tf.DataSet` for easy use in training:

```
tr_reviews, tr_segments, tr_masks = np.split(x_train, 3, axis=1)
val_reviews, val_segments, val_masks = np.split(x_val, 3, axis=1)

tr_reviews = tr_reviews.squeeze()
tr_segments = tr_segments.squeeze()
tr_masks = tr_masks.squeeze()

val_reviews = val_reviews.squeeze()
val_segments = val_segments.squeeze()
val_masks = val_masks.squeeze()
```

These training and validation sequences are converted into a dataset like so:

```
def example_to_features(input_ids,attention_masks,token_type_ids,y):
    return {"input_ids": input_ids,
            "attention_mask": attention_masks,
            "token_type_ids": token_type_ids},y
```

```
train_ds = tf.data.Dataset.from_tensor_slices((tr_reviews,
tr_masks, tr_segments, y_train)).\
            map(example_to_features).shuffle(100).batch(16)
```

```
valid_ds = tf.data.Dataset.from_tensor_slices((val_reviews,
val_masks, val_segments, y_val)).\
            map(example_to_features).shuffle(100).batch(16)
```

A batch size of 16 has been used here. The memory of the GPU is the limiting factor here. Google Colab can support a batch length of 32. An 8 GB RAM GPU can support a batch size of 16. Now, we are ready to train a model using BERT for classification. We will see two approaches. The first approach will use a pre-built classification model on top of BERT. This is shown in the next section. The second approach will use the base BERT model and adds custom layers on top to accomplish the same task. This technique will be demonstrated in the section after.

Pre-built BERT classification model

Hugging Face libraries make it really easy to use a pre-built BERT model for classification by providing a class to do so:

```
from transformers import TFBertForSequenceClassification
bert_model = TFBertForSequenceClassification.from_pretrained(bert_name)
```

That was quite easy, wasn't it? Note that the instantiation of the model will require a download of the model from the cloud. However, these models are cached on the local machine if the code is being run from a local or dedicated machine. In the Google Colab environment, this download will be run every time a Colab instance is initialized. To use this model, we only need to provide an optimizer and a loss function and compile the model:

```
optimizer = tf.keras.optimizers.Aadam(learning_rate=2e-5)
loss = tf.keras.losses.BinaryCrossentropy(from_logits=True)

bert_model.compile(optimizer=optimizer, loss=loss, metrics=['accuracy'])
```

This model is actually quite simple in layout as its summary shows:

```
bert_model.summary()
```

```
Model: "tf_bert_for_sequence_classification_7"

Layer (type)                 Output Shape              Param #
=================================================================
bert (TFBertMainLayer)       multiple                  108310272

dropout_303 (Dropout)        multiple                  0

classifier (Dense)           multiple                  1538
=================================================================
Total params: 108,311,810
Trainable params: 108,311,810
Non-trainable params: 0
```

So, the model has the entire BERT model, a dropout layer, and a classifier layer on top. This is as simple as it gets.

 The BERT paper suggests some settings for fine-tuning. They suggest a batch size of 16 or 32, run for 2 to 4 epochs. Further, they suggest using one of the following learning rates for Adam: 5e-5, 3e-5, or 2e-5. Once this model is up and running in your environment, please feel free to train with different settings to see the impact on accuracy.

In the previous section, we batched the data into sets of 16. Here, the Adam optimizer is configured to use a learning rate of 2e-5. Let's train this model for 3 epochs. Note that training is going to be quite slow:

```
print("Fine-tuning BERT on IMDB")
bert_history = bert_model.fit(train_ds, epochs=3,
                              validation_data=valid_ds)
```

```
Fine-tuning BERT on IMDB
Train for 1250 steps, validate for 313 steps
Epoch 1/3
1250/1250 [==============================] - 480s 384ms/step - loss:
0.3567 - accuracy: 0.8320 - val_loss: 0.2654 - val_accuracy: 0.8813
Epoch 2/3
```

```
1250/1250 [==============================] - 469s 375ms/step - loss:
0.2009 - accuracy: 0.9188 - val_loss: 0.3571 - val_accuracy: 0.8576
Epoch 3/3
1250/1250 [==============================] - 470s 376ms/step - loss:
0.1056 - accuracy: 0.9613 - val_loss: 0.3387 - val_accuracy: 0.8883
```

The validation accuracy is quite impressive for the little work we have done here if it holds on the test set. That needs to be checked next. Using the convenience methods from the previous section, the test data will be tokenized and encoded in the right format:

```
# prep data for testing
bert_test = [bert_encoder(r) for r,l in imdb_test]
bert_tst_lbl = [l for r, l in imdb_test]

bert_test2 = np.array(bert_test)
bert_tst_lbl2 = tf.keras.utils.to_categorical (bert_tst_lbl,
                                                num_classes=2)

ts_reviews, ts_segments, ts_masks = np.split(bert_test2, 3, axis=1)
ts_reviews = ts_reviews.squeeze()
ts_segments = ts_segments.squeeze()
ts_masks = ts_masks.squeeze()

test_ds = tf.data.Dataset.from_tensor_slices((ts_reviews,
                    ts_masks, ts_segments, bert_tst_lbl2)).\
            map(example_to_features).shuffle(100).batch(16)
```

Evaluating the performance of this model on the test dataset, we get the following:

```
bert_model.evaluate(test_ds)
```

```
1563/1563 [==============================] - 202s 129ms/step - loss:
0.3647 - accuracy: 0.8799

[0.3646871318983454, 0.8799]
```

The model accuracy is almost 88%! This is higher than the best GloVe model shown previously, and it took much less code to implement.

In the next section, let's try to build custom layers on top of the BERT model to take transfer learning to the next level.

Custom model with BERT

The BERT model outputs contextual embeddings for all of the input tokens. The embedding corresponding to the [CLS] token is generally used for classification tasks, and it represents the entire document. The pre-built model from Hugging Face returns the embeddings for the entire sequence as well as this *pooled output*, which represents the entire document as the output of the model. This pooled output vector can be used in future layers to help with the classification task. This is the approach we will take in building a customer model.

> The code for this section is under the heading *Customer Model With BERT* in the same notebook as above.

The starting point for this exploration is the base TFBertModel. It can be imported and instantiated like so:

```
from transformers import TFBertModel
bert_name = 'bert-base-cased'
bert = TFBertModel.from_pretrained(bert_name)
bert.summary()
```

```
Model: "tf_bert_model"

Layer (type)                 Output Shape              Param #
=================================================================
bert (TFBertMainLayer)       multiple                  108310272
=================================================================
Total params: 108,310,272
Trainable params: 108,310,272
Non-trainable params: 0
```

Since we are using the same pre-trained model, the cased BERT-Base model, we can reuse the tokenized and prepared data from the section above. If you haven't already, take a moment to ensure the code in the *Tokenization and normalization with BERT* section has been run to prepare the data.

Now, the custom model needs to be defined. The first layer of this model is the BERT layer. This layer will take three inputs, namely the input tokens, attention masks, and token type IDs:

```
max_seq_len = 150
inp_ids = tf.keras.layers.Input((max_seq_len,), dtype=tf.int64,
name="input_ids")
att_mask = tf.keras.layers.Input((max_seq_len,), dtype=tf.int64,
name="attention_mask")
seg_ids = tf.keras.layers.Input((max_seq_len,), dtype=tf.int64,
name="token_type_ids")
```

These names need to match the dictionary defined in the training and testing dataset. This can be checked by printing the specification of the dataset:

```
train_ds.element_spec
```

```
({'input_ids': TensorSpec(shape=(None, 150), dtype=tf.int64,
name=None),
   'attention_mask': TensorSpec(shape=(None, 150), dtype=tf.int64,
name=None),
   'token_type_ids': TensorSpec(shape=(None, 150), dtype=tf.int64,
name=None)},
  TensorSpec(shape=(None, 2), dtype=tf.float32, name=None))
```

The BERT model expects these inputs in a dictionary. It can also accept the inputs as named arguments, but this approach is clearer and makes it easy to trace the inputs. Once the inputs are mapped, the output of the BERT model can be computed:

```
inp_dict = {"input_ids": inp_ids,
            "attention_mask": att_mask,
            "token_type_ids": seg_ids}
outputs = bert(inp_dict)
# let's see the output structure
outputs
```

```
(<tf.Tensor 'tf_bert_model_3/Identity:0' shape=(None, 150, 768)
dtype=float32>,
 <tf.Tensor 'tf_bert_model_3/Identity_1:0' shape=(None, 768)
dtype=float32>)
```

The first output has embeddings for each of the input tokens including the special tokens [CLS] and [SEP]. The second output corresponds to the output of the [CLS] token. This output will be used further in the model:

```
x = tf.keras.layers.Dropout(0.2)(outputs[1])
x = tf.keras.layers.Dense(200, activation='relu')(x)
x = tf.keras.layers.Dropout(0.2)(x)
x = tf.keras.layers.Dense(2, activation='sigmoid')(x)

custom_model = tf.keras.models.Model(inputs=inp_dict, outputs=x)
```

The model above is only illustrative, to demonstrate the technique. We add a dense layer and a couple of dropout layers before an output layer. Now, the customer model is ready for training. The model needs to be compiled with an optimizer, loss function, and metrics to watch for:

```
optimizer = tf.keras.optimizers.Adam(learning_rate=2e-5)
loss = tf.keras.losses.BinaryCrossentropy(from_logits=True)
custom_model.compile(optimizer=optimizer, loss=loss, metrics=['accuracy'])
```

Here is what this model looks like:

```
custom_model.summary()
```

```
Model: "model_2"
_____
Layer (type)                   Output Shape           Param #      Connected to
=========================================================================================
attention_mask (InputLayer)    [(None, 150)]          0

input_ids (InputLayer)         [(None, 150)]          0

token_type_ids (InputLayer)    [(None, 150)]          0

tf_bert_model (TFBertModel)    ((None, 150, 768), (   108310272    attention_mask[0][0]
                                                                   input_ids[0][0]
                                                                   token_type_ids[0][0]

dropout_345 (Dropout)          (None, 768)            0            tf_bert_model[3][1]

dense_4 (Dense)                (None, 200)            153800       dropout_345[0][0]

dropout_346 (Dropout)          (None, 200)            0            dense_4[0][0]

dense_5 (Dense)                (None, 2)              402          dropout_346[0][0]
=========================================================================================
Total params: 108,464,474
Trainable params: 108,464,474
Non-trainable params: 0
_____
```

This custom model has 154,202 additional trainable parameters in addition to the BERT parameters. The model is ready to be trained. We will use the same settings from the previous BERT section and train the model for 3 epochs:

```
print("Custom Model: Fine-tuning BERT on IMDB")
custom_history = custom_model.fit(train_ds, epochs=3,
                                  validation_data=valid_ds)
```

```
Custom Model: Fine-tuning BERT on IMDB
Train for 1250 steps, validate for 313 steps
Epoch 1/3
1250/1250 [==============================] - 477s 381ms/step - loss:
0.5912 - accuracy: 0.8069 - val_loss: 0.6009 - val_accuracy: 0.8020
Epoch 2/3
1250/1250 [==============================] - 469s 375ms/step - loss:
0.5696 - accuracy: 0.8570 - val_loss: 0.5643 - val_accuracy: 0.8646
Epoch 3/3
1250/1250 [==============================] - 470s 376ms/step - loss:
0.5559 - accuracy: 0.8883 - val_loss: 0.5647 - val_accuracy: 0.8669
```

Evaluating on the test set gives an accuracy of 86.29%. Note that the test data encoding steps used in the pretrained BERT model section are used here as well:

```
custom_model.evaluate(test_ds)
```

```
1563/1563 [==============================] - 201s 128ms/step - loss:
0.5667 - accuracy: 0.8629
```

Fine-tuning of BERT is run for a small number of epochs with a small value for Adam's learning rate. If a lot of fine-tuning is done, then there is a risk of BERT forgetting its pretrained parameters. This can be a limitation while building custom models on top as a few epochs may not be sufficient to train the layers that have been added. In this case, the BERT model layer can be frozen, and training can be continued further. Freezing the BERT layer is fairly easy, though it needs the re-compilation of the model:

```
bert.trainable = False                  # don't train BERT any more
optimizer = tf.keras.optimizers.Adam()  # standard learning rate
custom_model.compile(optimizer=optimizer, loss=loss, metrics=['accuracy'])
```

We can check the model summary to verify that the number of trainable parameters has changed to reflect the BERT layer being frozen:

```
custom_model.summary()
```

```
Model: "model_2"

Layer (type)                    Output Shape         Param #     Connected to
=================================================================================
attention_mask (InputLayer)     [(None, 150)]        0

input_ids (InputLayer)          [(None, 150)]        0

token_type_ids (InputLayer)     [(None, 150)]        0

tf_bert_model (TFBertModel)     ((None, 150, 768), ( 108310272   attention_mask[0][0]
                                                                 input_ids[0][0]
                                                                 token_type_ids[0][0]

dropout_345 (Dropout)           (None, 768)          0           tf_bert_model[3][1]

dense_4 (Dense)                 (None, 200)          153800      dropout_345[0][0]

dropout_346 (Dropout)           (None, 200)          0           dense_4[0][0]

dense_5 (Dense)                 (None, 2)            402         dropout_346[0][0]
=================================================================================
Total params: 108,464,474
Trainable params: 154,202
Non-trainable params: 108,310,272
```

Figure 4.8: Model summary

We can see that all the BERT parameters are now set to non-trainable. Since the model was being recompiled, we also took the opportunity to change the learning rate.

> Changing the sequence length and learning rate during training are advanced techniques in TensorFlow. The BERT model also used 128 as the sequence length for initial epochs, which was changed to 512 later in training. It is also common to see a learning rate increase for the first few epochs and then decrease as training proceeds.

Now, training can be continued for a number of epochs like so:

```
print("Custom Model: Keep training custom model on IMDB")
custom_history = custom_model.fit(train_ds, epochs=10,
                                  validation_data=valid_ds)
```

The training output has not been shown for brevity. Checking the model on the test set yields 86.96% accuracy:

```
custom_model.evaluate(test_ds)
```

```
1563/1563 [==============================] - 195s 125ms/step - loss:
0.5657 - accuracy: 0.8696
```

If you are contemplating whether the accuracy of this custom model is lower than the pre-trained model, then it is a fair question to ponder over. A bigger network is not always better, and overtraining can lead to a reduction in model performance due to overfitting. Something to try in the custom model is to use the output encodings of all the input tokens and pass them through an LSTM layer or concatenate them together to pass through dense layers and then make the prediction.

Having done the tour of the encoder side of the Transformer architecture, we are ready to look into the decoder side of the architecture, which is used for text generation. That will be the focus of the next chapter. Before we go there, let's review everything we covered in this chapter.

Summary

Transfer learning has made a lot of progress possible in the world of NLP, where data is readily available, but labeled data is a challenge. We covered different types of transfer learning first. Then, we took pre-trained GloVe embeddings and applied them to the IMDb sentiment analysis problem, seeing comparable accuracy with a much smaller model that takes much less time to train.

Next, we learned about seminal moments in the evolution of NLP models, starting from encoder-decoder architectures, attention, and Transformer models, before understanding the BERT model. Using the Hugging Face library, we used a pre-trained BERT model and a custom model built on top of BERT for the purpose of sentiment classification of IMDb reviews.

BERT only uses the encoder part of the Transformer model. The decoder side of the stack is used in text generation. The next two chapters will focus on completing the understanding of the Transformer model. The next chapter will use the decoder side of the stack to perform text generation and sentence completion. The chapter after that will use the full encoder-decoder network architecture for text summarization.

Thus far, we have trained embeddings for tokens in the models. A considerable amount of lift can be achieved by using pre-trained embeddings. The next chapter will focus on the concept of transfer learning and the use of pre-trained embeddings like BERT.

5
Generating Text with RNNs and GPT-2

When your mobile phone completes a word as you type a message or when Gmail suggests a short reply or completes a sentence as you reply to an email, a text generation model is working in the background. The Transformer architecture forms the basis of state-of-the-art text generation models. BERT, as explained in the previous chapter, uses only the encoder part of the Transformer architecture.

However, BERT, being bi-directional, is not suitable for the generation of text. A left-to-right (or right-to-left, depending on the language) language model built on the decoder part of the Transformer architecture is the foundation of text generation models today.

Text can be generated a character at a time or with words and sentences together. Both of these approaches are shown in this chapter. Specifically, we will cover the following topics:

- Generating text with:
    - Character-based RNNs for generating news headlines and completing text messages
    - GPT-2 to generate full sentences

- Improving the quality of text generation using techniques such as:
  - Greedy search
  - Beam search
  - Top-K sampling
- Using advanced techniques such as learning rate annealing and checkpointing to enable long training times:
- Details of the Transformer decoder architecture
- Details of the GPT and GPT-2 models

A character-based approach for generating text is shown first. Such models can be quite useful for generating completions of a partially typed word in a sentence on a messaging platform, for example.

Generating text – one character at a time

Text generation yields a window into whether deep learning models are learning about the underlying structure of language. Text will be generated using two different approaches in this chapter. The first approach is an RNN-based model that generates a character at a time.

In the previous chapters, we have seen different tokenization methods based on words and sub-words. Text is tokenized into characters, which include capital and small letters, punctuation symbols, and digits. There are 96 tokens in total. This tokenization is an extreme example to test how much a model can learn about the language structure. The model will be trained to predict the next character based on a given set of input characters. If there is indeed an underlying structure in the language, the model should pick it up and generate reasonable-looking sentences.

Generating coherent sentences one character at a time is a very challenging task. The model does not have a dictionary or vocabulary, and it has no sense of capitalization of nouns or any grammar rules. Yet, we are expecting it to generate reasonable-looking sentences. The structure of words and their order in a sentence is not random but driven by grammar rules in a language. Words have some structure, based on parts of speech and word roots. A character-based model has the smallest possible vocabulary, but we hope that the model learns a lot about the use of the letters. This may seem like a tall order but be prepared to be surprised. Let's get started with the data loading and pre-processing steps.

Data loading and pre-processing

For this particular example, we are going to use data from a constrained domain – a set of news headlines. The hypothesis is that news headlines are usually short and follow a particular structure. These headlines are usually a summary of an article and contain a large number of proper nouns like names of companies and celebrities. For this particular task, data from two different datasets are joined together and used. The first dataset is called the News Aggregator dataset generated by the Artificial Intelligence Lab, part of the Faculty of Engineering at Roma Tre University in Italy. The University of California, Irvine, has made the dataset available for download from `https://archive.ics.uci.edu/ml/datasets/News+Aggregator`. This dataset has over 420,000 news article titles, URLs, and other information. The second dataset is a set of over 200,000 news articles from The Huffington Post, called the News Category dataset, collected by Rishabh Mishra and posted on Kaggle at `https://www.kaggle.com/rmisra/news-category-dataset`.

News article headlines from both datasets are extracted and compiled into one file. This step is already done to save time. The compressed output file is called `news-headlines.tsv.zip` and is located in the `chapter5-nlg-with-transformer-gpt/char-rnn` GitHub folder corresponding to this chapter. The folder is located inside the GitHub repository for this book. The format of this file is pretty simple. It has two columns separated by a tab. The first column is the original headline, and the second column is an uncased version of the same headline. This example uses the first column of the file only.

However, you can try the uncased version to see how the results differ. Training such models usually takes a lot of time, often several hours. Training in an IPython notebook can be difficult as a number of issues, such as the loss of the connection to the kernel or the kernel process dying, can result in the loss of the trained model. What we are attempting to do in this example is akin to training BERT from scratch. Don't worry; we train the model for a much shorter time than it took to train BERT. Running long training loops runs the risk of training loops crashing in the middle. In such a case, we don't want to restart training from scratch. The model is checkpointed frequently during training so that the model state can be restored from the last checkpoint if a failure occurs. Then, training can be restarted from the last checkpoint. Python files executed from the command line give the most control when running long training loops.

The command-line instructions shown in this example were tested on an Ubuntu 18.04 LTS machine. These commands should work as is on a macOS command line but may need some adjustments. Windows users may need to translate these commands for their operating system. Windows 10 power users should be able to use the **Windows Subsystem for Linux (WSL)** capabilities to execute the same commands.

Going back to the data format, all that needs to be done for loading the data is to unzip the prepared headline file. Navigate to the folder where the ZIP file has been pulled down from GitHub. The compressed file of headlines can be unzipped and inspected:

```
$ unzip news-headlines.tsv.zip
Archive:  news-headlines.tsv.zip
  inflating: news-headlines.tsv
```

Let's inspect the contents of the file to get a sense of the data:

```
$ head -3 news-headlines.tsv
There Were 2 Mass Shootings In Texas Last Week, But Only 1 On TV there
were 2 mass shootings in texas last week, but only 1 on tv
Will Smith Joins Diplo And Nicky Jam For The 2018 World Cup's Official
Song will smith joins diplo and nicky jam for the 2018 world cup's
official song
Hugh Grant Marries For The First Time At Age 57 hugh grant marries for
the first time at age 57
```

The model is trained on the headlines shown above. We are ready to move on to the next step and load the file to perform normalization and tokenization.

Data normalization and tokenization

As discussed above, this model uses a token per character. So, each letter, including punctuation, numbers, and space, becomes a token. Three additional tokens are added. These are:

- <EOS>: Denotes end of sentences. The model can use this token to indicate that the generation of text is complete. All headlines end with this token.

- <UNK>: While this is a character-level model, it is possible to have different characters from other languages or character sets in the dataset. When a character is detected that is not present in our set of 96 characters, this token is used. This approach is consistent with word-based vocabulary approaches where it is common to replace out-of-vocabulary words with a special token.

- <PAD>: This is a unique padding token used to pad all headlines to the same length. Padding is done by hand in this example as opposed to using TensorFlow methods, which we have seen previously.

All the code in this section will refer to the rnn-train.py file from the chapter5-nlg-with-transformer-gpt folder of the GitHub repo of the book. The first part of this file has the imports and optional instructions for setting up a GPU. Ignore this section if your setup does not use a GPU.

 A GPU is an excellent investment for deep learning engineers and researchers. A GPU could speed up your training times by orders of magnitude or more! It would be worthwhile to outfit your deep learning setup with a GPU like the Nvidia GeForce RTX 2070.

The code for data normalization and tokenization is between lines 32 and 90 of this file. To start, the tokenization function needs to be set up:

```
chars = sorted(set("abcdefghijklmnopqrstuvwxyz0123456789
-,;.!?:'''/\|_@#$%^&*~'+-=()[]{}' ABCDEFGHIJKLMNOPQRSTUVWXYZ"))
chars = list(chars)
EOS = '<EOS>'
UNK = "<UNK>"
PAD = "<PAD>"          # need to move mask to '0'index for Embedding Layer
chars.append(UNK)
chars.append(EOS)  # end of sentence

chars.insert(0, PAD)  # now padding should get index of 0
```

Once the token list is ready, methods need to be defined for converting characters to tokens and vice versa. Creating mapping is relatively straightforward:

```
# Creating a mapping from unique characters to indices
char2idx = {u:i for i, u in enumerate(chars)}
idx2char = np.array(chars)

def char_idx(c):
    # takes a character and returns an index
    # if character is not in list, returns the unknown token
```

```
    if c in chars:
        return char2idx[c]

    return char2idx[UNK]
```

Now, the data needs can be read in from the TSV file. A maximum length of 75 characters is used for the headlines. If the headlines are shorter than this length, they are padded. Any headlines longer than 75 characters are snipped. The <EOS> token is appended to the end of every headline. Let's set this up:

```
data = []       # load into this list of lists
MAX_LEN = 75  # maximum length of a headline

with open("news-headlines.tsv", "r") as file:
    lines = csv.reader(file, delimiter='\t')
    for line in lines:
        hdln = line[0]
        cnvrtd = [char_idx(c) for c in hdln[:-1]]
        if len(cnvrtd) >= MAX_LEN:
            cnvrtd = cnvrtd[0:MAX_LEN-1]
            cnvrtd.append(char2idx[EOS])
        else:
            cnvrtd.append(char2idx[EOS])
            # add padding tokens
            remain = MAX_LEN - len(cnvrtd)
            if remain > 0:
                for i in range(remain):
                    cnvrtd.append(char2idx[PAD])
        data.append(cnvrtd)
print("**** Data file loaded ****")
```

All the data is loaded into a list with the code above. You may be wondering about the ground truth here for training as we only have a line of text. Since we want this model to generate text, the objective can be reduced to predicting the next character given a set of characters. Hence, a trick will be used to construct the ground truth – we will just shift the input sequence by one character and set it as the expected output. This transformation is quite easy do with numpy:

```
# now convert to numpy array
np_data = np.array(data)

# for training, we use one character shifted data
np_data_in = np_data[:, :-1]
np_data_out = np_data[:, 1:]
```

With this nifty trick, we have both inputs and expected outputs ready for training. The final step is to convert it into `tf.Data.DataSet` for ease of batching and shuffling:

```
# Create TF dataset
x = tf.data.Dataset.from_tensor_slices((np_data_in, np_data_out))
```

Now everything is ready to start training.

Training the model

The code for model training starts at line 90 in the `rnn-train.py` file. The model is quite simple. It has an embedding layer, followed by a GRU layer and a dense layer. The size of the vocabulary, the number of RNN units, and the size of the embeddings are set up:

```
# Length of the vocabulary in chars
vocab_size = len(chars)

# The embedding dimension
embedding_dim = 256

# Number of RNN units
rnn_units = 1024

# batch size
BATCH_SIZE=256
```

With the batch size being defined, training data can be batched and ready for use by the model:

```
# create tf.DataSet
x_train = x.shuffle(100000, reshuffle_each_iteration=True).batch(BATCH_
SIZE, drop_remainder=True)
```

Similar to code in previous chapters, a convenience method to build models is defined like so:

```
# define the model
def build_model(vocab_size, embedding_dim, rnn_units, batch_size):
  model = tf.keras.Sequential([
    tf.keras.layers.Embedding(vocab_size, embedding_dim,
                      mask_zero=True,
                      batch_input_shape=[batch_size, None]),
    tf.keras.layers.GRU(rnn_units,
```

```
                              return_sequences=True,
                              stateful=True,
                              recurrent_initializer='glorot_uniform'),
    tf.keras.layers.Dropout(0.1),
    tf.keras.layers.Dense(vocab_size)
])
return model
```

A model can be instantiated with this method:

```
model = build_model(
                  vocab_size = vocab_size,
                  embedding_dim=embedding_dim,
                  rnn_units=rnn_units,
                  batch_size=BATCH_SIZE)


print("**** Model Instantiated ****")
print(model.summary())
```

```
**** Model Instantiated ****
Model: "sequential"

_____
Layer (type)                 Output Shape              Param #
=================================================================
embedding (Embedding)        (256, None, 256)          24576

gru (GRU)                    (256, None, 1024)         3938304

dropout (Dropout)            (256, None, 1024)         0

dense (Dense)                (256, None, 96)           98400
=================================================================
Total params: 4,061,280
Trainable params: 4,061,280
Non-trainable params: 0
_____
```

There are just over 4 million trainable parameters in this model. The Adam optimizer, with a sparse categorical loss function, is used for training this model:

```
loss = tf.keras.losses.SparseCategoricalCrossentropy(from_logits=True)
model.compile(optimizer = 'adam', loss = loss)
```

Since training is potentially going to take a long time, we need to set up checkpoints along with the training. If there is any problem in training and training stops, these checkpoints can be used to restart the training from the last saved checkpoint. A directory is created using the current timestamp for saving these checkpoints:

```
# Setup checkpoints
# dynamically build folder names
dt = datetime.datetime.today().strftime("%Y-%b-%d-%H-%M-%S")

# Directory where the checkpoints will be saved
checkpoint_dir = './training_checkpoints/'+dt

# Name of the checkpoint files
checkpoint_prefix = os.path.join(checkpoint_dir, "ckpt_{epoch}")

checkpoint_callback=tf.keras.callbacks.ModelCheckpoint(
    filepath=checkpoint_prefix,
    save_weights_only=True)
```

A custom callback that saves checkpoints during training is defined in the last line of code above. This is passed to the `model.fit()` function to be called at the end of every epoch. Starting the training loop is straightforward:

```
print("**** Start Training ****")
EPOCHS=25
start = time.time()
history = model.fit(x_train, epochs=EPOCHS,
                    callbacks=[checkpoint_callback])
print("**** End Training ****")
print("Training time: ", time.time()- start)
```

The model will be trained for 25 epochs. The time taken in training will be logged as well in the code above. The final piece of code uses the history to plot the loss and save it as a PNG file in the same directory:

```
# Plot accuracies
lossplot = "loss-" + dt + ".png"
plt.plot(history.history['loss'])
plt.title('model loss')
plt.xlabel('epoch')
plt.ylabel('loss')
plt.savefig(lossplot)

print("Saved loss to: ", lossplot)
```

The best way to start training is to start the Python process so that it can run in the background without needing a Terminal or command-line. On Unix systems, this can be done with the nohup command:

```
$ nohup python rnn-train.py > training.log &
```

This command line starts the process in a way that disconnecting the Terminal would not interrupt the training process. On my machine, this training took approximately 1 hour and 43 minutes. Let's check out the loss curve:

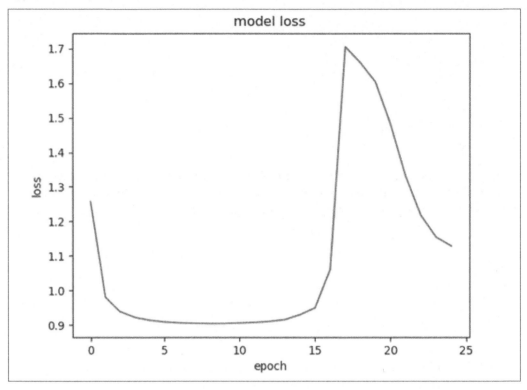

Figure 5.1: Loss curve

As we can see, the loss decreases to a point and then shoots up. The standard expectation is that loss would monotonically decrease as the model was trained for more epochs. In the case shown above, the loss suddenly shoots up. In other cases, you may observe a NaN, or Not-A-Number, error. NaNs result from the exploding gradient problem during backpropagation through RNNs. The gradient direction causes weights to grow very large quickly and overflow, resulting in NaNs. Given how prevalent this is, there are quite a few jokes about NLP engineers and Indian food to go with the nans (referring to a type of Indian bread).

The primary reason behind these occurrences is gradient descent overshooting the minima and starting to climb the slope before reducing again. This happens when the steps gradient descent is taking are too large. Another way to prevent the NaN issue is gradient clipping where gradients are clipped to an absolute maximum, preventing loss from exploding. In the RNN model above, a scheme needs to be used that reduces the learning rate over time. Reducing the learning rate over epochs reduces the chances for gradient descent to overshoot the minima. This technique of reducing the learning rate over time is called **learning rate annealing** or **learning rate decay**. The next section walks through implementing learning rate decay while training the model.

Implementing learning rate decay as custom callback

There are two ways to implement learning rate decay in TensorFlow. The first way is to use one of the prebuilt schedulers that are part of the tf.keras.optimizers.schedulers package and use a configured instance with the optimizer. An example of a prebuilt scheduler is InverseTimeDecay, and it can be set up as shown below:

```
lr_schedule = tf.keras.optimizers.schedules.InverseTimeDecay(
    0.001,
    decay_steps=STEPS_PER_EPOCH*(EPOCHS/10),
    decay_rate=2,
    staircase=False)
```

The first parameter, 0.001 in the example above, is the initial learning rate. The number of steps per epoch can be calculated by dividing the number of training examples by batch size. The number of decay steps determines how the learning rate is reduced. The equation used to compute the learning rate is:

$$new\_rate = \frac{initial\_rate}{1 + decay\_rate * (\frac{step}{decay\_step})}$$

After being set up, all this function needs is the step number for computing the new learning rate. Once the schedule is set up, it can be passed to the optimizer:

```
optimizer = tf.keras.optimizers.Adam(lr_schedule)
```

That's it! The rest of the training loop code is unchanged. However, this learning rate scheduler starts reducing the learning rate from the first epoch itself. A lower learning rate increases the amount of training time. Ideally, we would keep the learning rate unchanged for the first few epochs and then reduce it.

Looking at *Figure 5.1* above, the learning rate is probably effective until about the tenth epoch. BERT also uses **learning rate warmup** before learning rate decay. Learning rate warmup generally refers to increasing the learning rate for a few epochs. BERT was trained for 1,000,000 steps, which roughly translates to 40 epochs. For the first 10,000 steps, the learning rate was increased, and then it was linearly decayed. Implementing such a learning rate schedule is better accomplished by a custom callback.

Custom callbacks in TensorFlow enable the execution of custom logic at various points during training and inference. We saw an example of a prebuilt callback that saves checkpoints during training. A custom callback provides hooks that enable desired logic that can be executed at various points during training. This main step is to define a subclass of `tf.keras.callbacks.Callback`. Then, one or more of the following functions can be implemented to hook onto the events exposed by TensorFlow:

- `on_[train,test,predict]_begin` / `on_[train,test,predict]_end`: This callback happens at the start of training or the end of the training. There are methods for training, testing, and prediction loops. Names for these methods can be constructed using the appropriate stage name from the possibilities shown in brackets. The method naming convention is a common pattern across other methods in the rest of the list.

- `on_[train,test,predict]_batch_begin` / `on_[train,test,predict] _batch_ end`: These callbacks happen when training for a specific batch starts or ends.

- `on_epoch_begin` / `on_epoch_end`: This is a training-specific function called at the start or end of an epoch.

We will implement a callback for the start of the epoch that adjusts that epoch's learning rate. Our implementation will keep the learning rate constant for a configurable number of initial epochs and then reduce the learning rate in a fashion similar to the inverse time decay function described above. This learning rate would look like the following *Figure 5.2*:

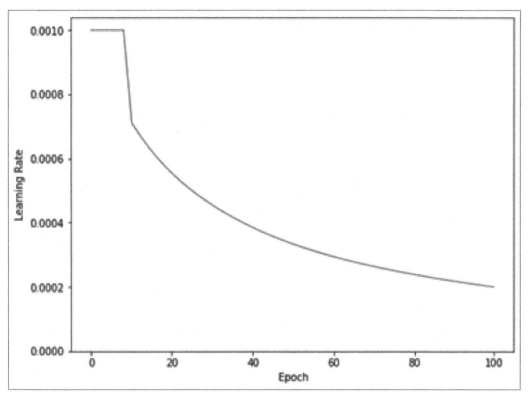

Figure 5.2: Custom learning rate decay function

First, a subclass is created with the function defined in it. The best place to put this in rnn_train.py is just around the checkpoint callback, before the start of training. This class definition is shown below:

```
class LearningRateScheduler(tf.keras.callbacks.Callback):
    """Learning rate scheduler which decays the learning rate"""

    def __init__(self, init_lr, decay, steps, start_epoch):
        super().__init__()
        self.init_lr = init_lr          # initial learning rate
        self.decay = decay              # how sharply to decay
        self.steps = steps              # total number of steps of decay
        self.start_epoch = start_epoch  # which epoch to start decaying

    def on_epoch_begin(self, epoch, logs=None):
        if not hasattr(self.model.optimizer, 'lr'):
            raise ValueError('Optimizer must have a "lr" attribute.')
        # Get the current learning rate
```

```
    lr = float(tf.keras.backend.get_value(self.model.optimizer.lr))
    if(epoch >= self.start_epoch):
        # Get the scheduled learning rate.
        scheduled_lr = self.init_lr / (1 + self.decay * (epoch / self.
steps))
        # Set the new learning rate
        tf.keras.backend.set_value(self.model.optimizer.lr,
                                    scheduled_lr)
    print('\nEpoch %05d: Learning rate is %6.4f.' % (epoch, scheduled_lr))
```

Using this callback in the training loop requires the instantiation of the callback. The following parameters are set while instantiating the callback:

- The initial learning rate is set to 0.001.
- The decay rate is set to 4. Please feel free to play around with different settings.
- The number of steps is set to the number of epochs. The model is trained for 150 epochs.
- Learning rate decay should start after epoch 10, so the start epoch is set to 10.

The training loop is updated to include the callback like so:

```
print("**** Start Training ****")
EPOCHS=150
lr_decay = LearningRateScheduler(0.001, 4., EPOCHS, 10)
start = time.time()
history = model.fit(x_train, epochs=EPOCHS,
                    callbacks=[checkpoint_callback, lr_decay])
print("**** End Training ****")
print("Training time: ", time.time()- start)
print("Checkpoint directory: ", checkpoint_dir)
```

Changes are highlighted above. Now, the model is ready to be trained using the command shown above. Training 150 epochs took over 10 hours on the GPU-capable machine. The loss surface is shown in *Figure 5.3*:

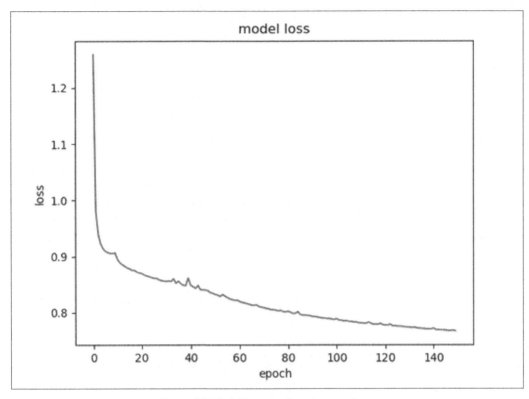

Figure 5.3: Model loss after learning rate decay

In the figure above, the loss drops very fast for the first few epochs before plateauing near epoch 10. Learning rate decay kicks in at that point, and the loss starts to fall again. This can be verified from a snippet of the log file:

```
...
Epoch 8/150
2434/2434 [==================] - 249s 102ms/step - loss: 0.9055
Epoch 9/150
2434/2434 [==================] - 249s 102ms/step - loss: 0.9052
Epoch 10/150
2434/2434 [==================] - 249s 102ms/step - loss: 0.9064

Epoch 00010: Learning rate is 0.00078947.
Epoch 11/150
2434/2434 [==================] - 249s 102ms/step - loss: 0.8949

Epoch 00011: Learning rate is 0.00077320.
Epoch 12/150
```

```
2434/2434 [==================] - 249s 102ms/step - loss: 0.8888
...
Epoch 00149: Learning rate is 0.00020107.
Epoch 150/150
2434/2434 [==================] - 249s 102ms/step - loss: 0.7667
**** End Training ****
Training time:  37361.16723680496
Checkpoint directory:  ./training_checkpoints/2021-Jan-01-09-55-03
Saved loss to:  loss-2021-Jan-01-09-55-03.png
```

Note the highlighted loss above. The loss slightly increased around epoch 10 as learning rate decay kicked in, and the loss started falling again. The small bumps in the loss that can be seen in *Figure 5.3* correlate with places where the learning rate was higher than needed, and learning rate decay kicked it down to make the loss go lower. The learning rate started at 0.001 and ended at a fifth of that at 0.0002.

Training this model took much time and advanced tricks like learning rate decay to train. But how does this model do in terms of generating text? That is the focus of the next section.

Generating text with greedy search

Checkpoints were taken during the training process at the end of every epoch. These checkpoints are used to load a trained model for generating text. This part of the code is implemented in an IPython notebook. The code for this section is found in the charRNN-text-generation.ipynb file in this chapter's folder in GitHub. The generation of text is dependent on the same normalization and tokenization logic used during training. The *Setup Tokenization* section of the notebook has this code replicated.

There are two main steps in generating text. The first step is restoring a trained model from the checkpoint. The second step is generating a character at a time from a trained model until a specific end condition is met.

The *Load the Model* section of the notebook has the code to define the model. Since the checkpoints only stored the weights for the layers, defining the model structure is important. The main difference from the training network is the batch size. We want to generate a sentence at a time, so we set the batch size as 1:

```
# Length of the vocabulary in chars
vocab_size = len(chars)

# The embedding dimension
```

```
embedding_dim = 256

# Number of RNN units
rnn_units = 1024

# Batch size
BATCH_SIZE=1
```

A convenience function for setting up the model structure is defined like so:

```
# this one is without padding masking or dropout layer
def build_gen_model(vocab_size, embedding_dim, rnn_units, batch_size):
  model = tf.keras.Sequential([
    tf.keras.layers.Embedding(vocab_size, embedding_dim,
                        batch_input_shape=[batch_size, None]),
    tf.keras.layers.GRU(rnn_units,
                    return_sequences=True,
                    stateful=True,
                    recurrent_initializer='glorot_uniform'),
    tf.keras.layers.Dense(vocab_size)
  ])
  return model

gen_model = build_gen_model(vocab_size, embedding_dim, rnn_units,
                      BATCH_SIZE)
```

Note that the embedding layer does not use masking because, in text generation, we are not passing an entire sequence but only part of a sequence that needs to be completed. Now that the model is defined, the weights for the layers can be loaded in from the checkpoint. Please remember to replace the checkpoint directory with your local directory containing the checkpoints from training:

```
checkpoint_dir = './training_checkpoints/<YOUR-CHECKPOINT-DIR>'

gen_model.load_weights(tf.train.latest_checkpoint(checkpoint_dir))

gen_model.build(tf.TensorShape([1, None]))
```

The second main step is to generate text a character at a time. Generating text needs a seed or a starting few letters, which are completed by the model into a sentence. The process of generation is encapsulated in the function below:

```python
def generate_text(model, start_string, temperature=0.7, num_
generate=75):
    # Low temperatures results in more predictable text.
    # Higher temperatures results in more surprising text.
    # Experiment to find the best setting.

    # Converting our start string to numbers (vectorizing)
    input_eval = [char2idx[s] for s in start_string]
    input_eval = tf.expand_dims(input_eval, 0)

    # Empty string to store our results
    text_generated = []

    # Here batch size == 1
    for i in range(num_generate):
        predictions = model(input_eval)
        # remove the batch dimension
        predictions = tf.squeeze(predictions, 0)

        # using a categorical distribution to predict the
        # word returned by the model
        predictions = predictions / temperature
        predicted_id = tf.random.categorical(predictions,
                            num_samples=1)[-1,0].numpy()

        # We pass the predicted word as the next input to the model
        # along with the previous hidden state
        input_eval = tf.expand_dims([predicted_id], 0)

        text_generated.append(idx2char[predicted_id])
        # Lets break is <EOS> token is generated
        # if idx2char[predicted_id] == EOS:
        # break #end of a sentence reached, let's stop

    return (start_string + ''.join(text_generated))
```

The generation method takes in a seed string that is used as the starting point for the generation. This seed string is vectorized. The actual generation happens in a loop, where one character is generated at a time and appended to the sequence generated. At every point, the character with the highest likelihood is chosen. Choosing the next letter with the highest probability is called **greedy search**. However, there is a configuration parameter called **temperature**, which can be used to adjust the predictability of the generated text.

Once probabilities for all characters are predicted, dividing the probabilities by the temperature changes the distribution of the generated characters. Smaller values of the temperature generate text that is closer to the original text. Larger values of the temperature generate more creative text. Here, a value of 0.7 is chosen to bias more on the surprising side.

To generate the text, all that is needed is one line of code:

```
print(generate_text(gen_model, start_string=u"Google"))
```

```
Google plans to release the Xbox One vs. Samsung Galaxy
Gea<EOS><PAD>ote on Mother's Day
```

Each execution of the command may generate slightly different results. The line generated above, while obviously nonsensical, is pretty well structured. The model has learned capitalization rules and headline structure. Normally, we would not generate text beyond the <EOS> token, but all 75 characters are generated here for the sake of understanding the model output.

Note that the output shown for text generation is indicative. You may see a different output for the same prompt. There is some inherent randomness that is built into this process, which we can try and control by setting random seeds. When a model is retrained, it may end up on a slightly different point on the loss surface, where even though the loss numbers look similar, there may be slight differences in the model weights. Please take the outputs presented in the entire chapter as indicative versus actual.

Here are some other examples of seed strings and model outputs, snipped after the end-of-sentence tag:

Seed	Generated Sentence
S&P	S&P 500 closes above 190<EOS>
	S&P: Russell Slive to again find any business manufacture<EOS>
	S&P closes above 2000 for first tim<EOS>
Beyonce	Beyonce and Solange pose together for 'American Idol' contes<EOS>
	Beyonce's sister Solange rules' Dawn of the Planet of the Apes' report<EOS>
	Beyonce & Jay Z Get Married<EOS>

Note the model's use of quotes in the first two sentences for *Beyonce* as the seed word. The following table shows the impact of different temperature settings for similar seed words:

Seed	Temperature	Generated Sentence
S&P	0.1	S&P 500 Closes Above 1900 For First Tim<EOS>
	0.3	S&P Close to $5.7 Billion Deal to Buy Beats Electronic<EOS>
	0.5	S&P 500 index slips to 7.2%, signaling a strong retail sale<EOS>
	0.9	
		S&P, Ack Factors at Risk of what you see This Ma<EOS>
Kim	0.1	Kim Kardashian and Kanye West wedding photos release<EOS>
	0.3	
		Kim Kardashian Shares Her Best And Worst Of His First Look At The Met Gala<EOS>
	0.5	Kim Kardashian Wedding Dress Dress In The Works From Fia<EOS>
	0.9	Kim Kardashian's en<EOS>

Generally, the quality of the text goes down at higher values of temperature. All these examples were generated by passing in the different temperature values to the generation function.

A practical application of such a character-based model is to complete words in a text messaging or email app. By default, the generate_text() method is generating 75 characters to complete the headline. It is easy to pass in much shorter lengths to see what the model proposes as the next few letters or words.

The table below shows some experiments of trying to complete the next 10 characters of text fragments. These completions were generated using:

```
print(generate_text(gen_model, start_string=u"Lets meet tom",
                    temperature=0.7, num_generate=10))
```

```
Lets meet tomorrow to t
```

Prompt	Completion
I need some money from ba	I need some money from bank chairma
Swimming in the p	Swimming in the profitabili
Can you give me a	Can you give me a Letter to
are you fr	are you from around
The meeting is	The meeting is back in ex
Lets have coffee at S	Lets have coffee at Samsung hea
	Lets have coffee at Staples stor
	Lets have coffee at San Diego Z

Given that the dataset used was only from news headlines, it is biased toward certain types of activities. For example, the second sentence could be completed with *pool* instead of the model trying to fill it in with profitability. If a more general text dataset was used, then this model could do quite well at generating completions for partially typed words at the end of the sentence. However, there is one limitation that this text generation method has – the use of the greedy search algorithm.

The greedy search process is a crucial part of the text generation above. It is one of several ways to generate text. Let's take an example to understand this process. For this example, bigram frequencies were analyzed by Peter Norvig and published on `http://norvig.com/mayzner.html`. Over 743 billion English words were analyzed in this work. With 26 characters in an uncased model, there are theoretically 26 x 26 = 676 bigram combinations. However, the article reports that the following bigrams were never seen in roughly 2.8 trillion bigram instances: JQ, QG, QK, QY, QZ, WQ, and WZ.

The *Greedy Search with Bigrams* section of the notebook has code to download and process the full dataset and show the process of greedy search. After downloading the set of all n-grams, bigrams are extracted. A set of dictionaries is constructed to help look up the highest-probability next letter given a starting letter. Then, using some recursive code, a tree is constructed, picking the top three choices for the next letter. In the generation code above, only the top letter is chosen. However, the top three letters are chosen to show how greedy search works and its shortcomings.

Using the nifty anytree Python package, a nicely formatted tree can be visualized. This tree is shown in the following figure:

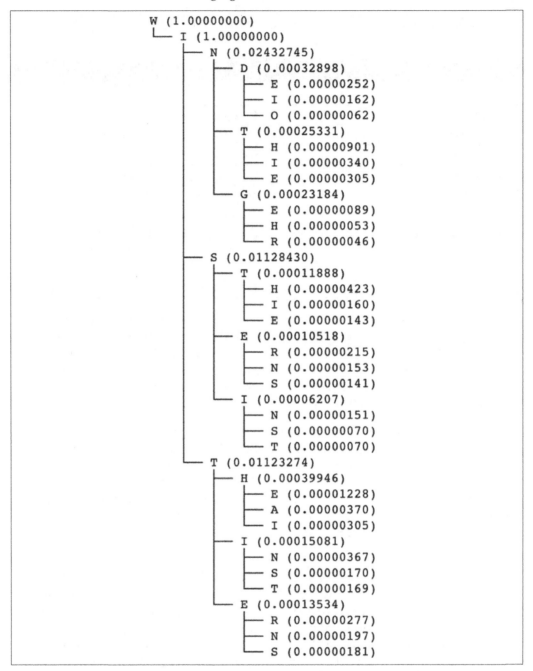

Figure 5.4: Greedy search tree starting with WI

The algorithm was given the task of completing **WI** in a total of five characters. The preceding tree shows cumulative probabilities for a given path. More than one path is shown so that the branches not taken by greedy search can also be seen. If a three-character word was being built, the highest probability choice is **WIN** with a probability of 0.243, followed by **WIS** at 0.01128. If four-letter words are considered, then the greedy search would consider only those words that start with **WIN** as that was the path with the highest probability considering the first three letters. **WIND** has the highest probability of 0.000329 in this path. However, a quick scan across all four-letter words shows that the highest probability word should be **WITH** having a probability of 0.000399.

This, in essence, is the challenge of the greedy search algorithm for text generation. Higher-probability options considering joint probabilities are hidden due to optimization at each character instead of cumulative probability. Whether the text is generated a character or a word at a time, greedy search suffers from the same issue.

An alternative algorithm, called **beam search**, allows tracking multiple options, and pruning out the lower-probability options as generation proceeds. The tree shown in *Figure 5.4* can also be seen as an illustration of tracking beams of probabilities. To see the power of this technique, a more sophisticated model for generating text would be better. The **GPT-2**, or **Generative Pre-Training**, based model published by OpenAI set many benchmarks including in open-ended text generation. This is the subject of the next half of this chapter, where the GPT-2 model is explained first. The next topic is fine-tuning a GPT-2 model for completing email messages. Beam search and other options to improve the quality of the generated text are also shown.

Generative Pre-Training (GPT-2) model

OpenAI released the first version of the GPT model in June 2018. They followed up with GPT-2 in February 2019. This paper attracted much attention as full details of the large GPT-2 model were not released with the paper due to concerns of nefarious uses. The large GPT-2 model was released subsequently in November 2019. The GPT-3 model is the most recent, released in May 2020.

Figure 5.5 shows the number of parameters in the largest of each of these models:

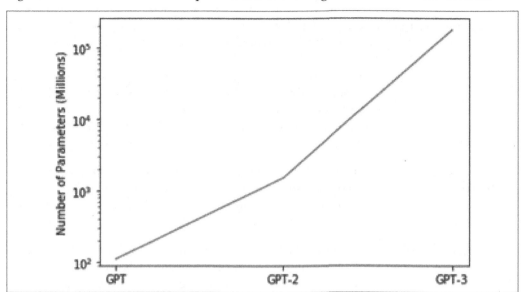

Figure 5.5: Parameters in different GPT models

The first model used the standard Transformer decoder architecture with twelve layers, each with twelve attention heads and 768-dimensional embeddings, for a total of approximately 110 million parameters, which is very similar to the BERT model. The largest GPT-2 has over 1.5 billion parameters, and the most recently released GPT-3 model's largest variant has over 175 billion parameters!

Cost of training language models

As the number of parameters and dataset sizes increase, the time taken for training also increases. As per a Lambda Labs article, If the GPT-3 model were to be trained on a single Nvidia V100 GPU, it would take 342 years. Using stock Microsoft Azure pricing, this would cost over $3 million. GPT-2 model training is estimated to run to $256 per hour. Assuming a similar running time as BERT, which is about four days, that would cost about $25,000. If the cost of training multiple models during research is factored in, the overall cost can easily increase ten-fold.

At such costs, training these models from scratch is out of reach for individuals and even most companies. Transfer learning and the availability of pre-trained models from companies like Hugging Face make it possible for the general public to use these models.

The base architecture of GPT models uses the decoder part of the Transformer architecture. The decoder is a *left-to-right* language model. The BERT model, in contrast, is a bidirectional model. A left-to-right model is autoregressive, that is, it uses tokens generated thus far to generate the next token. Since it cannot see future tokens like a bi-directional model, this language model is ideal for text generation.

Figure 5.6 shows the full Transformer architecture with the encoder blocks on the left and decoder blocks on the right:

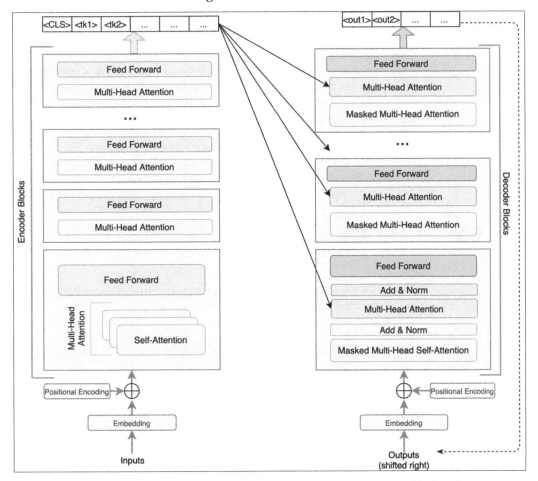

Figure 5.6: Full Transformer architecture with encoder and decoder blocks

The left side of *Figure 5.6* should be familiar – it is essentially *Figure 4.6* from the *Transformer model* section of the previous chapter. The encoder blocks shown are the same as the BERT model. The decoder blocks are very similar to the encoder blocks with a couple of notable differences.

In the encoder block, there is only one source of input – the input sequence and all of the input tokens are available for the multi-head attention to operate on. This enables the encoder to understand the context of the token from both the left and right sides.

In the decoder block, there are two inputs to each block. The outputs generated by the encoder blocks are available to all the decoder blocks and fed to the middle of the decoder block through multi-head attention and layer norms.

What is layer normalization?

Large deep neural networks are trained using the **Stochastic Gradient Descent (SGD)** optimizer or a variant like Adam. Training large models on big datasets can take a significant amount of time for the model to converge. Techniques such as weight normalization, batch normalization, and layer normalization are aimed at reducing training time by helping models to converge faster while also acting as a regularizer. The idea behind layer normalization is to scale the inputs of a given hidden layer with the mean and standard deviation of the inputs. First, the mean and standard deviation are computed:

$$\mu^l = \frac{1}{H}\sum_{i=1}^{H} a_i^l \qquad \sigma^l = \sqrt{\frac{1}{H}\sum_{i=1}^{H}(a_i^l - \mu^l)^2}$$

H denotes the number of hidden units in layer l. Inputs to the layer are normalized using the above-calculated values:

$$\overline{a}_i^l = \frac{g_i^l}{\sigma_i^l}(a_i^l - \mu_i^l)$$

where g is a gain parameter. Note that the formulation of the mean and standard deviation is not dependent on the size of the mini-batches or dataset size. Hence, this type of normalization can be used for RNNs and other sequence modeling problems.

However, the tokens generated by the decoder thus far are fed back through a masked multi-head self-attention and added to the output from the encoder blocks. Masked here refers to the fact that tokens to the right of the token being generated are masked, and the decoder cannot see them. Similar to the encoder, there are several such blocks stacked on top of each other. However, GPT architecture is only one half of the Transformer. This requires some modifications to the architecture.

The modified architecture for GPT is shown in *Figure 5.7*. Since there is no encoder block to feed the representation of the input sequence, the multi-head layer is no longer required. The outputs generated by the model are recursively fed back to generate the next token.

The smallest GPT-2 model has twelve layers and 768 dimensions for each token. The largest GPT-2 model has 48 layers and 1,600 dimensions per token. To pre-train models of this size, the authors of GPT-2 needed to create a new dataset. Web pages provide a great source of text, but the text comes with quality issues. To solve this challenge, they scraped all outbound links from Reddit, which had received at least three karma points. The assumption made by the authors is that karma points are an indicator of the quality of the web page being linked. This assumption allows scraping a huge set of text data. The resulting dataset was approximately 45 million links.

To extract text from the HTML on the web pages, two Python libraries were used: Dragnet and Newspaper. After some quality checks and deduplication, the final dataset was about 8 million documents with 40 GB of text. One exciting thing that the authors did was to remove any Wikipedia documents as they felt many of the test datasets used Wikipedia, and adding these pages would cause an overlap between test and training data sets. The pre-training objective is a standard LM training objective of predicting the next word given a set of previous words:

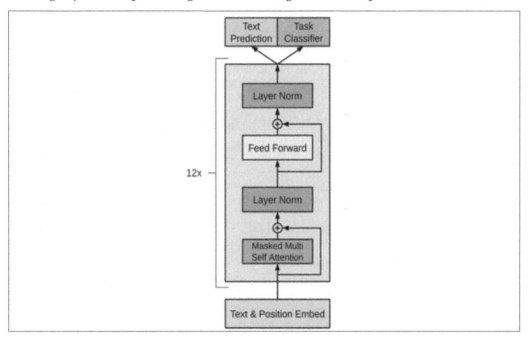

Figure 5.7: GPT architecture
(Source: Improving Language Understanding by Generative Pre-Training by Radford et al.)

During pre-training, the GPT-2 model is trained with a maximum sequence length of 1,024 tokens. A **Byte Pair Encoding (BPE)** algorithm is used for tokenization, with a vocabulary size of about 50,000 tokens. GPT-2 uses byte sequences rather than Unicode code points for the byte pair merges. If GPT-2 only used bytes for encoding, then the vocabulary would only be 256 tokens. On the other hand, using Unicode code points would yield a vocabulary of over 130,000 tokens. By cleverly using bytes in BPE, GPT-2 is able to keep the vocabulary size to a manageable 50,257 tokens.

Another peculiarity of the tokenizer in GPT-2 is that it converts all text to lowercase and uses spaCy and `ftfy` tokenizers prior to using BPE. The `ftfy` library is quite useful for fixing Unicode issues. If these two are not available, then the basic BERT tokenizer is used.

There are several ways to encode the inputs to solve various problems, even though the left-to-right model may seem limiting. These are shown in *Figure 5.8*:

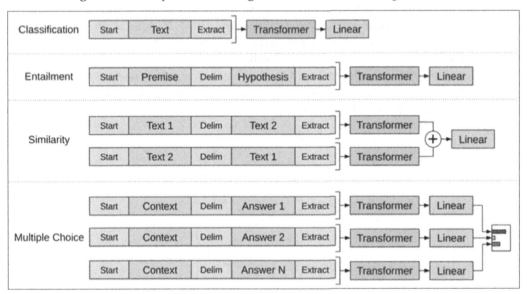

Figure 5.8: Input transformations in GPT-2 for different problems
(Source: Improving Language Understanding by Generative Pre-Training by Radford et al.)

The figure above shows how a pre-trained GPT-2 model can be used for a variety of tasks other than text generation. In each instance, start and end tokens are added before and after the input sequence. In all cases, a linear layer is added to the end that is trained during model fine-tuning. The major advantage being claimed is that many different types of tasks can be accomplished using the same architecture. The topmost architecture in *Figure 5.8* shows how it can be used for classification. GPT-2 could be used for IMDb sentiment analysis using this approach, for example.

The second example is of textual entailment. Textual entailment is an NLP task where the relationship between two fragments of text needs to be established. The first text fragment is called a premise, and the second fragment is called the hypothesis. Different relationships can exist between the premise and hypothesis. The premise can validate or contradict the hypothesis, or they may be unrelated.

Let's say the premise is *Exercising every day is an important part of a healthy lifestyle and longevity*. If the hypothesis is *exercise increases lifespan*, then the premise *entails* or *validates* the hypothesis. Alternatively, if the hypothesis is *Running has no benefits*, then the premise *contradicts* the hypothesis. Lastly, if the hypothesis is that *lifting weights can build a six-pack*, then the premise neither entails nor contradicts the hypothesis. To perform entailment with GPT-2, the premise and hypothesis are concatenated with a delimiter, usually $, in between them.

For text similarity, two input sequences are constructed, one with the first text sequence first and the second with the second text sequence first. The output from the GPT model is added together and fed to the linear layer. A similar approach is used for multiple-choice questions. However, our focus in this chapter is text generation.

Generating text with GPT-2

Hugging Face's transformers library simplifies the process of generating text with GPT-2. Similar to the pre-trained BERT model, as shown in the previous chapter, Hugging Face provides pre-trained GPT and GPT-2 models. These pre-trained models are used in the rest of the chapter. Code for this and the rest of the sections of this chapter can be found in the IPython notebook named `text-generation-with-GPT-2.ipynb`. After running the setup, scoot over to the *Generating Text with GPT-2* section. A section showing the generation of text with GPT is also provided for reference. The first step in generating text is to download the pre-trained model, and its corresponding tokenizer:

```
from transformers import TFGPT2LMHeadModel, GPT2Tokenizer

gpt2tokenizer = GPT2Tokenizer.from_pretrained("gpt2")

# add the EOS token as PAD token to avoid warnings
gpt2 = TFGPT2LMHeadModel.from_pretrained("gpt2",
                        pad_token_id=gpt2tokenizer.eos_token_id)
```

This may take a few minutes as the models need to be downloaded. You may see a warning if spaCy and ftfy are not available in your environment. These two libraries are not mandatory for text generation. The following code can be used to generate text using a greedy search algorithm:

```
# encode context the generation is conditioned on
input_ids = gpt2tokenizer.encode('Robotics is the domain of ', return_
tensors='tf')

# generate text until the output length
# (which includes the context length) reaches 50
greedy_output = gpt2.generate(input_ids, max_length=50)

print("Output:\n" + 50 * '-')
print(gpt2tokenizer.decode(greedy_output[0], skip_special_tokens=True))
```

```
Output:
--------------------------------------------------
Robotics is the domain of the United States Government.

The United States Government is the primary source of information on
the use of drones in the United States.

The United States Government is the primary source of information on
the use of drones
```

A prompt was supplied for the model to complete. The model started in a promising manner but soon resorted to repeating the same output.

 Note that the output shown for text generation is indicative. You may see different outputs for the same prompt. There are a few different reasons for this. There is some inherent randomness that is built into this process, which we can try and control by setting random seeds. The models themselves may be retrained periodically by the Hugging Face team and may evolve with newer versions.

Issues with the greedy search were noted in the previous section. Beam search can be considered as an alternative. At each step of generating a token, a set of top probability tokens are kept as part of the beam instead of just the highest-probability token. The sequence with the highest overall probability is returned at the end of the generation. *Figure 5.4*, in the previous section with a greedy search, can be considered as the output of a beam search algorithm with a beam size of 3.

Generating text using beam search is trivial:

```
# BEAM SEARCH
# activate beam search and early_stopping
beam_output = gpt2.generate(
    input_ids,
    max_length=50,
    num_beams=5,
    early_stopping=True
)

print("Output:\n" + 50 * '-')
print(gpt2tokenizer.decode(beam_output[0], skip_special_tokens=True))
```

```
Output:
--------------------------------------------------
Robotics is the domain of science and technology. It is the domain of
science and technology. It is the domain of science and technology. It
is the domain of science and technology. It is the domain of science
and technology. It is the domain
```

Qualitatively, the first sentence makes a lot more sense than the one generated by the greedy search. The `early_stopping` parameter signals generation to stop when all beams reach the EOS token. However, there is still much repetition going on. One parameter that can be used to control the repetition is by setting a limit on n-grams being repeated:

```
# set no_repeat_ngram_size to 2
beam_output = gpt2.generate(
    input_ids,
    max_length=50,
    num_beams=5,
    no_repeat_ngram_size=3,
    early_stopping=True
)

print("Output:\n" + 50 * '-')
print(gpt2tokenizer.decode(beam_output[0], skip_special_tokens=True))
```

```
Output:
--------------------------------------------------
Robotics is the domain of science and technology.

In this article, we will look at some of the most important aspects of
```

```
robotics and how they can be used to improve the lives of people around
the world. We will also take a look
```

This has made a considerable difference in the quality of the generated text. The no_
repeat_ngram_size parameter prevents the model from generating any 3-grams or
triplets of tokens more than once. While this improves the quality of the text, using
the n-gram constraint can have a significant impact on the quality of the generated
text. If the generated text is about *The White House*, then these three words can only
be used once in the entire generated text. In such a case, using the n-gram constraint
will be counter-productive.

To beam or not to beam

Beam search works well in cases where the generated sequence
is of a restricted length. As the length of the sequence increases,
the number of beams to be maintained and computed increases
significantly. Consequently, beam search works well in tasks like
summarization and translation but performs poorly in open-ended
text generation. Further, beam search, by trying to maximize the
cumulative probability, generates more predictable text. The text
feels less natural. The following piece of code can be used to get
a feel for the various beams being generated. Just make sure that
the number of beams is greater than or equal to the number of
sequences to be returned:

```
# Returning multiple beams
beam_outputs = gpt2.generate(
    input_ids,
    max_length=50,
    num_beams=7,
    no_repeat_ngram_size=3,
    num_return_sequences=3,
    early_stopping=True,
    temperature=0.7
)

print("Output:\n" + 50 * '-')
for i, beam_output in enumerate(beam_outputs):
  print("\n{}: {}".format(i,
                    gpt2tokenizer.decode(beam_output,
                        skip_special_tokens=True)))
```

```
Output:
--------------------------------------------------
0: Robotics is the domain of the U.S. Department of
Homeland Security. The agency is responsible for
the security of the United States and its allies,
including the United Kingdom, Canada, Australia, New
Zealand, and the European Union.
1: Robotics is the domain of the U.S. Department of
Homeland Security. The agency is responsible for
the security of the United States and its allies,
including the United Kingdom, France, Germany,
Italy, Japan, and the European Union.

2: Robotics is the domain of the U.S. Department of
Homeland Security. The agency is responsible for
the security of the United States and its allies,
including the United Kingdom, Canada, Australia, New
Zealand, the European Union, and the United
The text generated is very similar but differs near
the end. Also, note that temperature is available to
control the creativity of the generated text.
```

There is another method for improving the coherence and creativity of the text being generated called Top-K sampling. This is the preferred method in GPT-2 and plays an essential role in the success of GPT-2 in story generation. Before explaining how this works, let's try it out and see the output:

```
# Top-K sampling
tf.random.set_seed(42)  # for reproducible results
beam_output = gpt2.generate(
    input_ids,
    max_length=50,
    do_sample=True,
    top_k=25,
    temperature=2
)

print("Output:\n" + 50 * '-')
print(gpt2tokenizer.decode(beam_output[0], skip_special_tokens=True))
```

```
Output:
--------------------------------------------------
Robotics is the domain of people with multiple careers working with
robotics systems. The purpose of Robotics & Machine Learning in Science
```

```
and engineering research is not necessarily different for any given
research type because the results would be much more diverse.


Our team uses
```

The above sample was generated by selecting a high temperature value. A random seed was set to ensure repeatable results. The Top-K sampling method was published in a paper titled *Hierarchical Neural Story Generation* by Fan Lewis and Dauphin in 2018. The algorithm is relatively simple – at every step, it picks a token from the top *K* highest probability tokens. If *K* is set to 1, then this algorithm is identical to the greedy search.

In the code example above, the model looks at the 25 top tokens out of the 50,000+ tokens while generating text. Then, it picks a random word from these and continues the generation. Choosing larger values will result in more surprising or creative text. Choosing lower values of *K* will result in more predictable text. If you are a little underwhelmed by the results thus far, that is because the prompt selected is a really tough one. Consider this output generated with Top-K of 50 for the prompt *In the dark of the night, there was a*:

In the dark of the night, there was a sudden appearance of light.

Sighing, Xiao Chen slowly stood up and looked at Tian Cheng standing over. He took a step to look closely at Tian Cheng's left wrist and frowned.

Lin Feng was startled, and quickly took out a long sword!

Lin Feng didn't understand what sort of sword that Long Fei had wielded in the Black and Crystal Palace!

The Black and Crystal Palace was completely different than his original Black Stone City. Long Fei carried a sword as a souvenir, which had been placed on the back of his father's arm by Tian Cheng.

He drew the sword from his dad's arm again!

The black blade was one of the most valuable weapons within the Black and Crystal Palace. The sword was just as sharp as the sharpest of all weapons, which had been placed on Long Fei's father's arm by the Black Stone City's Black Ice, for him to

The above longer form text was generated by the smallest GPT-2 model, which has roughly 124 million parameters. Several different settings and model sizes are available for you to now play with. Remember, with great power comes great responsibility.

Between the last chapter and this one, we have covered both the encoder and decoder parts of the Transformer architecture conceptually. Now, we are ready to put both parts together in the next chapter. Let's quickly review what we covered in this chapter.

Summary

Generating text is a complicated task. There are practical uses that can make typing text messages or composing emails easier. On the other hand, there are creative uses, like generating stories. In this chapter, we covered a character-based RNN model to generate headlines one character at a time and noted that it picked up the structure, capitalization, and other things quite well. Even though the model was trained on a particular dataset, it showed promise in completing short sentences and partially typed words based on the context. The next section covered the state-of-the-art GPT-2 model, which is based on the Transformer decoder architecture. The previous chapter had covered the Transformer encoder architecture, which is used by BERT.

Generating text has many knobs to tune like temperature to resample distributions, greedy search, beam search, and Top-K sampling to balance the creativity and predictability of the generated text. We saw the impact of these settings on text generation and used a pre-trained GPT-2 model provided by Hugging Face to generate text.

Now that both the encoder and decoder parts of the Transformer architecture have been covered, the next chapter will use the full Transformer to build a text summarization model. Text summarization is at the cutting edge of NLP today. We will build a model that will read news articles and summarize them in a few sentences. Onward!

6

Text Summarization with Seq2seq Attention and Transformer Networks

Summarizing a piece of text challenges a deep learning model's understanding of language. Summarization can be considered a uniquely human ability, where the gist of a piece of text needs to be understood and phrased. In the previous chapters, we have built components that can help in summarization. First, we used BERT to encode text and perform sentiment analysis. Then, we used a decoder architecture with GPT-2 to generate text. Putting the Encoder and Decoder together yields a summarization model. In this chapter, we will implement a seq2seq Encoder-Decoder with Bahdanau Attention. Specifically, we will cover the following topics:

- Overview of extractive and abstractive text summarization
- Building a seq2seq model with attention to summarize text
- Improving summarization with beam search
- Addressing beam search issues with length normalizations
- Measuring the performance of summarization with ROUGE metrics
- A review of state-of-the-art summarization

The first step of this journey begins with understanding the main ideas behind text summarization. It is important to understand the task before building a model.

Overview of text summarization

The core idea in summarization is to condense long-form text or articles into a short representation. The shorter representation should contain the main idea of crucial information from the longer form. A single document can be summarized. This document could be long or may contain just a couple of sentences. An example of a short document summarization is generating a headline from the first few sentences of an article. This is called **sentence compression**. When multiple documents are being summarized, they are usually related. They could be the financial reports of a company or news reports about an event. The generated summary could itself be long or short. A shorter summary would be desirable when generating a headline. A lengthier summary would be something like an abstract and could have multiple sentences.

There are two main approaches when summarizing text:

- **Extractive summarization**: Phrases or sentences from the articles are selected and put together to create a summary. A mental model for this approach is using a highlighter on the long-form text, and the summary is the highlights put together. Extractive summarization is a more straightforward approach as sentences from the source text can be copied, which leads to fewer grammatical issues. The quality of the summarization is also easier to measure using metrics such as ROUGE. This metric is detailed later in this chapter. Extractive summarization was the predominant approach before deep learning and neural networks.

- **Abstractive summarization**: A person may use the full vocabulary available in a language while summarizing an article. They are not restricted to only using words from the article. The mental model is that the person is penning a new piece of text. The model must have some understanding of the meaning of different words so that the model can use them in the summary. Abstractive summarization is quite hard to implement and evaluate. The advent of the seq2seq architecture made significant improvements to the quality of abstractive summarization models.

This chapter focuses on abstractive summarization. Here are some examples of summaries that our model can generate:

Source text	Generated summary
american airlines group inc said on sunday it plans to raise ## billion by selling shares and convertible senior notes , to improve the airline's liquidity as it grapples with travel restrictions caused by the coronavirus .	american airlines to raise ## **bln** convertible **bond issue**
sales of newly-built single-family houses occurred at a seasonally adjusted annual rate of ## in may , that represented a #.#% increase from the downwardly revised pace of ## in april .	**new home** sales **rise** in may
jc penney will close another ## stores for good . the department store chain , which filed for bankruptcy last month , is inching toward its target of closing ## stores .	jc penney to close **more** stores

The source text was pre-processed to be all in lowercase, and numbers were replaced with placeholder tokens to prevent the model from inventing numbers in the summary. The generated summaries have some words highlighted. Those words were not present in the source text. The model was able to propose these words in the summary. Thus, the model is an abstractive summarization model. So, how can such a model be built?

One way of looking at the summarization problem is that the model is *translating* an input sequence of tokens into a smaller set of output tokens. The model learns the output lengths based on the supervised examples provided. Another well-known problem is mapping an input sequence to an output sequence – the problem of Neural Machine Translation or NMT. In NMT, the input sequence could be a sentence from the source language, and the output could be a sequence of tokens in the target language. The process for translation is as follows:

1. Convert the input text into tokens
2. Learn embeddings for these tokens
3. Pass the token embeddings through an encoder to calculate the hidden states and outputs
4. Use the hidden states with the attention mechanism for generating a context vector for the inputs
5. Pass encoder outputs, hidden states, and context vectors to the decoder part of the network
6. Generate the outputs from left to right using an autoregressive model

Google AI published a tutorial on NMT using a seq2seq attention model in July 2017. This model uses a left-to-right encoder with GRU cells. The Decoder also uses GRU cells. In summarization, the piece of text to be summarized is a prerequisite. This may or may not be valid for machine translation. In some cases, the translation is performed on the fly. In that case, a left-to-right encoder is useful. However, if the entire text to be translated or summarized is available from the outset, a bi-directional Encoder can encode context from both sides of a given token. BiRNN in the Encoder leads to much better performance of the overall model. The NMT tutorial code serves as inspiration for the seq2seq attention model and the attention tutorial referenced previously. Before we work on the model, let's look at the datasets that are used for this purpose.

Data loading and pre-processing

There are several summarization-related datasets available for training. These datasets are available through the TensorFlow Datasets or `tfds` package, which we have used in the previous chapters as well. The datasets that are available differ in length and style. The CNN/DailyMail dataset is one of the most commonly used datasets. It was published in 2015, with approximately a total of 1 million news articles. Articles from CNN, starting in 2007, and Daily Mail, starting in 2010, were collected until 2015. The summaries are usually multi-sentence. The Newsroom dataset, available from `https://summari.es`, contains over 1.3 million news articles from 38 publications. However, this dataset requires that you register to download it, which is why it is not used in this book. The wikiHow data set contains full Wikipedia article pages and the summary sentences for those articles. The LCSTS data set contains Chinese language data collected from Sina Weibo with paragraphs and their one-sentence summaries.

Another popular dataset is the Gigaword dataset. It provides the first one or two sentences of a news story and has the headline of the story as the summary. This dataset is quite large, with just under 4 million rows. This dataset was published in a paper titled *Annotated Gigaword* by Napoles et al. in 2011. It is quite easy to import this dataset using `tfds`. Given the large size of the dataset and long training times for the model, the training code is stored in Python files, while the inference code is in an IPython notebook. This pattern was used in the previous chapter as well. The code for training is in the `s2s-training.py` file. The top part of the file contains the imports and a method called `setupGPU()` to initialize the GPU. The file contains a main function, which provides the control flow, and several functions that perform specific actions.

The dataset needs to be loaded first. The code for loading the data is in the `load_data()` function:

```
def load_data():
    print(" Loading the dataset")
    (ds_train, ds_val, ds_test), ds_info = tfds.load(
        'gigaword',
        split=['train', 'validation', 'test'],
        shuffle_files=True,
        as_supervised=True,
        with_info=True,
    )
    return ds_train, ds_val, ds_test
```

The corresponding section in the main function looks like this:

```
if __name__ == "__main__":
    setupGPU()  # OPTIONAL - only if using GPU
    ds_train, _, _ = load_data()
```

Only the training dataset is being loaded. The validation dataset contains approximately 190,000 examples, while the test split contains over 1,900 examples. In contrast, the training set contains over 3.8 million examples. Depending on the internet connection, downloading the dataset may take a while:

```
Downloading and preparing dataset gigaword/1.2.0 (download: 551.61
MiB, generated: Unknown size, total: 551.61 MiB) to /xxx/tensorflow_
datasets/gigaword/1.2.0...
/xxx/anaconda3/envs/tf21g/lib/python3.7/site-packages/urllib3/
connectionpool.py:986: InsecureRequestWarning: Unverified HTTPS
request is being made to host 'drive.google.com'. Adding certificate
verification is strongly advised. See: https://urllib3.readthedocs.io/
en/latest/advanced-usage.html#ssl-warnings
  InsecureRequestWarning,
  InsecureRequestWarning,

Shuffling and writing examples to /xxx/tensorflow_datasets/
gigaword/1.2.0.incomplete1FP5M4/gigaword-train.tfrecord
100%
<snip/>
100%
1950/1951 [00:00<00:00, 45393.40 examples/s]
Dataset gigaword downloaded and prepared to /xxx/tensorflow_datasets/
gigaword/1.2.0. Subsequent calls will reuse this data.
```

The warning about insecure requests can be safely ignored. The data is now ready to be tokenized and vectorized.

Data tokenization and vectorization

The Gigaword dataset has been already cleaned, normalized, and tokenized using the StanfordNLP tokenizer. All the data is converted into lowercase and normalized using the StanfordNLP tokenizer, as seen in the preceding examples. The main task in this step is to create a vocabulary. A word-based tokenizer is the most common choice in summarization. However, we will use a subword tokenizer in this chapter. A subword tokenizer provides the benefit of limiting the size of the vocabulary while minimizing the number of unknown words. *Chapter 3, Named Entity Recognition (NER) with BiLSTMs, CRFs, and Viterbi Decoding,* on BERT, described different types of tokenizers. Consequently, models such specifically the part as BERT and GPT-2 use some variant of a subword tokenizer. The `tfds` package provides a way for us to create a subword tokenizer, initialized from a corpus of text. Since generating the vocabulary requires running it over all of the training data, this process can be slow. After initialization, the tokenizer can be persisted to disk for future use. The code for this process is defined in the `get_tokenizer()` function:

```
def get_tokenizer(data, file="gigaword32k.enc"):
    if os.path.exists(file+.subwords):
        # data has already been tokenized - just load and return
        tokenizer = \
tfds.features.text.SubwordTextEncoder.load_from_file(file)
    else:
        # This takes a while
        tokenizer = \
tfds.features.text.SubwordTextEncoder.build_from_corpus(
        ((art.numpy() + b" " + smm.numpy()) for art, smm in data),
        target_vocab_size=2**15
        )  # End tokenizer construction

        tokenizer.save_to_file(file)  # save for future iterations

    print("Tokenizer ready. Total vocabulary size: ", tokenizer.vocab_size)
    return tokenizer
```

This method checks to see if a subword tokenizer is saved and loads it. If no tokenizer exists on disk, it creates one by feeding in the articles and summaries combined. Note that creating a new tokenizer took over 20 minutes on my machine.

Hence, it is a good idea to do this process only once and persist the results for future use. The GitHub folder for this chapter contains a saved version of the tokenizer to save some of your time.

Two additional tokens that denote the start and end of a sequence are added to the vocabulary after its creation. These tokens help the model start and end the inputs and outputs. The end of sequence token provides a way for the Decoder, which generates the summary, to signal the end of the summary. The main method at this point looks like so:

```
if __name__ == "__main__":
    setupGPU()  # OPTIONAL - only if using GPU
    ds_train, _, _ = load_data()
    tokenizer = get_tokenizer(ds_train)
    # Test tokenizer
    txt = "Coronavirus spread surprised everyone"
    print(txt, " => ", tokenizer.encode(txt.lower()))

    for ts in tokenizer.encode(txt.lower()):
        print ('{} ----> {}'.format(ts, tokenizer.decode([ts])))

    # add start and end of sentence tokens
    start = tokenizer.vocab_size + 1
    end = tokenizer.vocab_size
    vocab_size = end + 2
```

Articles and their summaries can be tokenized using the tokenizer. Articles can be of varying lengths and will need to be truncated at a maximum length. A maximum token length of 128 has been chosen as the Gigaword dataset only contains a few sentences from the article. Note that 128 tokens are not the same as 128 words due to the subword tokenizer. Using a subword tokenizer minimizes the presence of unknown tokens during summary generation.

Once the tokenizer is ready, both the article and summary texts need to be tokenized. Since the summary will be fed to the Decoder one token at a time, the provided summary text will be shifted right by adding a start token, as shown previously. An end token will be appended to the summary to let the Decoder learn how to signal the end of the summary's generation. The encode() method in the file seq2seq.py defines the vectorization step:

```
def encode(article, summary, start=start, end=end,
           tokenizer=tokenizer, art_max_len=128,
           smry_max_len=50):
    # vectorize article
```

```
        tokens = tokenizer.encode(article.numpy())
        if len(tokens) > art_max_len:
            tokens = tokens[:art_max_len]
        art_enc = sequence.pad_sequences([tokens], padding='post',
                            maxlen=art_max_len).squeeze()
        # vectorize summary
        tokens = [start] + tokenizer.encode(summary.numpy())
        if len(tokens) > smry_max_len:
            tokens = tokens[:smry_max_len]
        else:
            tokens = tokens + [end]

        smry_enc = sequence.pad_sequences([tokens], padding='post',
                            maxlen=smry_max_len).squeeze()


        return art_enc, smry_enc
```

Since this is a Python function working on the contents of the text of tensors, another function needs to be defined. This can be passed to the dataset to be applied to all the rows of the data. This function is also defined in the same file as the encode function:

```
def tf_encode(article, summary):
    art_enc, smry_enc = tf.py_function(encode, [article, summary],
                            [tf.int64, tf.int64])
    art_enc.set_shape([None])
    smry_enc.set_shape([None])
    return art_enc, smry_enc
```

Going back to the main function in the s2s-training.py file, the dataset can be vectorized with the help of the preceding functions like so:

```
BUFFER_SIZE = 1500000  # dataset is 3.8M samples, using less
BATCH_SIZE = 64  # try bigger batch for faster training

train = ds_train.take(BUFFER_SIZE)  # 1.5M samples
print("Dataset sample taken")
train_dataset = train.map(s2s.tf_encode)

# train_dataset = train_dataset.shuffle(BUFFER_SIZE) - optional
train_dataset = train_dataset.batch(BATCH_SIZE,
drop_remainder=True)
print("Dataset batching done")
```

Note that shuffling the dataset is recommended. By shuffling the dataset, it is easier for the model to converge and not overfit to batches. However, this adds to the training time. This has been commented out here as this is an optional step. Shuffling records in batches while training models for production use cases is recommended. The last step in preparing the data is batching it, as shown in the last step here. Now, we are ready to build the model and train it.

Seq2seq model with attention

The summarization model has an Encoder part with a bidirectional RNN and a unidirectional decoder part. There is an attention layer that helps the Decoder focus on specific parts of the input while generating an output token. The overall architecture is shown in the following diagram:

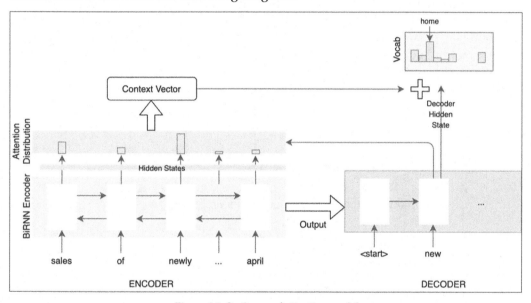

Figure 6.1: Seq2seq and attention model

These layers are detailed in the following subsections. All the code for these parts of the model are in the file `seq2seq.py`. All the layers use common hyperparameters specified in the main function in the `s2s-training.py` file:

```
embedding_dim = 128
units = 256  # from pointer generator paper
```

The code and architecture for this section have been inspired by the paper titled *Get To The Point: Summarization with Pointer-Generator Networks* by Abigail See, Peter Liu, and Chris Manning, published in April 2017. The fundamental architecture is easy to follow and provides impressive performance for a model that can be trained on a desktop with a commodity GPU.

Encoder model

The detailed architecture of the Encoder layer is shown in the following diagram. Tokenized and vectorized input is fed through an embedding layer. Embeddings for the tokens generated by the tokenizer are learned from scratch. It is possible to use a set of pre-trained embeddings like GloVe and use the corresponding tokenizer. While using a pre-trained set of embeddings can help with the accuracy of the model, a word-based vocabulary would have many unknown tokens, as we saw in the IMDb example and GloVe vectors earlier. The unknown tokens would impact the ability of the model to create summaries with words it hasn't seen before. If the summarization model is used on daily news, there can be several unknown words, like names of people, places, or new products:

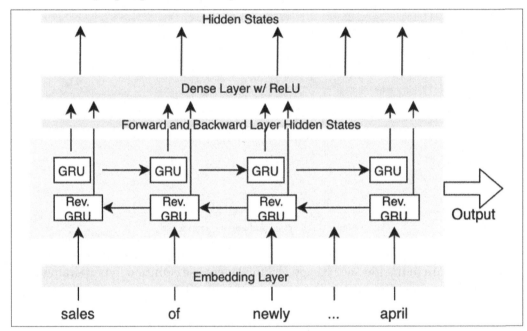

Figure 6.2: Encoder architecture

The embedding layer has a dimension of 128, as configured in the hyperparameters. These hyperparameters have been chosen to resemble those in the paper. We then create an embedding singleton that can be used by both the Encoder and the Decoder. The code for the class is in the `seq2seq.py` file:

```
class Embedding(object):
    embedding = None  # singleton

    @classmethod
    def get_embedding(self, vocab_size, embedding_dim):
        if self.embedding is None:
            self.embedding = tf.keras.layers.Embedding(vocab_size,
                                                       embedding_dim,
                                                       mask_zero=True)
        return self.embedding
```

Input sequences will be padded to a fixed length of 128. Hence, a masking parameter is passed to the embedding layer so that the embedding layer ignores the mask tokens. Next, let's define an `Encoder` class and instantiate the embedding layer in the constructor:

```
# Encoder
class Encoder(tf.keras.Model):
    def __init__(self, vocab_size, embedding_dim, enc_units, batch_size):
        super(Encoder, self).__init__()
        self.batch_size = batch_size
        self.enc_units = enc_units
        # Shared embedding layer
        self.embedding = Embedding.get_embedding(vocab_size,
                                                 embedding_dim)
```

The constructor takes a number of parameters:

- **Size of the vocabulary**: In the present case, this is 32,899 tokens.

- **Embedding dimensions**: This is 128 dimensions. Feel free to experiment with a larger or smaller embedding dimension. Smaller dimensions would reduce the model's size and memory required for training the model.

- **Encoder units**: The number of forward and backward units in the bidirectional layer. 256 units will be used for a total of 512 units.

- **Batch size**: The size of the input batches. 64 records will be in one batch. A larger batch would make training go faster but would need more memory on the GPU. So, this number can be adjusted based on the capacity of the training hardware.

The output of the embedding layer is fed to a bidirectional RNN layer. There are 256 GRU units in each direction. The bidirectional layer in Keras provides options on how to combine the output of the forward and backward layer. In this case, we concatenate the outputs of the forward and backward GRU cells. Hence, the output will be 512-dimensional. Furthermore, the hidden states are also needed for the attention mechanism to work, so a parameter is passed to retrieve the output states. The bidirectional GRU layer is configured like so:

```
self.bigru = Bidirectional(GRU(self.enc_units,
                    return_sequences=True,
                    return_state=True,
                    recurrent_initializer='glorot_uniform'),
                  merge_mode='concat'
              )
self.relu = Dense(self.enc_units, activation='relu')
```

A dense layer with ReLU activation is also set up. The two layers return their hidden layers. However, the Decoder and attention layers require one vector of hidden states. We pass the hidden states through the dense layer and convert the dimensions from 512 into 256, which is expected by the Decoder and attention modules. This completes the constructor for the Encoder class. Given this is a custom model with specific ways to compute the model, a `call()` method is defined that operates on a batch of inputs to produce the output and hidden states. This method takes in hidden states to seed the bidirectional layer:

```
def call(self, x, hidden):
    x = self.embedding(x)  # We are using a mask

    output, forward_state, backward_state = self.bigru(x, initial_
state = hidden)
# now, concat the hidden states through the dense ReLU
# layer
    hidden_states = tf.concat([forward_state, backward_state],
                        axis=1)
    output_state = self.relu(hidden_states)

    return output, output_state
```

First, the input is passed through the embedding layer. The output is fed to the bidirectional layer, and the output and hidden states are retrieved. The two hidden states are concatenated and fed through the dense layer to create the output hidden state. Lastly, a utility method to return initial hidden states is defined:

```
def initialize_hidden_state(self):
        return [tf.zeros((self.batch_size, self.enc_units))
                for i in range(2)]
```

This completes the code for the Encoder. Before going into the Decoder, an attention layer needs to be defined, which will be used in the Decoder. Bahdanau's attention formulation will be used for this. Note that TensorFlow/Keras does not provide an attention layer out of the box. However, this simple attention layer code should be entirely reusable.

Bahdanau attention layer

Bahdanau et al. published this form of global attention in 2015. It has been widely used in Transformer models, as we saw in the previous chapters. Now, we are going to implement an attention layer from scratch. This part of the code is inspired by the NMT tutorial published by the TensorFlow team.

The core idea behind attention is to let the Decoder see all the inputs and focus on the most relevant inputs while predicting the output token. A global attention mechanism allows the Decoder to see all the inputs. This global version of the attention mechanism will be implemented. At an abstract level, the purpose of the attention mechanism maps a set of values to a given query. It does this by providing a relevance score of each of these values for a given query.

In our case, the query is the Decoder's hidden state, and the values are the Encoder outputs. We are interested in figuring out which inputs can best help in generating the next token from the Decoder. The first step is computing a score using the Encoder output and the Decoder's previous hidden state. If this is the first step of decoding, then the hidden states from the Encoder are used to seed the Decoder. A corresponding weight matrix is multiplied by the Encoder's output and Decoder's hidden state. The output is passed through a *tanh* activation function and multiplied by another weight matrix to produce the final score. The following equation shows this formulation:

$$score = V \cdot \tanh(W_1 \cdot hidden_{decoder} + W_2 \cdot output_{encoder} + bias)$$

Matrices V, W_1, and W_2 are trainable. Then, to understand the alignment between the Decoder output and the Encoder outputs, a softmax is computed:

$$attention_{weights} = softmax(score)$$

The last step is to produce a context vector. The context vector is produced by multiplying the attention weights by the Encoder outputs:

$$context_{vector} = attentention_{weights} \cdot output_{encoder}$$

These are all the computations in the attention layer.

The first step is setting up the constructor for the attention class:

```
class BahdanauAttention(tf.keras.layers.Layer):
    def __init__(self, units):
        super(BahdanauAttention, self).__init__()
        self.W1 = tf.keras.layers.Dense(units)
        self.W2 = tf.keras.layers.Dense(units)
        self.V = tf.keras.layers.Dense(1)
```

The `call()` method of the `BahdanauAttention` class implements the equations shown previously with some additional code to manage the tensor shapes. This is shown here:

```
def call(self, decoder_hidden, enc_output):
    # decoder hidden state shape == (64, 256)
    # [batch size, decoder units]
    # encoder output shape == (64, 128, 256)
    # which is [batch size, max sequence length, encoder units]
    query = decoder_hidden # to map our code to generic
    # form of attention
    values = enc_output

    # query_with_time_axis shape == (batch_size, 1, hidden size)
    # we are doing this to broadcast addition along the time axis
    query_with_time_axis = tf.expand_dims(query, 1)

    # score shape == (batch_size, max_length, 1)
    score = self.V(tf.nn.tanh(
        self.W1(query_with_time_axis) + self.W2(values)))

    # attention_weights shape == (batch_size, max_length, 1)
```

```
attention_weights = tf.nn.softmax(score, axis=1)

# context_vector shape after sum == (batch_size, hidden_size)
context_vector = attention_weights * values
context_vector = tf.reduce_sum(context_vector, axis=1)

return context_vector, attention_weights
```

The only thing we have left to do is implement the Decoder model.

Decoder model

The detailed Decoder model is shown in the following diagram:

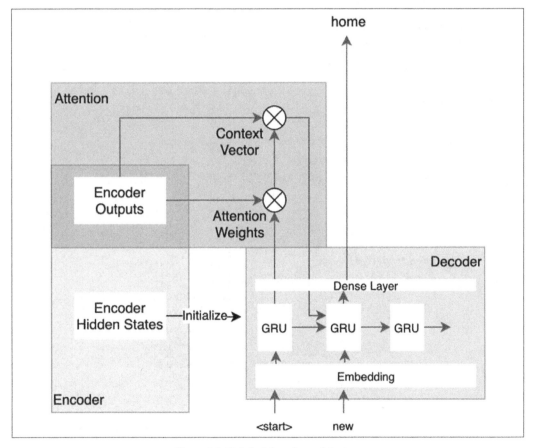

Figure 6.3: Detailed decoder architecture

Hidden states from the Encoder are used to initialize the hidden states of the Decoder. The start token initiates the summaries being generated. The hidden states of the Decoder, along with the Encoder output, are used to compute the attention weights and the context vector. The context vector, along with the embeddings of the output token, are concatenated and passed through the unidirectional GRU cell. The output of the GRU cell is passed through a dense layer, with a softmax activation function to get the output token. This process is repeated token by token.

Note that the Decoder functions differently during training and inference. During training, the output token from the Decoder is used to calculate the loss but is not fed back into the Decoder to produce the next token. Instead, the next token from the ground truth is fed into the Decoder at each time step. This process is called **teacher forcing**. The output tokens generated by the Decoder are only fed back in during inference when summaries are being generated.

A `Decoder` class is defined in the `seq2seq.py` file. The constructor for this class sets up the dimensions and the various layers:

```
class Decoder(tf.keras.Model):
    def __init__(self, vocab_size, embedding_dim, dec_units, batch_sz):
        super(Decoder, self).__init__()
        self.batch_sz = batch_sz
        self.dec_units = dec_units
        # Unique embedding layer
        self.embedding = tf.keras.layers.Embedding(vocab_size,
                                                   embedding_dim,
                                                   mask_zero=True)
        # Shared embedding layer
        # self.embedding = Embedding.get_embedding(vocab_size,
        # embedding_dim)
        self.gru = tf.keras.layers.GRU(self.dec_units,
                                       return_sequences=True,
                                       return_state=True,
                                       recurrent_initializer=\
                                       'glorot_uniform')
        self.fc1 = tf.keras.layers.Dense(vocab_size,
                             activation='softmax')

        # used for attention
        self.attention = BahdanauAttention(self.dec_units)
```

The embedding layer in the Decoder is not shared with the Encoder. This is a design choice. It is common in summarization to use a shared embedding layer. The structure of the articles and their summaries is slightly different in the Gigaword dataset as news headlines are not proper sentences but fragments of sentences. During training, using different embedding layers gave better results than shared embeddings. It is possible that, on the CNN/DailyMail dataset, shared embeddings give better results than on the Gigaword dataset. In the case of machine translation, the Encoder and Decoder are seeing different languages, so having separate embedding layers is a best practice. You are encouraged to try out both versions on different datasets and build your own intuition. The preceding commented code makes it easy to switch back and forth between shared and separate embeddings between the Encoder and Decoder.

The next part of the Decoder is the computation that calculates the output:

```
def call(self, x, hidden, enc_output):
    # enc_output shape == (batch_size, max_length, hidden_size)
    context_vector, attention_weights = self.attention(hidden,
                                                       enc_output)

    # x shape after passing through embedding
    # == (batch_size, 1, embedding_dim)
    x = self.embedding(x)

    x = tf.concat([tf.expand_dims(context_vector, 1), x], axis=-1)

    # passing the concatenated vector to the GRU
    output, state = self.gru(x)

    output = tf.reshape(output, (-1, output.shape[2]))

    x = self.fc1(output)

    return x, state, attention_weights
```

The computation is fairly straightforward. The model looks like this:

```
Model: "encoder"

Layer (type)                 Output Shape              Param #
=================================================================
embedding (Embedding)        multiple                  4211072
```

```
bidirectional (Bidirectional multiple              592896

dense (Dense)                 multiple             131328
=================================================================
Total params: 4,935,296
Trainable params: 4,935,296
Non-trainable params: 0

Model: "decoder"

Layer (type)                  Output Shape         Param #
=================================================================
embedding_1 (Embedding)       multiple             4211072

gru_1 (GRU)                   multiple             689664

dense_1 (Dense)               multiple             8455043

bahdanau_attention (Bahdanau multiple              197377
=================================================================
Total params: 13,553,156
Trainable params: 13,553,156
Non-trainable params: 0
```

The Encoder model contains 4.9M parameters, while the Decoder model contains 13.5M parameters for a total of 18.4M parameters. Now, we are ready to train the model.

Training the model

There are a number of steps to be performed in training that require a custom training loop. First, let's define a method that executes one step of the training loop. This method is defined in the s2s-training.py file:

```python
@tf.function
def train_step(inp, targ, enc_hidden, max_gradient_norm=5):
    loss = 0

    with tf.GradientTape() as tape:
        # print("inside gradient tape")
        enc_output, enc_hidden = encoder(inp, enc_hidden)
```

```
            dec_hidden = enc_hidden
            dec_input = tf.expand_dims([start] * BATCH_SIZE, 1)

            # Teacher forcing - feeding the target as the next input
            for t in range(1, targ.shape[1]):
                # passing enc_output to the decoder
                predictions, dec_hidden, _ = decoder(dec_input,
                                          dec_hidden, enc_output)

                loss += s2s.loss_function(targ[:, t], predictions)
                # using teacher forcing
                dec_input = tf.expand_dims(targ[:, t], 1)

        batch_loss = (loss / int(targ.shape[1]))

        variables = encoder.trainable_variables + \
    decoder.trainable_variables
        gradients = tape.gradient(loss, variables)

        # Gradient clipping
        clipped_gradients, _ = tf.clip_by_global_norm(
                                    gradients, max_gradient_norm)

        optimizer.apply_gradients(zip(clipped_gradients, variables))

        return batch_loss
```

This is a custom training loop that uses `GradientTape`, which tracks the different variables of the model and calculates the gradients. The preceding function runs once for each batch of inputs. Inputs are passed through the Encoder to get the final encoding and the last hidden state. The Decoder is initialized with the last Encoder hidden state, and summaries are generated one token at a time. However, the generated token is not fed back into the Decoder. Instead, the actual token is fed back. This method is known as **Teacher Forcing**. A custom loss function is defined in the `seq2seq.py` file:

```
  loss_object = tf.keras.losses.SparseCategoricalCrossentropy(
                  from_logits=False, reduction='none')


  def loss_function(real, pred):
      mask = tf.math.logical_not(tf.math.equal(real, 0))
      loss_ = loss_object(real, pred)
```

```
    mask = tf.cast(mask, dtype=loss_.dtype)
    loss_ *= mask

    return tf.reduce_mean(loss_)
```

The key to the loss function is to use a mask to handle summaries of varying lengths. The last part of the model is using an optimizer. The Adam optimizer is being used here, with a learning rate schedule that reduces the learning rate over epochs of training. The concept of learning rate annealing was covered in previous chapters. The code for the optimizer is inside the main function in the s2s-training.py file:

```
steps_per_epoch = BUFFER_SIZE // BATCH_SIZE
embedding_dim = 128
units = 256  # from pointer generator paper
EPOCHS = 16

encoder = s2s.Encoder(vocab_size, embedding_dim, units, BATCH_SIZE)
decoder = s2s.Decoder(vocab_size, embedding_dim, units, BATCH_SIZE)

# Learning rate scheduler
lr_schedule = tf.keras.optimizers.schedules.InverseTimeDecay(
                0.001,
                decay_steps=steps_per_epoch*(EPOCHS/2),
                decay_rate=2,
                staircase=False)

optimizer = tf.keras.optimizers.Adam(lr_schedule)
```

Since the model is going to be trained for a long time, it is important to set up checkpoints that can be used to restart training in case issues occur. Checkpoints also provide us with an opportunity to adjust some of the training parameters across runs. The next part of the main function sets up the checkpointing system. We looked at checkpoints in the previous chapter. We will extend what we've learned and set up an optional command-line argument that specifies if training needs to be restarted from a specific checkpoint:

```
if args.checkpoint is None:
    dt = datetime.datetime.today().strftime("%Y-%b-%d-%H-%M-%S")
    checkpoint_dir = './training_checkpoints-' + dt
else:
    checkpoint_dir = args.checkpoint
```

```
checkpoint_prefix = os.path.join(checkpoint_dir, "ckpt")
checkpoint = tf.train.Checkpoint(optimizer=optimizer,
                                    encoder=encoder,
                                    decoder=decoder)
if args.checkpoint is not None:
    # restore last model
    print("Checkpoint being restored: ",
 tf.train.latest_checkpoint(checkpoint_dir))
    chkpt_status = checkpoint.restore(
tf.train.latest_checkpoint(checkpoint_dir))
    # to check loading worked
 chkpt_status.assert_existing_objects_matched()
else:
    print("Starting new training run from scratch")

 print("New checkpoints will be stored in: ", checkpoint_dir)
```

If training needs to be restarted from a checkpoint, then a command-line argument in the form ``--checkpoint <dir>`` can be specified while invoking the training script. If no argument is supplied, then a new checkpoint directory will be created. Training with 1.5M records takes over 3 hours. Running 10 iterations will take over a day and a half. The Pointer-Generator model we referenced earlier in this chapter was trained for 33 epochs, which took over 4 days of training. However, it is possible to see some results after 4 epochs of training.

Now, the last part of the main function is to start the training process:

```
print("Starting Training. Total number of steps / epoch: ", steps_per_
epoch)

    for epoch in range(EPOCHS):
        start_tm = time.time()
        enc_hidden = encoder.initialize_hidden_state()
        total_loss = 0
        for (batch, (art, smry)) in enumerate(train_dataset.take(steps_
per_epoch)):
            batch_loss = train_step(art, smry, enc_hidden)
            total_loss += batch_loss
            if batch % 100 == 0:
                ts = datetime.datetime.now().\
strftime("%d-%b-%Y (%H:%M:%S)")
                print('[{}] Epoch {} Batch {} Loss {:.6f}'.\
                    format(ts,epoch + 1, batch,
```

```
                    batch_loss.numpy())) # end print

    # saving (checkpoint) the model every 2 epochs
    if (epoch + 1) % 2 == 0:
        checkpoint.save(file_prefix = checkpoint_prefix)
    print('Epoch {} Loss {:.6f}'.\
            format(epoch + 1, total_loss / steps_per_epoch))

    print('Time taken for 1 epoch {} sec\n'.\
            format(time.time() - start_tm))
```

The training loop prints the loss every 100 batches and saves a checkpoint every second epoch. Feel free to adjust these settings as needed. The following command can be used to start training:

```
$ python s2s-training.py
```

The output of this script should be something similar to:

```
Loading the dataset
Tokenizer ready. Total vocabulary size:  32897
Coronavirus spread surprised everyone  => [16166, 2342, 1980, 7546,
21092]
16166 ----> corona
2342 ----> virus
1980 ----> spread
7546 ----> surprised
21092 ----> everyone
Dataset sample taken
Dataset batching done
Starting new training run from scratch
New checkpoints will be stored in:  ./training_checkpoints-2021-
Jan-04-04-33-42
Starting Training. Total number of steps / epoch:  31
[04-Jan-2021 (04:34:45)] Epoch 1 Batch 0 Loss 2.063991
...
Epoch 1 Loss 1.921176
Time taken for 1 epoch 83.241370677948 sec
[04-Jan-2021 (04:35:06)] Epoch 2 Batch 0 Loss 1.487815
Epoch 2 Loss 1.496654
Time taken for 1 epoch 21.058568954467773 sec
```

This sample run used only 2,000 samples since we edited this line:

```
BUFFER_SIZE = 2000  # 3500000 takes 7hr/epoch
```

If training is being restarted from a checkpoint, then the command line will be:

```
$ python s2s-trainingo.py --checkpoint training_checkpoints-2021-
Jan-04-04-33-42
```

With this comment, the model is hydrated from the checkpoint directory we used in the training step. Training continues from that point. Once the model has finished training, we are ready to generate the summaries. Note that the model we'll be using in the next section was trained for 8 epochs with 1.5M records. Using all 3.8M records and training for more epochs would give better results.

Generating summaries

The critical thing to note while generating summaries is that a new inference loop will need to be built. Recall that *teacher forcing* was used during training, and the output of the Decoder was not used in predicting the next token. While generating summaries, we would like to use the generated tokens in predicting the next token. Since we would like to play with various input texts and generate summaries, we will use the code in the generating-summaries.ipynb IPython notebook. After importing and setting everything up, the tokenizer needs to be instantiated. The *Setup Tokenization* section of the notebook loads the tokenizers and sets up the vocabulary by adding start and end token IDs. Similar to when we loaded the data, the data encoding method is set up to encode the input articles.

Now, we must hydrate the model from the saved checkpoint. All of the model objects are created first:

```
BATCH_SIZE = 1  # for inference
embedding_dim = 128
units = 256  # from pointer generator paper
vocab_size = end + 2

# Create encoder and decoder objects
encoder = s2s.Encoder(vocab_size, embedding_dim, units,
                      BATCH_SIZE)
decoder = s2s.Decoder(vocab_size, embedding_dim, units,
                      BATCH_SIZE)
optimizer = tf.keras.optimizers.Adam()
```

Next, a checkpoint with the appropriate checkpoint directory is defined:

```
# Hydrate the model from saved checkpoint
checkpoint_dir = 'training_checkpoints-2021-Jan-25-09-26-31'
checkpoint_prefix = os.path.join(checkpoint_dir, "ckpt")

checkpoint = tf.train.Checkpoint(optimizer=optimizer,
                                 encoder=encoder,
                                 decoder=decoder)
```

Then, the last checkpoint is checked:

```
# The last training checkpoint
tf.train.latest_checkpoint(checkpoint_dir)
```

```
'training_checkpoints-2021-Jan-25-09-26-31/ckpt-11'
```

Since checkpoints are stored after every alternate epoch, this checkpoint corresponds to 8 epochs of training. Checkpoints can be loaded and tested with the following code:

```
chkpt_status = checkpoint.restore(
                        tf.train.latest_checkpoint(checkpoint_dir))
chkpt_status.assert_existing_objects_matched()
```

```
<tensorflow.python.training.tracking.util.CheckpointLoadStatus at
0x7f603ae03c90>
```

That's it! The model is now ready for inference.

Checkpoints and variable names

It is possible that the second command may give an error if it cannot match the names of the variables in the checkpoint with the names in the model. This can happen as we did not explicitly name the layers when they were instantiated in the model. TensorFlow will provide a dynamically generated name for the layer when the model is instantiated:

```
for layer in decoder.layers:
    print(layer.name)
```

```
embedding_1
gru_1
fc1
```

Variable names in the checkpoint can be inspected with:

```
tf.train.list_variables(
        tf.train.latest_checkpoint('./<chkpt_dir>/')
)
```

If the model is instantiated again, these names may change, and restore from checkpoint may fail. There are two solutions to prevent this. A quick fix is to restart the notebook kernel. A better fix is to edit the code and add names to each layer in the Encoder and Decoder constructors before training. This ensures that checkpoints will always find the variables. An example of this approach is shown for the `fc1` layer in the Decoder:

```
self.fc1 = tf.keras.layers.Dense(
                vocab_size, activation='softmax',
                name='fc1')
```

Inference can be done via the greedy search or beam search algorithms. Both of these methods will be demonstrated here. Before going into the code for generating summaries, a convenience method for plotting attention weights will be defined. This helps in providing some intuition on what inputs contributed to a given token being generated in the summary:

```
# function for plotting the attention weights
def plot_attention(attention, article, summary):
    fig = plt.figure(figsize=(10,10))
    ax = fig.add_subplot(1, 1, 1)
    # https://matplotlib.org/3.1.0/tutorials/colors/colormaps.html
    # for scales
    ax.matshow(attention, cmap='cividis')

    fontdict = {'fontsize': 14}

    ax.set_xticklabels([''] + article, fontdict=fontdict, rotation=90)

    ax.set_yticklabels([''] + summary, fontdict=fontdict)

    ax.xaxis.set_major_locator(ticker.MultipleLocator(1))
    ax.yaxis.set_major_locator(ticker.MultipleLocator(1))

    plt.show()
```

A plot is configured with the input sequence as the columns and the output summary tokens as the rows. Feel free to play with different color scales to get a better idea of the strength of the association between the tokens.

We have covered much ground and possibly trained a network for hours. It is time to see the fruits of our labor!

Greedy search

Greedy search uses the highest probability token at each time step to construct the sequence. The predicted token is fed back into the model to generate the next token. This is the same model that was used in the previous chapter while generating characters in the char-RNN model:

```python
art_max_len = 128
smry_max_len = 50

def greedy_search(article):
    # To store attention plots of the output
    attention_plot = np.zeros((smry_max_len, art_max_len))

    tokens = tokenizer.encode(article)
    if len(tokens) > art_max_len:
        tokens = tokens[:art_max_len]

    inputs = sequence.pad_sequences([tokens], padding='post',
                                maxlen=art_max_len).squeeze()
    inputs = tf.expand_dims(tf.convert_to_tensor(inputs), 0)

    # output summary tokens will be stored in this
    summary = "

    hidden = [tf.zeros((1, units)) for i in range(2)] #BiRNN
    enc_out, enc_hidden = encoder(inputs, hidden)
    dec_hidden = enc_hidden
    dec_input = tf.expand_dims([start], 0)

    for t in range(smry_max_len):
        predictions, dec_hidden, attention_weights = \
    decoder(dec_input, dec_hidden, enc_out)

        predicted_id = tf.argmax(predictions[0]).numpy()
```

```
    if predicted_id == end:
        return summary, article, attention_plot
    # storing the attention weights to plot later on
    attention_weights = tf.reshape(attention_weights, (-1, ))
    attention_plot[t] = attention_weights.numpy()

    summary += tokenizer.decode([predicted_id])
    # the predicted ID is fed back into the model
    dec_input = tf.expand_dims([predicted_id], 0)


  return summary, article, attention_plot
```

The first part of the code encodes the inputs the same way they were encoded during training. These inputs are passed through the Encoder to the final encoder output and the last hidden state. The Decoder's initial hidden state is set to the last hidden state of the Encoder. Now, the process of generating the output tokens begins. First, the inputs are fed to the Decoder, which generates a prediction, the hidden state, and the attention weights. Attention weights are added to a running list of attention weights per time step. This generation continues until whichever comes earlier; producing an end-of-sequence token, or producing 50 tokens. The resulting summary and attention plot are returned. A summarization method is defined, which calls this greedy search algorithm, plots the attention weights, and converts the generated tokens into proper words:

```
# Summarize
def summarize(article, algo='greedy'):
    if algo == 'greedy':
        summary, article, attention_plot = greedy_search(article)
    else:
        print("Algorithm {} not implemented".format(algo))
        return

    print('Input: %s' % (article))
    print('** Predicted Summary: {}'.format(summary))

    attention_plot = \
  attention_plot[:len(summary.split(' ')), :len(article.split(' '))]

    plot_attention(attention_plot, article.split(' '),
                     summary.split(' '))
```

The preceding method has a spot where we can plug in beam search later. Let's test the model:

```
# Test Summarization
txt = "president georgi parvanov summoned france 's ambassador on
wednesday in a show of displeasure over comments from french president
jacques chirac chiding east european nations for their support of
washington on the issue of iraq ."
summarize(txt.lower())
```

```
Input: president georgi parvanov summoned france's ambassador on
wednesday in a show of displeasure over comments from french president
jacques chirac chiding east european nations for their support of
washington on the issue of iraq .
** Predicted Summary: bulgarian president summons french ambassador
over remarks on iraq
```

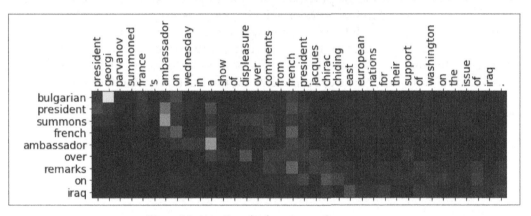

Figure 6.4: Attention plot for an example summary

Let's take a look at the generated summary:

bulgarian president summons french ambassador over remarks on iraq

It is a pretty good summary! The most surprising part is that the model was able to identify the Bulgarian president, even though Bulgaria is not mentioned anywhere in the source text. It contains other words not found in the original text. These are highlighted in the preceding output. The model was able to change the tense of the word *summoned* to *summons*. The word *remarks* never appears in the source text. The model was able to infer this from a number of input tokens. The notebook contains many examples, both good and bad, of summaries generated by the model.

Here is an example of a piece of challenging text for the model:

- **Input**: *charles kennedy , leader of britain's third-ranked liberal democrats , announced saturday he was quitting with immediate effect and would not stand in a new leadership election . us president george w. bush on saturday called for extending tax cuts adopted in his first term , which he said had bolstered economic growth.*
- **Predicted summary**: *kennedy quits to be a step toward new term*

In this article, there are two seemingly unrelated sentences. The model is trying to make sense of them but messes it up. There are other examples where the model doesn't do so well:

- **Input**: *jc penney will close another ## stores for good . the department store chain , which filed for bankruptcy last month , is inching toward its target of closing ## stores.*
- **Predicted summary**: *jc penney to close another ## stores for #nd stores*

In this example, the model repeats itself, attending to the same positions. In fact, this is a common problem with summarization models. One solution to prevent repetition is to add coverage loss. Coverage loss keeps a running total of the attention weights across time steps and feeds it back to the attention mechanism, as a way to clue it in to previously attended positions. Furthermore, coverage loss terms are added to the overall loss equation to penalize repetition. Training the model for much longer would also help in this particular case. Note that Transformer-based models suffer a little less from repetition.

The second example is the model inventing something:

- **Input**: *the german engineering giant siemens is working on a revamped version of its defective tram car , of which the ### units sold so far worldwide are being recalled owing to a technical fault , a company spokeswoman said on tuesday.*
- **Predicted summary**: *siemens to launch reb-made cars*

The model invents *reb-made*, which is incorrect:

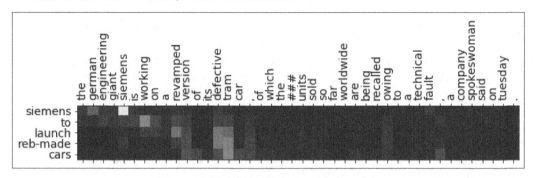

Figure 6.5: Model invents the word "reb-made"

Looking at the preceding attention plot, the new word is being generated by attending to *revamped*, *version*, *defective*, and *tram*. This made-up word garbles the summary generated.

As noted earlier, using beam search can help in further improving the accuracy of the translations. We will try some of these challenging examples after implementing the beam search algorithm.

Beam search

Beam search uses multiple paths or beams to generate tokens and tries to minimize the overall conditional probability. At each time step, all the options are evaluated, and the cumulative conditional probabilities are evaluated over all the time steps so far. Only the top k beams, where k is the beam width, are kept; the rest are pruned for the next time step. Greedy search is a special case of beam search with a beam width of 1. In fact, this property serves as a test case for the beam search algorithm. The code for this section can be found in the *Beam Search* section of the IPython notebook.

A new method called beam_search() is defined. The first part of this method is similar to greedy search, where inputs are tokenized and passed through the Encoder. The main difference between this algorithm and the greedy search algorithm is the core loop, which processes one token at a time. In beam search, a token needs to be generated for every beam. This makes beam search slower than greedy search, and running time increases in proportion to beam width. At each time step, for each of the k beams, the top k tokens are generated, sorted, and pruned back to k items. This step is performed until each beam generates an end of sequence token or has generated the maximum number of tokens. If there are m tokens to be generated, then beam search would require $k * m$ runs of the Decoder to generate the output sequence. The main loop is shown in the following code:

```python
# initial beam with (tokens, last hidden state, attn, score)
start_pt = [([start], dec_hidden, attention_plot, 0.0)]  # initial beam

for t in range(smry_max_len):
    options = list() # empty list to store candidates
    for row in start_pt:
        # handle beams emitting end signal
        allend = True
        dec_input = row[0][-1]
        if dec_input != end_tk:
            # last token
            dec_input = tf.expand_dims([dec_input], 0)

            dec_hidden = row[1]  # second item is hidden states
            attn_plt = np.zeros((smry_max_len, art_max_len)) +\
                    row[2] # new attn vector

            predictions, dec_hidden, attention_weights = \
decoder(dec_input, dec_hidden, enc_out)

            # storing the attention weights to plot later on
            attention_weights = tf.reshape(attention_weights, (-1, ))
            attn_plt[t] = attention_weights.numpy()

            # take top-K in this beam
            values, indices = tf.math.top_k(predictions[0],
                                            k=beam_width)

            for tokid, scre in zip(indices, values):
                score = row[3] - np.log(scre)
                options.append((row[0]+[tokid], dec_hidden,
                                attn_plt, score))
            allend=False
        else:
            options.append(row)  # add ended beams back in

    if allend:
        break # end for loop as all sequences have ended

    start_pt = sorted(options, key=lambda tup:tup[3])[:beam_width]
```

At the start, there is only one beam within the start token. A list to keep track of the beams generated is then defined. The list of tuples stores the attention plots, tokens, last hidden state, and the overall cost of the beam. Conditional probability requires a product of all probabilities. Given that all probabilities are numbers between 0 and 1, the conditional probability could become very small. Instead, logs of the probabilities are added together, as shown in the preceding highlighted code. The best beams minimize this score. Finally, a small section is inserted that prints all the top beams with their scores once the function completes its execution. This part is optional and can be removed:

```
if verbose:  # to control output
    # print all the final summaries
    for idx, row in enumerate(start_pt):
        tokens = [x for x in row[0] if x < end_tk]
        print("Summary {} with {:5f}: {}".format(idx, row[3],
                                  tokenizer.decode(tokens)))
```

At the end, the function returns the best beam:

```
# return final sequence
summary = tokenizer.decode([x for x in start_pt[0][0] if x < end_
tk])
attention_plot = start_pt[0][2] # third item in tuple
return summary, article, attention_plot
```

The `summarize()` method is extended so that you can generate greedy and beam search, like so:

```
# Summarize
def summarize(article, algo='greedy', beam_width=3, verbose=True):
    if algo == 'greedy':
        summary, article, attention_plot = greedy_search(article)
    elif algo=='beam':
        summary, article, attention_plot = beam_search(article,
                                      beam_width=beam_width,
                                      verbose=verbose)
    else:
        print("Algorithm {} not implemented".format(algo))
        return

    print('Input: %s' % (article))
    print('** Predicted Summary: {}'.format(summary))
```

```
attention_plot = attention_plot[:len(summary.split(' ')),
                                 :len(article.split(' '))]
plot_attention(attention_plot, article.split(' '),
               summary.split(' '))
```

Let's re-run the Siemens tram car example:

- **Greedy search summary**: *siemens to launch reb-made cars*
- **Beam search summary**: *siemens working on revamped european tram car*

The beam search summary contains more detail and represents the text better. It introduces a new word, *european*, which may or may not be accurate in the current context. Contrast the following attention plot with the one shown previously:

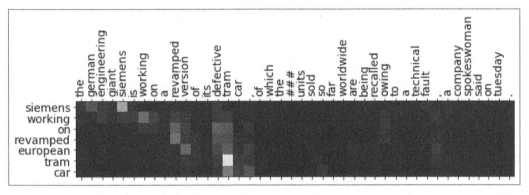

Figure 6.6: Attention plot of summary generated by beam search

The summary generated by beam search covers more concepts from the source text. For the JC Penney example, beam search makes the output better:

- **Greedy search summary**: *jc penney to close another ## stores stores for #nd stores*
- **Beam search summary**: *jc penney to close ## more stores*

The beam search summary is more concise and grammatically correct. These examples were generated with a beam width of 3. The notebook contains several other examples for you to play with. You will notice that generally, beam search improves the results, but it reduces the length of the output. Beam search suffers from issues where the score of sequences is not normalized for the sequence length, and repeatedly attending to the same input tokens has no penalty.

The most significant improvement at this point will come from training the model for longer and on more examples. The model that was used for these examples was trained for 22 epochs on 1.5M samples out of 3.8M from the Gigaword dataset. However, it is important to have beam search and various penalties in your back pocket to improve the quality of your model.

There are two specific penalties that address these issues, both of which will be discussed in the next section.

Decoding penalties with beam search

Wu et al. proposed two penalties in the seminal paper *Google's Neural Machine Translation System*, published in 2016. These penalties are:

- **Length normalization**: Aimed at encouraging longer or short summaries.

- **Coverage normalization**: Aimed at penalizing generation if the output focuses too much on the same part of the input sequence. As per the pointer-generator paper, this is best added during training for the last few iterations of training. This will not be implemented in this section.

These methods are inspired by NMT and must be adapted for the needs of summarization. At a high level, the score can be represented by the following formula:

$$score_{norm} = \frac{score}{length\_penalty} + coverage\_penalty$$

For example, the beam search algorithm naturally produces shorter sequences. The length penalty is important for NMT as the output sequence should address the input text. This is different from summarization, where shorter outputs are preferred. Length normalization computes a factor based on a parameter and the current token number. The cost of the beam is divided by this factor to calculate a length-normalized score. The paper proposes the following empirical formula:

$$length\_penalty(Y) = \frac{(5 + |Y|)^{\alpha}}{(5 + 1)^{\alpha}}$$

Smaller values of alpha produce shorter sequences, and larger values produce longer sequences. Values of α are between 0 and 1. The conditional probability score is divided by the preceding quantity to give the normalized score for a beam. The `length_wu()` method normalizes the score using this parameter.

Note that all the code for this part is in the *Beam Search with Length Normalizations* section of the notebook:

```
def length_wu(step, score, alpha=0.):
    # NMT length re-ranking score from
    # "Google's Neural Machine Translation System" paper by Wu et al
    modifier = (((5 + step) ** alpha) /
                ((5 + 1) ** alpha))
    return (score / modifier)
```

It is easy to implement in the code. A new beam search method with normalizations is created. Most of the code is the same as in the previous implementation. The key change for enabling length normalization involves adding an alpha parameter to the method signature and updating the computation of the score so that it uses the aforementioned method:

```
# Beam search implementation with normalization
def beam_search_norm(article, beam_width=3,
                     art_max_len=128,
                     smry_max_len=50,
                     end_tk=end,
                     alpha=0.,
                     verbose=True)
```

Next, the score is normalized like so (around line 60 in the code):

```
for tokid, scre in zip(indices, values):
    score = row[3] - np.log(scre)
    score = length_wu(t, score, alpha)
```

Let's try the settings out on some examples. First, we will try placing a length normalization penalty on the Siemens example:

- **Greedy search**: *siemens to launch reb-made cars*
- **Beam search**: *siemens working on revamped european tram car*
- **Beam search with length penalties**: *siemens working on new version of defective tram car*

A beam size of 5 and an alpha of 0.8 was used to generate the preceding example. Length normalization generates longer summaries, which corrects some of the challenges that are faced by the summaries generated purely by beam search:

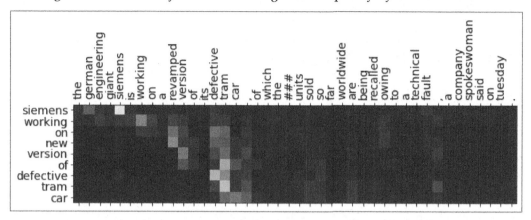

Figure 6.7: Beam search with length normalization produces a great summary

Now, let's take a look at a more complex contemporary example, which is not in the training set at all:

- **Input**: *the uk on friday said that it would allow a quarantine-free international travel to some low-risk countries falling in its green zone list of an estimated ## nations . uk transport secretary said that the us will fall within the red zone*

- **Greedy search**: *uk to allow free travel to low-risk countries*

- **Beam search**: *britain to allow free travel to low-risk countries*

- **Beam search with length normalization**: *britain to allow quarantines free travel to low-risk countries*

The best summary uses beam search and length normalization. Note that beam search alone was removing a very important word, "quarantines", before "free travel." This changed the meaning of the summary. With length normalization, the summary contains all the right details. Note that the Gigaword dataset has very short summaries in general, and beam search is making them even shorter. Hence, we use larger values of alpha. Generally, smaller values of alpha are used for summarization and larger values for NMT. You can try different values of the length normalization parameter and beam width to build some intuition. Note that the formulation for the length penalty was empirical. It should also be experimented with.

The penalty adds a new parameter that needs to be tuned in addition to beam size. Selecting the right parameters requires a better way of evaluating summaries than human inspection. This is the focus of the next section.

Evaluating summaries

When people write summaries, they use inventive language. Human-written summaries often use words that are not present in the vocabulary of the text being summarized. When models generate abstractive summaries, they may also use words that are different from the words used in the ground truth summaries provided. There is no real way to do an effective semantic comparison of the ground truth summary and the generated summary. In summarization problems, a human evaluation step is often involved, which is where a qualitative check of the generated summaries is done. This method is both unscalable and expensive. There are approximations that uses n-gram overlaps and the longest common subsequence matches after stemming and lemmatization. The hope is that such pre-processing helps bring ground truth and generated summaries closer together for evaluation. The most common metric used for evaluating summaries is **Recall-Oriented Understudy for Gisting Evaluation**, also referred to as **ROUGE**. In machine translation, metrics such as **Bilingual Evaluation Understudy (BLEU)** and **Metric for Evaluation of Translation with Explicit Ordering (METEOR)** are used. BLEU relies mainly on precision, as precision is very important for translation. In summarization, recall is more important. Consequently, ROUGE is the metric of choice for evaluating summarization models. It was proposed by Chin-Yew Lin in 2004 in a paper titled *Rouge: A Package for Automatic Evaluation of Summaries*.

ROUGE metric evaluation

A summary that's generated by a model should be readable, coherent, and factually correct. In addition, it should be grammatically correct. Human evaluation of summaries can be a mammoth task. If a person took 30 seconds to evaluate one summary in the Gigaword dataset, then it would take over 26 hours for one person to check the validation set. Since abstractive summaries are being generated, this human evaluation work will need to be done every time summaries are produced. The ROUGE metric tries to measure various aspects of an abstractive summary. It is a collection of four metrics:

- **ROUGE-N** is the n-gram recall between a generated summary and the ground truth or reference summary. "N" at the end of the name specifies the length of the n-gram. It is common to report ROUGE-1 and ROUGE-2. The metric is calculated as the ratio of matching n-grams between the ground truth summary and the generated summary, divided by the total number of n-grams in the ground truth. This formulation is oriented toward recall. If multiple reference summaries exist, the ROUGE-N metric is calculated pairwise for each reference summary, and the maximum score is taken. In our example, only one reference summary exists.

- **ROUGE-L** uses the **longest common subsequence (LCS)** between the generated summary and the ground truth to calculate the metric. Often, the sequences are stemmed prior to computing the LCS. Once the length of the LCS is known, precision is calculated by dividing it by the length of the reference summary; recall is calculated by dividing by the length of the generated score. The F1 score, which is the harmonic mean of precision and recall, is also calculated and reported. The F1 score provides a way for us to balance precision and recall. Since the LCS already includes common n-grams, choosing an n-gram length is not required. This particular version of ROUGE-L is called the sentence-level LCS score. There is a summary-level score as well, for cases when the summary contains more than one sentence. It is used for the CNN and DailyMail datasets, among others. The summary-level score matches each sentence in the ground truth with all the generated sentences to calculate the union LCS precision and recall. Details of the method can be found in the paper referenced previously.

- **ROUGE-W** is a weighted version of the previous metric, where contiguous matches in the LCS are weighted higher than if the tokens were separated by some other tokens in the middle.

- **ROUGE-S** uses skip-bigram co-occurrence statistics. A skip-bigram allows there to be arbitrary gaps between two tokens. Precision and recall are calculated using this measure.

The paper that proposed these metrics also contained code, in Perl, for calculating these metrics. This requires generating text files with references and generating summaries. Google Research has published a full Python implementation that is available from their GitHub repository: https://github.com/google-research/google-research. The rouge/ directory contains the code for these metrics. Please follow the installation instructions from the repository. Once installed, we can evaluate greedy search, beam search, and beam search with length normalization to judge their quality using the ROUGE-L metric. The code for this part is in the ROUGE Evaluation section.

The scorer library can be imported and initialized like so:

```
from rouge_score import rouge_scorer as rs
scorer = rs.RougeScorer(['rougeL'], use_stemmer=True)
```

A version of the summarize() method, called summarize_quietly(), is used to summarize pieces of text without printing any outputs like attention plots. Random samples from the validation test will be used to measure the performance. The code for loading the data and the quiet summarization method can be found in the notebook and should be run prior to running metrics. Evaluation can be run using a greedy search, as shown in the following code fragment:

```
# total eval size: 189651
articles = 1000
f1 = 0.
prec = 0.
rec = 0.
beam_width = 1

for art, smm in ds_val.take(articles):
    summ = summarize_quietly(str(art.numpy()), algo='beam-norm',
                             beam_width=1, verbose=False)

    score = scorer.score(str(smm.numpy()), summ)
    f1 += score['rougeL'].fmeasure / articles
    prec += score['rougeL'].precision / articles
    rec += score['rougeL'].recall / articles

    # see if a sample needs to be printed
    if random.choices((True, False), [1, 99])[0] is True:
    # 1% samples printed out
        print("Article: ", art.numpy())
        print("Ground Truth: ", smm.numpy())
        print("Greedy Summary: ", summarize_quietly(str(art.numpy()),
            algo='beam-norm',
            beam_width=1, verbose=False))
        print("Beam Search Summary :", summ, "\n")

print("Precision: {:.6f}, Recall: {:.6f}, F1-Score: {:.6f}".
format(prec, rec, f1))
```

While the validation set contains close to 190,000 records, the preceding code runs metrics on 1,000 records. The code also randomly prints out summaries for about 1% of the samples. The results of this evaluation should look similar to these:

```
Precision: 0.344725, Recall: 0.249029, F1-Score: 0.266480
```

This is not a bad start since we have high precision, but the recall is low. The current leaderboard for the Gigaword dataset has 36.74 as the highest ROUGE-L F1 score, as per paperswithcode.com. Let's run the same test with beam search and see the results. The code here is identical to the preceding code, with the only difference being that a beam width of 3 is being used:

```
Precision: 0.382001, Recall: 0.226766, F1-Score: 0.260703
```

It seems that the precision has improved considerably at the expense of recall. Overall, the F1 score shows a slight decrease. Beam search does produce shorter summaries, which could be the reason for the decrease in recall. Adjusting length normalization could help with this. Another hypothesis could be to try bigger beams. Trying a bigger beam size of 5 produces this result:

```
Precision: 0.400730, Recall: 0.219472, F1-Score: 0.258531
```

There is a significant improvement in precision and a further decrease in recall. Now, let's try some length normalization. Running beam search with an alpha of 0.7 gives us the following:

```
Precision: 0.356155, Recall: 0.253459, F1-Score: 0.271813
```

By running a larger beam width of 5 with the same alpha, we obtain this result:

```
Precision: 0.356993, Recall: 0.252384, F1-Score: 0.273171
```

There is a considerable increase in recall due to there being a decline in precision. Overall, for a basic model trained only on a slice of data, the performance is quite good. A score of 27.3 would yield a spot on the top 20 of the leaderboard.

Seq2seq-based text summarization was the main approach prior to the advent of Transformer-based models. Now, Transformer-based models, which include both the Encoder and Decoder parts, are used for summarization. The next section reviews state-of-the-art approaches to summarization.

Summarization – state of the art

Today, the predominant approach to summarization uses the full Transformer architecture. Such models are quite big, often ranging from 223M parameters to over a billion in the case of GPT-3. Google Research published a paper at ICML in June 2020 titled *PEGASUS: Pre-training with Extracted Gap-sentences for Abstractive Summarization*. This paper sets the benchmark for state-of-the-art results as of the time of writing. The key innovation proposed by this model is a specific pre-training objective for summarization. Recall that BERT was pre-trained using a **masked language model** (**MLM**) objective, where tokens were randomly masked and the model had to predict them. The PEGASUS model proposed a **Gap Sentence Generation** (**GSG**) pre-training objective, where important sentences are completely replaced with a special masking token, and the model has to generate the sequence.

The importance of the sentence is judged using the ROUGE1-F1 score of a given score compared to the entire document. A certain number of top-scoring sentences are masked from the input, and the model needs to predict them. Additional details can be found in the aforementioned paper. The base Transformer model is very similar to the BERT configurations. The pre-training objective makes a significant difference to the ROUGE1/2/L-F1 scores and sets new records on many of the datasets.

These models are quite large and training them on a desktop is not realistic. Often, the models are pre-trained on humongous datasets for several days at a time. Thankfully, pre-trained versions of such models are available through libraries like HuggingFace.

Summary

Summarizing text is considered a uniquely human trait. Deep learning NLP models have made great strides in this area in the past 2-3 years. Summarization remains a very hot area of research within many applications. In this chapter, we built a seq2seq model from scratch that can summarize sentences from news articles and generate a headline. This model obtains fairly good results due to its simplicity. We were able to train the model for a long period of time due to learning rate annealing. By checkpointing the model, training was made resilient as it could be restarted from the last checkpoint in case of failure. Post-training, we improved our generated summaries through a custom implementation of beam search. As beam search has a tendency to provide short summaries, length normalization techniques were used to make the summaries even better.

Measuring the quality of generated summaries is a challenge in abstractive summarization. Here is a random example from the validation dataset:

- **Input**: *the french soccer star david ginola on saturday launched his anti-land mines campaign on behalf of the international committee for the red cross which has taken him on as a sort of poster boy for the cause .*
- **Ground truth**: *soccer star joins red cross effort against land mines*
- **Beam search (5/0.7)**: *former french star ginola launches anti-land mine campaign*

The generated summary is very comparable to the ground truth. However, matching token by token would give us a very low score. ROUGE metrics that use n-grams and the LCS allow us to measure the quality of the summaries.

Finally, we took a quick look at the current state-of-the-art models for summarization. Large models that are pre-trained on even larger datasets are ruling the roost. Unfortunately, training a model of such size is often beyond the resources of a single individual.

Now, we will move on to a very new and exciting area of research – multi-modal networks. Thus far, we have only treated text in isolation. But is a picture really worth a thousand words? We shall find out when we try to caption images and answer questions about them in the next chapter.

7

Multi-Modal Networks and Image Captioning with ResNets and Transformer Networks

"A picture is worth a thousand words" is a famous adage. In this chapter, we'll put this adage to the test and generate captions for an image. In doing so, we'll work with **multi-modal** networks. Thus far, we have operated on text as input. Humans can handle multiple sensory inputs together to make sense of the environment around them. We can watch a video with subtitles and combine the information provided to understand the scene. We can use facial expressions and lip movement along with sounds to understand speech. We can recognize text in an image, and we can answer natural language questions about images. In other words, we have the ability to process information from different modalities at the same time, and then put them together to understand the world around us. The future of artificial intelligence and deep learning is in building multi-modal networks as they closely mimic human cognitive functions.

Recent advances in image, speech, and text processing lay a solid foundation for multi-modal networks. This chapter transitions you from the world of NLP to the world of multi-modal learning, where we will combine visual and textual features using the familiar Transformer architecture.

We will cover the following topics in this chapter:

- Overview of multi-modal deep learning
- Vision and language tasks
- Detailed overview of the Image Captioning task and the MS-COCO dataset
- Architecture of a residual network, specifically ResNet
- Extracting features from images using pre-trained ResNet50
- Building a full Transformer model from scratch
- Ideas for improving the performance of image captioning

Our journey starts with an overview of the various tasks in the visual understanding domain, with a focus on tasks that combine language and images.

Multi-modal deep learning

The dictionary definition of "modality" states that it is "a particular mode in which something exists or is experienced or expressed." Sensory modalities, like touch, taste, smell, vision, and sound, allow humans to experience the world around them. Suppose you are out at the farm picking strawberries, and your friend tells you to pick ripe and red strawberries. The instruction, *ripe and red strawberries*, is processed and converted into a visual and haptic criterion. As you see strawberries and feel them, you know instinctively if they match the criteria of *ripe and red*. This task is an example of multiple modalities working together for a task. As you can imagine, these capabilities are essential for robotics.

As a direct application of the preceding example, consider a harvesting robot that needs to pick ripe and ready fruit. In December 1976, Harry McGurk and John MacDonald published a piece of research titled *Hearing lips and seeing voices* (`https://www.nature.com/articles/264746a0`) in the reputed journal, Nature. They recorded a video of a young woman talking, where utterances of the syllable *ba* had been dubbed onto the lip movement of the syllable *ga*. When this video was played back to adults, people repeated hearing the syllable *da*. When the audio track was played without the video, the right syllable was reported. This research paper highlighted the role of vision in speech recognition. Speech recognition models using lip-reading information were developed in the field of **Audio-Visual Speech Recognition (AVSR)**. There are several exciting applications of multi-modal deep learning models in medical devices and diagnosis, learning technology, and other **Artificial Intelligence (AI)** areas.

Let's drill down into the specific interaction of vision and language and the various tasks we can perform.

Vision and language tasks

A combination of **Computer Vision (CV)** and **Natural Language Processing (NLP)** allows us to build smart AI systems that can see and talk. CV and NLP together produce interesting tasks for model development. Taking an image and generating a caption for it is a well-known task. A practical application of this task is generating alt-text tags for images on web pages. Visually impaired readers use screen readers, which can read these tags while reading the page, improving the accessibility of web pages. Other topics in this area include video captioning and storytelling – composing a story from a sequence of images. The following image shows some examples of images and captions. Our primary focus in this chapter is on image captioning:

Figure 7.1: Example images with captions

Visual Question Answering (VQA) is the challenging task of answering questions about objects in the image. The following image shows some examples from the VQA dataset. Compared to image captioning, where prominent objects are reflected in the caption, VQA is a more complex task. Answering the question may also require some reasoning.

Consider the bottom-right panel in the following image. Answering the question, "Does this person have 20/20 vision?" requires reasoning. Datasets for VQA are available at `visualqa.org`:

Figure 7.2: Examples from the VQA Dataset
(Source: VQA: Visual Question Answering by Agrawal et al.)

Reasoning leads to another challenging but fascinating task – **Visual Commonsense Reasoning (VCR)**. When we look at an image, we can guess emotions, actions, and frame a hypothesis of what is happening. Such a task is quite easy for people and may even happen without conscious effort. The aim of the VCR task is to build models that can perform such a task. These models should also be able to explain or choose an appropriate reason for the logical inference that's been made. The following image shows an example from the VCR dataset. More details on the VCR dataset can be found at `visualcommonsense.com`:

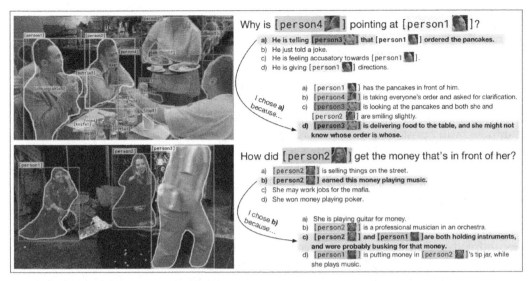

Figure 7.3: VCR example (Source: From Recognition to
Cognition: Visual Commonsense Reasoning by Zellers et al.)

Thus far, we have gone from images to text. The reverse is also possible and is
an active area of research. In this task, images or videos are generated from text
using GANs and other generative architectures. Imagine being able to generate an
illustrative comic book from the text of a story! This particular task is at the forefront
of research currently.

A critical concept in this area is **visual grounding**. Grounding enables tying concepts
in language to the real world. Simply put, it matches words to objects in a picture. By
combining vision and language, we can ground concepts from languages to parts of
an image. For example, mapping the word "basketball" to something that looks like
one in an image is called visual grounding. There can be more abstract concepts that
can be grounded. For example, a short elephant and a short person have different
measurements. Grounding provides us with a way to see what models are learning
and helps us guide them in the right direction.

Now that we have a proper perspective on vision and language tasks, let's dive deep
into an image captioning task.

Image captioning

Image captioning is all about describing the contents of an image in a sentence. Captions can help in content-based image retrieval and visual search. We already discussed how captions could improve the accessibility of websites by making it easier for screen readers to summarize the content of an image. A caption can be considered a summary of the image. Once we frame the problem as an image summarization problem, we can adapt the seq2seq model from the previous chapter to solve this problem. In text summarization, the input is a sequence of the long-form article, and the output is a short sequence summarizing the content. In image captioning, the output is similar in format to summarization. However, it may not be obvious how to structure an image that consists of pixels as a sequence of embeddings to be fed into the Encoder.

Secondly, the summarization architecture used **Bi-directional Long Short-Term Memory networks (BiLSTMs)**, with the underlying principle that words that are closer together to each other are similar to each other in meaning. BiLSTMs exploited this property by looking at the input sequence from both sides and generated encoded representations. Generating a representation for an image that works for the Encoder requires some thought.

A naïve solution for representing images as a sequence could be expressing them as a list of pixels. So, an image of size 28x28 pixels becomes a sequence of 784 tokens. When the tokens represent text, an Embedding layer learns the representation of each token. If this Embedding layer had a dimension of 64, then each token would be represented by a 64-dimensional vector. This embedding vector was learned during training. Extending our analogy of using a pixel as a token, a straightforward solution is to use the value of the Red/Green/Blue channels of the pixel in an image to generate a three-dimensional embedding. However, training these three dimensions does not sound like a logical approach. More importantly, pixels are laid out in a 2D representation, while the text is laid out in a 1D representation. This concept is illustrated in the following image. Words are related to words next to each other. When pixels are laid out in a sequence, the **data locality** of these pixels is broken since the content of a pixel is related to the pixels all around it, not just to the left and right of it. This idea is shown by the following super zoomed in image of a tulip:

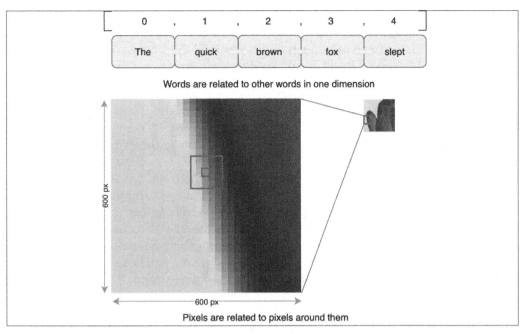

Figure 7.4: Data locality in text versus images

Data locality and translation invariance are two critical properties of images. Translation invariance is the idea that an object can appear in various spots in an image. In a fully connected model, the model would try to learn the position of the object, which would prevent the model from generalizing. The specialized architecture of **Convolutional Neural Networks (CNNs)** can be used to exploit these properties and extract signals from the image. At a high level, we use CNNs, specifically the **ResNet50** architecture, to convert the image into a tensor that can be fed to a seq2seq architecture. Our model will combine the best of CNNs and RNNs to handle the image and text parts under the seq2seq model. The following diagram shows our architecture at a very high level:

Figure 7.5: High-level image captioning model architecture

While a comprehensive explanation of CNNs is beyond the scope of this book, we will review the key concepts in short. Since we will be using a pre-trained CNN model, we won't have to go into much depth about CNNs. *Python Machine Learning, Third Edition*, published by Packt, is an excellent resource for reading up on CNNs.

In the previous chapter on text summarization, we built a seq2seq model with attention. In this chapter, we will build a Transformer model. Transformer models are currently state of the art in NLP. The Encoder part of the Transformer is the core of the **Bidirectional Encoder Representations from Transformers (BERT)** architecture. The Decoder part of the Transformer is the core of the **Generative Pre-trained Transformer (GPT)** family of architectures. There is a specific advantage of the Transformer architecture that is relevant to the image captioning problem. In the seq2seq architecture, we used BiLSTMS, which tries to learn relationships via co-occurrence. In the Transformer architecture, there is no recurrence. Instead, positional encodings and self-attention model relationships are made between inputs. This change enables us to feed in processed image patches as input and hope that the relationships between the image patches will be learned.

Implementing the image captioning model requires a large amount of code as we will implement several pieces, like pre-processing images, with ResNet50 and a complete implementation of Transformer architecture from scratch. This chapter contains much more code than the other chapters. We will rely on code fragments to highlight the most important aspects of the code rather than going over every line of code in detail, as we have been doing so far.

The main steps of building our model are summarized here:

1. **Downloading the data**: Given the large size of the dataset, this is a time-consuming activity.

2. **Pre-processing captions**: Since the captions are in JSON format, they are flattened into a CSV for easier processing.

3. **Feature extraction**: We pass the image files through ResNet50 to extract features and save them to speed up training.

4. **Transformer training**: A full Transformer model with positional encoding, multi-head attention, an Encoder, and a Decoder is trained on the processed data.

5. **Inference**: Use the trained model to caption some images!

6. **Evaluating performance**: **Bilingual Evaluation Understudy (BLEU)** scores are used to compare the trained models with ground truth data.

Let's start with the dataset first.

MS-COCO dataset for image captioning

Microsoft published the **Common Objects in Context** or COCO dataset in 2014. All the versions of the dataset can be found at cocodataset.org. The COCO dataset is a big dataset that's used for object detection, segmentation, and captioning, among other annotations. Our focus will be on the 2014 training and validation images, where five captions per image are available. There are roughly 83K images in the training set and 41K images in the validation set. The training and validation images and captions need to be downloaded from the COCO website.

Large download warning: The training image dataset is approximately 13 GB, while the validation dataset is over 6 GB. The annotations for the image files, which include captions, are about 214 MB in size. Please be careful of your internet bandwidth usage and potential costs as you download this dataset.

Google has also published a new Conceptual Captions dataset at https://ai.google.com/research/ConceptualCaptions. It contains over 3M images. Having a large dataset allows deep models to train better. There is a corresponding competition where you can submit your models and see how they compete with others.

Given that these are large downloads, you may wish to use the download that's the most comfortable to you. If wget is available on your environment, you could use it to download the files, like so:

```
$ wget http://images.cocodataset.org/zips/train2014.zip
$ wget http://images.cocodataset.org/zips/val2014.zip
$ wget http://images.cocodataset.org/annotations/annotations_
trainval2014.zip
```

Note that the annotations for the training and validation sets are in one compressed archive. Once the files have been downloaded, they need to be unzipped. Each of these compressed files creates its own folder and puts the contents in there. We will create a folder called data and move all the expanded contents inside it:

```
$ mkdir data
$ mv train2014 data/
$ mv val2014 data/
$ mv annotations data/
```

All the images are either in the `train2014` or `val2014` folder. The code for the initial pre-processing of the data is in the `data-download-preprocess.py` file. Captions for the training and validation images can be found in the `captions_train2014.json` or `captions_val2014.json` JSON file inside the `annotations` subfolder. Both of these files are in a similar format. The files have four main keys – info, image, license, and annotation. The image key contains a record per image, along with information about the size, URL, name, and a unique ID that is used to refer to that image in the dataset. Captions are stored as a tuple of the image ID and caption text, along with a unique ID for the caption. We use the Python `json` module to read and process these files:

```
valcaptions = json.load(open(
    './data/annotations/captions_val2014.json', 'r'))
trcaptions = json.load(open(
    './data/annotations/captions_train2014.json', 'r'))

# inspect the annotations
print(trcaptions.keys())

dict_keys(['info', 'images', 'licenses', 'annotations'])
```

Our objective is to produce a single simple file with two columns – one for the image file name and another containing the caption for that file. Note that the validation set contains half the number of images of the training set. In a seminal paper on captioning titled *Deep Visual-Semantic Alignment for Generating Image Descriptions*, Andrej Karpathy and Fei-Fei Li proposed training on all the training and validation images after reserving 5,000 images from the validation set for testing. We will follow this approach by processing the image names and IDs into a dictionary:

```
prefix = "./data/"
val_prefix = prefix + 'val2014/'
train_prefix = prefix + 'train2014/'

# training images
trimages = {x['id']: x['file_name'] for x in trcaptions['images']}

# validation images
# take all images from validation except 5k - karpathy split
valset = len(valcaptions['images']) - 5000 # leave last 5k
valimages = {x['id']: x['file_name'] for x in valcaptions['images']
[:valset]}

truevalimg = {x['id']: x['file_name'] for x in valcaptions['images']
[valset:]}
```

Since each image has five captions, the validation set cannot be split based on captions. Otherwise, there will be leakage of data from the training set into the validation/test set. In the preceding code, we reserved the last 5K images for the validation set.

Now, let's go over the captions for the training and validation images and create a combined list. We will create empty lists to store the tuples of image paths and captions:

```
# we flatten to (caption, image_path) structure
data = list()
errors = list()
validation = list()
```

Next, we will process all the training captions:

```
for item in trcaptions['annotations']:
    if int(item['image_id']) in trimages:
        fpath = train_prefix + trimages[int(item['image_id'])]
        caption = item['caption']
        data.append((caption, fpath))
    else:
        errors.append(item)
```

For the validation captions, the logic is similar, but we need to ensure that no captions are included for the images that have been reserved:

```
for item in valcaptions['annotations']:
    caption = item['caption']
    if int(item['image_id']) in valimages:
        fpath = val_prefix + valimages[int(item['image_id'])]
        data.append((caption, fpath))
    elif int(item['image_id']) in truevalimg: # reserved
        fpath = val_prefix + truevalimg[int(item['image_id'])]
        validation.append((caption, fpath))
    else:
        errors.append(item)
```

Hopefully, there should not be any errors. If you encounter errors, this could be due to corrupted downloads or errors while unzipping the files. The training dataset is shuffled to aid in training. Finally, two CSV files are persisted with the training and testing data:

```
# persist for future use
```

```
with open(prefix + 'data.csv', 'w') as file:
    writer = csv.writer(file, quoting=csv.QUOTE_ALL)
    writer.writerows(data)

# persist for future use
with open(prefix + 'validation.csv', 'w') as file:
    writer = csv.writer(file, quoting=csv.QUOTE_ALL)
    writer.writerows(validation)

print("TRAINING: Total Number of Captions: {},  Total Number of Images:
{}".format(
    len(data), len(trimages) + len(valimages)))

print("VALIDATION/TESTING: Total Number of Captions: {},  Total Number
of Images: {}".format(
    len(validation), len(truevalimg)))

print("Errors: ", errors)
```

```
TRAINING: Total Number of Captions: 591751,  Total Number of Images:
118287
VALIDATION/TESTING: Total Number of Captions: 25016,  Total Number of
Images: 5000
Errors:  []
```

At this point, the data download and pre-processing phases are complete. The next step is to pre-process all the images using ResNet50 to extract features. Before we write the code for that, we will take a short detour and look at CNNs and the ResNet architecture. If you are already comfortable with CNNs, you may skip ahead to the code part.

Image processing with CNNs and ResNet50

In the world of deep learning, specific architectures have been developed to handle specific modalities. CNNs have been incredibly successful in processing images and are the standard architecture for CV tasks. A good mental model for using a pre-trained model for extracting features from images is that of using pre-trained word embeddings like GloVe for text. In this particular case, we use a specific architecture called ResNet50. While a comprehensive treatment of CNNs is outside the scope of this book, a brief overview of CNNs and ResNet will be provided in this section. If you are already comfortable with these concepts, you may skip ahead to the section titled *Image feature extraction with ResNet50*.

CNNs

CNNs are an architecture designed to learn from the following key properties, which are relevant to image recognition:

- **Data locality**: The pixels in an image are highly correlated to the pixels around them.

- **Translation invariance**: An object of interest, for example, a bird, may appear at different places in an image. The model should be able to identify the object, irrespective of the object's position in the image.

- **Scale invariance**: An object of interest may have a smaller or large size, depending on the zoom. Ideally, the model should be able to identify objects of interest in an image, irrespective of their size.

Convolution and pooling layers are key components that aid CNNs in extracting features from images.

Convolutions

A convolution is a mathematical operation that is performed on patches taken from an image with a filter. A filter is a matrix, usually square and with 3x3, 5x5, and 7x7 as common dimensions. The following image shows an example of a 3x3 convolution matrix applied to a 5x5 image. The image patches are taken from left to right and then top to bottom. The number of pixels this patch shifts by every step is called the **stride length**. A stride length of 1 in a horizontal and vertical direction reduces a 5x5 image to a 3x3 image, as shown here:

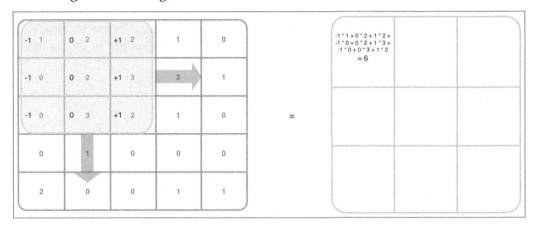

Figure 7.6: Example of a convolution operation

The specific filter that was applied here is an edge detection filter. Prior to CNNs, CV relied heavily on handcrafted filters. Sobel filters are an example of a special filter for the purpose of edge detection. The `convolution-example.ipynb` notebook provides an example of detecting edges using the Sobel filter. The code is quite straightforward. After the imports, the image file is loaded and converted into a grayscale image:

```
tulip = Image.open("chap7-tulip.jpg")

# convert to gray scale image
tulip_grey = tulip.convert('L')
tulip_ar = np.array(tulip_grey)
```

Next, we define and apply the Sobel filters to the image:

```
# Sobel Filter
kernel_1 = np.array([[1, 0, -1],
                     [2, 0, -2],
                     [1, 0, -1]])          # Vertical edge
kernel_2 = np.array([[1, 2, 1],
```

```
                          [0, 0, 0],
                          [-1, -2, -1]])      # Horizontal edge
    out1 = convolve2d(tulip_ar, kernel_1)    # vertical filter
    out2 = convolve2d(tulip_ar, kernel_2)    # horizontal filter
    # Create a composite image from the two edge detectors
    out3 = np.sqrt(out1**2 + out2**2)
```

The original image, along with the intermediate versions, are shown in the following image:

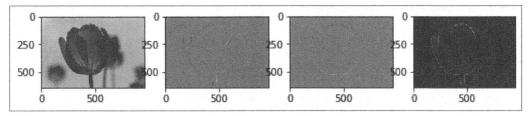

Figure 7.7: Edge detection using Sobel filters

Constructing such filters is very tedious. However, CNNs can learn many such filters by treating the filter matrices as learnable parameters. CNNs often pass an image through hundreds or thousands of such filters, referred to as channels, and stack them together. You can think of each filter as detecting some features, like vertical lines, horizontal lines, arcs, circles, trapezoids, and so on. However, the magic happens when multiple such layers are put together. Stacking multiple layers leads to learning hierarchical representations. An easy way to understand this concept is by imagining that earlier layers are learning simple shapes like lines and arcs, middle layers are learning shapes like circles and hexagons, and the top layers are learning complex objects like stop signs and steering wheels. The convolution operation is the key innovation that exploits data locality and extracts features that enable translation invariance.

A consequence of this layering is the amount of data flowing through the model increasing. Pooling is an operation that helps reduce the dimensions of the data flowing through and further highlights these features.

Pooling

Once the values from the convolution operation have been computed, a pooling operation can be applied to patches to further concentrate the signal in the image. The most common form of pooling is called **Max pooling** and is demonstrated in the following diagram. It is as simple as taking the maximum value in a patch.

The following diagram shows max pooling on non-overlapping 2x2 patches:

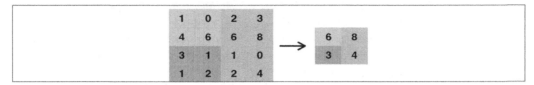

Figure 7.8: Max pooling operation

Another way to pool is by averaging the values. While pooling reduces the complexity and computation load, it also helps modestly with scale invariance. However, there is a chance that such a model overfits and does not generalize well. Dropout is a technique that helps with regularization and enables such models to generalize better.

Regularization with dropout

You may recall that we used dropout settings in previous chapters with the LSTM and BiLSTM settings. The core idea behind dropout is shown in the following diagram:

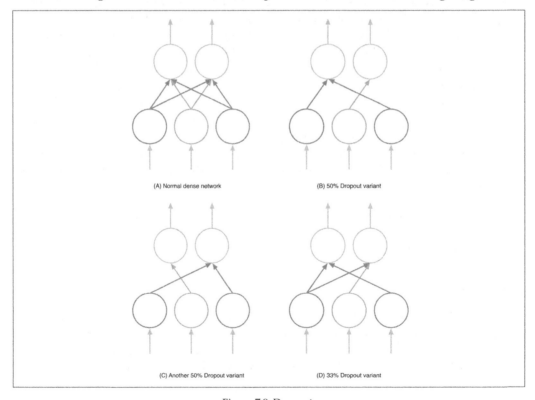

Figure 7.9: Dropout

Rather than connecting every unit from a lower layer to every unit in the next higher layer of the model, some of the connections are randomly dropped during training time. Inputs are dropped only during training time. Since dropping inputs reduces the total input reaching a node compared to test/inference time, inputs are upscaled in the proportion of dropout to ensure the relative magnitudes are preserved. Dropping some of the inputs during training forces the model to learn more from each of the inputs. This is because it cannot rely on the presence of a specific input. This helps the network build resilience to missing inputs and consequently helps generalize the models.

A combination of these techniques helped build deeper and deeper networks. A challenge that showed up as networks got deeper was that the signal from the inputs became quite small in the higher layers. Residual connections is a technique that helps deal with this problem.

Residual connections and ResNets

Intuition suggests that adding more layers should make performance better. A deeper network has more model capacity, so it should be able to model more complex distributions compared to shallower networks. As deeper and deeper models were built, a degradation in accuracy was observed. Since the reduction happened even on the training data, overfitting can be ruled out as a probable cause. As inputs pass through more and more layers, the optimizers have a harder time adjusting the gradients to the point where learning is impaired in the model. Kaiming He and his collaborators published the ResNet architecture in their seminal paper titled *Deep Residual Learning for Image Recognition*.

We must understand residual connections before understanding ResNets. The core concept of the residual connection is shown in the following diagram. In a regular dense layer, the input is first multiplied by the weights. Then, biases are added in, which is a linear operation. The output is passed through an activation function, like ReLU, which introduces non-linearity in the layer. The output from the activation function is the final output of the layer.

However, residual connections introduce a summation in-between the linear computation and the activation function, as shown on the right-hand side of the following diagram:

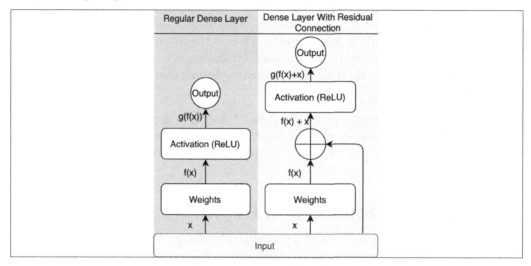

Figure 7.10: A conceptual residual connection

Note that the preceding diagram is only for illustrating the core concept behind residual connections. In ResNets, the residual connection is made between multiple blocks. The following diagram shows the basic building blocks of ResNet50, also referred to as the bottleneck design. This design is called the bottleneck design because the 1x1 convolution blocks reduce the dimensions of the inputs before passing them to the 3x3 convolution. The last 1x1 block scales the inputs out again for the next layer:

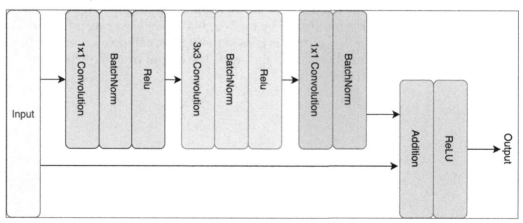

Figure 7.11: ResNet50 bottleneck building block

ResNet50 is composed of several such blocks stacked on top of each other. There are four groups, each consisting of three to seven such blocks. **BatchNorm** or batch normalization was proposed by Sergey Ioffe and Christian Szegedy in their paper titled *Batch Normalization: Accelerating Deep Network Training By Reducing Internal Covariate Shift* in 2015. Batch normalization aims to reduce the variance of the outputs coming from one layer being fed into the next layer. By reducing this variance, BatchNorm acts like L2 regularization, which attempts to do the same thing by adding the penalties of the magnitude of the weights to the cost function. The main motivation of BatchNorm is to efficiently backpropagate gradient updates through a large number of layers, while minimizing the risk that this update could result in divergence. In stochastic gradient descent, gradients are used to update the weights of all the layers at the same time, assuming that the output of one layer doesn't impact any other layers. However, this is not a completely valid assumption. For an n-layer network, computing this would need nth order gradients, which is intractable. Instead, batch-norm is used, which works on one mini-batch at a time and the constraints of the updates to reduce this unwanted shift in the distribution of weights. It does this by normalizing the outputs before they are fed into the next layer.

The last two layers of ResNet50 are dense layers that classify the outputs from the last block into an object category. Covering ResNets comprehensively is a tough ask, but hopefully, this crash course on CNNs and ResNets has given you enough background on how they work. You are encouraged to read the referenced papers and *Deep Learning with TensorFlow 2 and Keras, Second Edition*, published by Packt, for a detailed treatment of this topic. Fortunately for us, TensorFlow provides a pre-trained ResNet50 model that is ready for use. In the next section, we'll use this pre-trained ResNet50 model for extracting image features.

Image feature extraction with ResNet50

ResNet50 models are trained on the ImageNet dataset. This dataset contains millions of images in over 20,000 categories. The large-scale visual recognition challenge, ILSVRC, focuses on the top 1,000 categories for models to compete on recognizing images. Consequently, the top layers of the ResNet50 that perform classification have a dimension of 1,000. The idea behind using a pre-trained ResNet50 model is that it is already able to parse out objects that may be useful in image captioning.

The `tensorflow.keras.applications` package provides pre-trained models like ResNet50. At the time of writing, all the pre-trained models provided are related to CV. Loading up the pre-trained model is quite easy. All the code for this section is in the `feature-extraction.py` file in this chapter's folder on GitHub. The main reason for using a separate file is that it gives us the ability to run feature extraction as a script.

Given that we will be processing over 100,000 images, this process may take a while. CNNs benefit greatly from a GPU in computation. Let's get into the code now. First, we must set up the paths for the CSV file we created from the JSON annotations in the previous chapter:

```
prefix = './data/'
save_prefix = prefix + "features/"  # for storing prefixes
annot = prefix + 'data.csv'
# Load the pre-processed file
inputs = pd.read_csv(annot, header=None, names=["caption", "image"])
```

ResNet50 expects each image to be 224x224 pixels with three channels. The input images from the COCO set have different sizes. Hence, we must convert the input files into the standard that ResNet was trained on:

```
# We are going to use the last residual block of
# the ResNet50 architecture
# which has dimension 7x7x2048 and store into individual file
def load_image(image_path, size=(224, 224)):
    # pre-processes images for ResNet50 in batches
    image = tf.io.read_file(image_path)
    image = tf.io.decode_jpeg(image, channels=3)
    image = tf.image.resize(image, size)
    image = preprocess_input(image)  # from keras.applications.ResNet50
    return image, image_path
```

The highlighted code shows a special pre-processing function provided by the ResNet50 package. The pixels in the input image are loaded into an array via the decode_jpeg() function. Each pixel has a value between 0 and 255 for each color channel. The preprocess_input() function normalizes the pixel values so that their mean is 0. Since each input image has five captions, we should only process the unique images in the dataset:

```
uniq_images = sorted(inputs['image'].unique())
print("Unique images: ", len(uniq_images))  # 118,287 images
```

Next, we must convert the dataset into a tf.dat.Dataset, which makes it easier to batch and process the input files using the convenience function defined previously:

```
image_dataset = tf.data.Dataset.from_tensor_slices(uniq_images)
image_dataset = image_dataset.map(
    load_image, num_parallel_calls=tf.data.experimental.AUTOTUNE).
batch(16)
```

For efficiently processing and generating features, we must process 16 image files at a time. The next step is loading a pre-trained ResNet50 model:

```
rs50 = tf.keras.applications.ResNet50(
    include_top=False,
    weights="imagenet",
    input_shape=(224, 224, 3)
)

new_input = rs50.input
hidden_layer = rs50.layers[-1].output

features_extract = tf.keras.Model(new_input, hidden_layer)
features_extract.summary()
```

```
Layer (type)                    Output Shape         Param #
Connected to
===================================================================
input_1 (InputLayer)            [(None, 224, 224, 3) 0

<CONV BLOCK 1>

<CONV BLOCK 2>

<CONV BLOCK 3>

<CONV BLOCK 4>

<CONV BLOCK 5>
===================================================================
Total params: 23,587,712
Trainable params: 23,534,592
Non-trainable params: 53,120
```

The preceding output has been abbreviated for brevity. The model contains over 23 million trainable parameters. We don't need the top classification layer as we are using the model for feature extraction. We defined a new model with the input and output layer. Here, we took the output from the last layer. We could take output from different parts of ResNet by changing the definition of the `hidden_layer` variable. In fact, this variable can be a list of layers, in which case the output of the `features_extract` model will be the output from each of the layers in the list.

Next, a directory must be set up to store the extracted features:

```
save_prefix = prefix + "features/"
try:
    # Create this directory
    os.mkdir(save_prefix)
except FileExistsError:
    pass # Directory already exists
```

The feature extraction model can work on batches of images and predict the output. The output is 2,048 patches of 7x7 pixels for each image. If a batch of 16 images is supplied, then the output from the model will be a tensor of dimensions [16, 7, 7, 2048]. We store the features of each image file as a separate file while flattening the dimensions to [49, 2048]. Each image has now been converted into a sequence of 49 pixels, with an embedding size of 2,048. The following code performs this action:

```
for img, path in tqdm(image_dataset):
    batch_features = features_extract(img)
    batch_features = tf.reshape(batch_features,
                            (batch_features.shape[0], -1,
                             batch_features.shape[3]))

    for feat, p in zip(batch_features, path):
        filepath = p.numpy().decode("utf-8")
        filepath = save_prefix + filepath.split('/')[-1][:-3] + "npy"
        np.save(filepath, feat.numpy())

print("Images saved as npy files")
```

This could be a time-consuming operation, depending on your computing environment. On my Ubuntu Linux box with an RTX 2070 GPU, this took ~23 minutes.

The last step in data pre-processing is to train the Subword Encoder. This part should be quite familiar to you as it is identical to what we've done in previous chapters:

```
# Now, read the labels and create a subword tokenizer with it
# ~8K vocab size
cap_tokenizer = tfds.features.text.SubwordTextEncoder.build_from_
corpus(
    inputs['caption'].map(lambda x: x.lower().strip()).tolist(),
    target_vocab_size=2**13, reserved_tokens=['<s>', '</s>'])
cap_tokenizer.save_to_file("captions")
```

Note that we included two special tokens to signal the start and end of the sequences. You may recall this technique from *Chapter 5, Generating Text with RNNs and GPT-2*. Here, we used a slightly different way of accomplishing the same technique to show how you can accomplish the same objective in different ways.

With that, pre-processing and feature extraction is complete. The next step is defining the Transformer model. Then, we will be ready to train the model.

The Transformer model

The Transformer model was discussed in *Chapter 4, Transfer Learning with BERT*. It was inspired by the seq2seq model and has an Encoder and a Decoder part. Since the Transformer model does not rely on RNNs, input sequences need to be annotated with positional encodings, which allow the model to learn about the relationships between inputs. Removing recurrence improves the speed of the model vastly while reducing the memory footprint. This innovation of the Transformer model has made very large-sized models such as BERT and GPT-3 possible. The Encoder part of the Transformer model was shown in the aforementioned chapter. The full Transformer model was shown in *Chapter 5, Generating Text with RNNs and GPT-2*. We will start with a modified version of the full Transformer. Specifically, we will modify the Encoder part of the Transformer to create a visual Encoder, which takes image data as input instead of text sequences. There are some other small modifications to be made to accommodate images as input to the Encoder. The Transformer model we are going to build is shown in the following diagram. The main difference here is how the input sequence is encoded. In the case of text, we will tokenize the text using a Subword Encoder and pass it through an Embedding layer, which is trainable.

As training proceeds, the embeddings of the tokens are also learned. In the case of image captioning, we will pre-process the images into a sequence of 49 pixels, each with an "embedding" size of 2,048. This actually simplifies padding the inputs. All the images are pre-processed so that they're the same length. Consequently, padding and masking the inputs is not required:

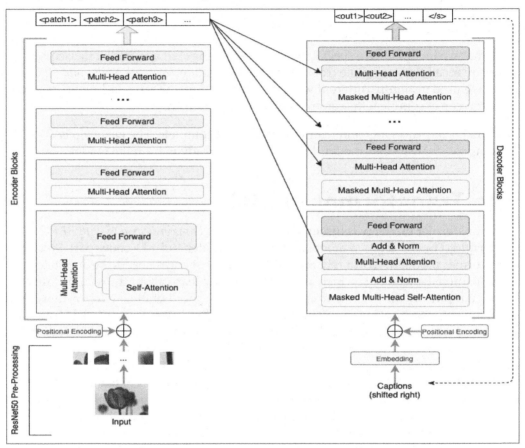

Figure 7.12: Transformer model with a visual Encoder

The following pieces of code need to be implemented to build the Transformer model:

- Positional encoding of the inputs, along with input and output masks. Our inputs are of a fixed length, but the output and captions are of a variable length.

- Scaled dot-product attention and multi-head attention to enable the Encoders and Decoders to focus on specific aspects of the data.

- An Encoder that consists of multiple repeating blocks.

- A Decoder that uses the outputs from the Encoder through its repeating blocks.

The code for the Transformer has been taken from the TensorFlow tutorial titled *Transformer model for language understanding*. We will be using this code as the base and adapting it for the image captioning use case. One of the beautiful things about the Transformer architecture is that if we can cast a problem as a sequence-to-sequence problem, then we can apply the Transformer model. As we describe the implementation, the main points of the code will be highlighted. Note that the code for this section is in the `visual_transformer.py` file.

Implementing the full Transformer model does take a little bit of code. If you are already familiar with the Transformer model or want to only know where our model differs from the standard Transformer model, please focus on the next section and the *VisualEncoder* section. You can read the rest of the sections at your leisure.

Positional encoding and masks

Transformer models don't use RNNs. This allows them to compute all the outputs in one step, leading to significant improvements in speed and also the ability to learn dependencies across long inputs. However, it comes at the cost of the model not knowing anything about the relationship between neighboring words or tokens. A positional encoding vector, with values for the odd and even positions of the tokens to help the model learn relationships between the positions of inputs, helps compensate for the lack of information about the ordering of tokens.

 Embeddings help place tokens that are similar in meaning close to each other in the embedding space. Positional encodings put tokens closer to each other based on their position in the sentence. Put together, the two are quite powerful.

In image captioning, this is important for captions. Technically, we don't need to provide these positional encodings for the image inputs as ResNet50 should have produced appropriate patches. Positional encoding can, however, still be used for the inputs as well. Positional encoding uses a *sin* function for even positions and a *cos* function for odd positions. The formula for computing the encodings for a position is:

$$PE_{pos} = \begin{cases} \sin(w_i \cdot pos) \, if \, i = 2k \\ \cos(w_i \cdot pos) \, if \, i = 2k + 1 \end{cases}$$

Here, w_i is defined as:

$$w_i = \frac{1}{1000^{2k/d\_model}}$$

In the preceding formula, *pos* refers to the position of a given token, d_{model} refers to the dimensions of the embeddings, and *i* is the specific dimension being computed. The positional encoding process produces a vector with the same dimensions as the embedding for each token. You may be wondering why this complex formulation is used for computing these positional encodings. Wouldn't numbering the tokens from one side to the other suffice? It turns out that the positional encoding algorithm must have a few characteristics. First, the values must generalize easily to sequences of a variable length. Using a straight-up numbering scheme would prevent inputs that have sequences longer than those in the training data. The output should be unique for each token's position. Furthermore, the distance between any two positions should be consistent across different lengths of input sequences. This formulation is relatively simple to implement. The code for this is in the Positional Encoder section of the file.

First, we must compute the *angle*, as shown in the preceding w_i formula, like so:

```
def get_angles(pos, i, d_model):
    angle_rates = 1 / np.power(10000, (2 * (i // 2)) / np.float32(d_
model))
    return pos * angle_rates
```

Then, we must compute the vector of positional encodings:

```
def positional_encoding(position, d_model):
    angle_rads = get_angles(np.arange(position)[:, np.newaxis],
                            np.arange(d_model)[np.newaxis, :],
                            d_model)

    # apply sin to even indices in the array; 2i
    angle_rads[:, 0::2] = np.sin(angle_rads[:, 0::2])

    # apply cos to odd indices in the array; 2i+1
    angle_rads[:, 1::2] = np.cos(angle_rads[:, 1::2])

    pos_encoding = angle_rads[np.newaxis, ...]

    return tf.cast(pos_encoding, dtype=tf.float32)
```

The next step is to compute the masks for input and output. Let's focus on the Decoder for a second. Since we are not using an RNN, the entire output is fed to the Decoder at once. However, we don't want the Decoder to look at data from future timesteps. So, the outputs must be masked. In terms of the Encoder, masks are needed if the input is padded to a fixed length. However, in our case, the inputs are always exactly a length of 49. So, the mask is a fixed vector of ones:

```
def create_padding_mask(seq):
    seq = tf.cast(tf.math.equal(seq, 0), tf.float32)

    # add extra dimensions to add the padding
    # to the attention logits.
    return seq[:, tf.newaxis, tf.newaxis, :]
    # (batch_size, 1, 1, seq_len)

# while decoding, we dont have recurrence and dont want Decoder
# to see tokens from the future

def create_look_ahead_mask(size):
    mask = 1 - tf.linalg.band_part(tf.ones((size, size)), -1, 0)
    return mask  # (seq_len, seq_len)
```

The first method is used to mask inputs if they are padded. This method has been included for the sake of completeness, but you will see later that we pass it a sequence of ones. So, all this method does is reshape the masks. The second mask function is used for masking Decoder inputs so that it can only see the positions it has generated.

The layers of the transfer Encoder and Decoder use a specific form of attention. This is a fundamental building block of the architecture and will be implemented next.

Scaled dot-product and multi-head attention

The purpose of the attention function is to match a query to a set of key-value pairs. The output is a sum of the values, weighted by the correspondence between the query and the key. multi-head attention learns multiple ways to compute the scaled dot-product attention and combines it.

Scaled dot-product attention is computed by multiplying the query vector by the key vector. This product is scaled by the square root of the dimensions of the query and key. Note that this formulation assumes that the key and query vectors have the same dimensions. Practically, the dimensions of the query, key, and value vectors are all set to the size of the embedding.

This was referred to as d_{model} in the position encoding. After computing the scaled product of the key and query vector, a softmax is applied, and the result of the softmax is multiplied by the value vector. A mask is used to mask the product of the query and keys:

```python
def scaled_dot_product_attention(q, k, v, mask):
    # (..., seq_len_q, seq_len_k)
    matmul_qk = tf.matmul(q, k, transpose_b=True)

    # scale matmul_qk
    dk = tf.cast(tf.shape(k)[-1], tf.float32)
    scaled_attention_logits = matmul_qk / tf.math.sqrt(dk)

    # add the mask to the scaled tensor.
    if mask is not None:
        scaled_attention_logits += (mask * -1e9)

    # softmax is normalized on the last axis (seq_len_k)
    # so that the scores
    # add up to 1.
    attention_weights = tf.nn.softmax(
                        scaled_attention_logits,
                        axis=-1)  # (..., seq_len_q, seq_len_k)

    output = tf.matmul(attention_weights, v)
    # (..., seq_len_q, depth_v)

    return output, attention_weights
```

Multi-ahead attention concatenates outputs from multiple scaled dot-product attention units and passes them through a linear layer. The dimensions of the embedding inputs are divided by the number of heads to compute the dimensions of the key and value vectors. Multi-head attention is implemented as a custom layer. First, we must create the constructor:

```python
class MultiHeadAttention(tf.keras.layers.Layer):
    def __init__(self, d_model, num_heads):
        super(MultiHeadAttention, self).__init__()
        self.num_heads = num_heads
        self.d_model = d_model

        assert d_model % self.num_heads == 0
```

```
self.depth = d_model // self.num_heads

self.wq = tf.keras.layers.Dense(d_model)
self.wk = tf.keras.layers.Dense(d_model)
self.wv = tf.keras.layers.Dense(d_model)

self.dense = tf.keras.layers.Dense(d_model)
```

Note the `assert` statement that is highlighted. When the Transformer model is instantiated, it is vital to choose some parameters so that the number of heads divides the model size or embedding dimensions completely. The main computation of this layer is in the `call()` function:

```
def call(self, v, k, q, mask):
    batch_size = tf.shape(q)[0]

    q = self.wq(q)  # (batch_size, seq_len, d_model)
    k = self.wk(k)  # (batch_size, seq_len, d_model)
    v = self.wv(v)  # (batch_size, seq_len, d_model)

    # (batch_size, num_heads, seq_len_q, depth)
    q = self.split_heads(q, batch_size)
    # (batch_size, num_heads, seq_len_k, depth)
    k = self.split_heads(k, batch_size)
    # (batch_size, num_heads, seq_len_v, depth)
    v = self.split_heads(v, batch_size)

    # scaled_attention.shape == (batch_size, num_heads,
    # seq_len_q, depth)
    # attention_weights.shape == (batch_size, num_heads,
    # seq_len_q, seq_len_k)
    scaled_attention, attention_weights = scaled_dot_product_
attention(q, k, v, mask)

    # (batch_size, seq_len_q, num_heads, depth)
    scaled_attention = tf.transpose(scaled_attention,
                                            perm=[0, 2, 1, 3])

    concat_attention = tf.reshape(scaled_attention,
                                    (batch_size, -1,
                        self.d_model))
    # (batch_size, seq_len_q, d_model)
```

```
        # (batch_size, seq_len_q, d_model)
        output = self.dense(concat_attention)

        return output, attention_weights
```

The three highlighted rows show splitting the vectors into multiple heads. split_heads() is defined like so:

```
    def split_heads(self, x, batch_size):
        """Split the last dimension into (num_heads, depth).
        Transpose the result such that the shape is (batch_size,
        num_heads, seq_len, depth)
        """
        x = tf.reshape(x, (batch_size, -1,
self.num_heads, self.depth))
        return tf.transpose(x, perm=[0, 2, 1, 3])
```

This completes the multi-head attention implementation. This is the key part of the Transformer model. There is a small detail surrounding a Dense layer, which is used to aggregate the outputs from multi-head attention. It is quite simple:

```
def point_wise_feed_forward_network(d_model, dff):
    return tf.keras.Sequential([
        # (batch_size, seq_len, dff)
        tf.keras.layers.Dense(dff, activation='relu'),
        tf.keras.layers.Dense(d_model)
        # (batch_size, seq_len, d_model)
    ])
```

Thus far, we have looked at the following parameters for specifying a Transformer mode:

- d_{model} is used for the size of the embeddings and primary flow of inputs
- d_{ff} is the size of the output from the intermediate Dense layer in the FeedForward part
- h specifies the number of heads for multi-head attention

Next, we will implement a visual Encoder, which has been modified to accommodate images as input.

VisualEncoder

The diagram shown in the *The Transformer model* section shows the Encoder's structure. The Encoder processes the inputs with positional encodings and masks, and then passes them through stacks of multi-head attention and feed-forward blocks. The implementation deviates from the TensorFlow tutorial as the input in the tutorial is text. In our case, we are passing 49x2,048 vectors that were generated by passing images through ResNet50. The main difference is in how the inputs are handled. VisualEncoder is built as a layer to allow composition into the eventual Transform model:

```python
class VisualEncoder(tf.keras.layers.Layer):
    def __init__(self, num_layers, d_model, num_heads, dff,
                 maximum_position_encoding=49, dropout_rate=0.1,
                 use_pe=True):
        # we have 7x7 images from ResNet50,
        # and each pixel is an input token
        # which has been embedded into 2048 dimensions by ResNet
        super(VisualEncoder, self).__init__()

        self.d_model = d_model
        self.num_layers = num_layers

        # FC layer replaces embedding layer in traditional encoder
        # this FC layers takes 49x2048 image
        # and projects into model dims
        self.fc = tf.keras.layers.Dense(d_model, activation='relu')
        self.pos_encoding = positional_encoding(
                                        maximum_position_encoding,
                                        self.d_model)

        self.enc_layers = [EncoderLayer(d_model, num_heads,
                                        dff, dropout_rate)
                           for _ in range(num_layers)]

        self.dropout = tf.keras.layers.Dropout(dropout_rate)

        self.use_pe = use_pe
```

The constructor is shown next. A new parameter that states the number of layers is introduced. The original paper used 6 layers, 512 as d_{model}, 8 multi-attention heads, and 2,048 as the size of the intermediate feed-forward output. Note the highlighted lines in the preceding code. The dimensions of the pre-processed images can vary depending on the layer of ResNet50 from which output is pulled. We pass the input through a dense layer, fc, to the size inputs according to the model. This allows us to experiment with different models to pre-process images such as VGG19 or Inception without changing the architecture. Also, note that the maximum position encoding is hardcoded to 49, since that is the dimension of the output of the ResNet50 model. Lastly, we add a flag that can switch positional encoding on or off in the Visual Encoder. You should experiment with training models with and without positional encodings in the input to see if this helps or hinders learning.

VisualEncoder is composed of multiple multi-head attention and feed-forward blocks. We can utilize a convenience class, EncoderLayer, to define one such block. A stack of these blocks is created based on the input parameters. We will examine the internals of EncoderLayer momentarily. First, let's see how inputs pass through VisualEncoder. The call() function is used to produce the outputs for the given inputs:

```
def call(self, x, training, mask):
    # all inp image sequences are always 49, so mask not needed
    seq_len = tf.shape(x)[1]

    # adding embedding and position encoding.
    # input size should be batch_size, 49, 2048)
    # output dims should be (batch_size, 49, d_model)
    x = self.fc(x)
    # scaled dot product attention
    x *= tf.math.sqrt(tf.cast(self.d_model, tf.float32))
    if self.use_pe:
        x += self.pos_encoding[:, :seq_len, :]

    x = self.dropout(x, training=training)

    for i in range(self.num_layers):
        x = self.enc_layers[i](
            x, training, mask)  # mask shouldnt be needed

    return x  # (batch_size, 49, d_model)
```

This code is fairly simple due to the abstractions defined previously. Note the use of the training flag to turn dropout on or off. Now, let's see how `EncoderLayer` is defined. Each Encoder building is composed of two sub-blocks. The first sub-block passes inputs through multi-head attention, while the second sub-block passes the output of the first sub-block through the 2-layer feed-forward layer:

```
class EncoderLayer(tf.keras.layers.Layer):
    def __init__(self, d_model, num_heads, dff, rate=0.1):
        super(EncoderLayer, self).__init__()

        self.mha = MultiHeadAttention(d_model, num_heads)
        self.ffn = point_wise_feed_forward_network(d_model, dff)

        self.layernorm1 = tf.keras.layers.LayerNormalization(
                                                epsilon=1e-6)
        self.layernorm2 = tf.keras.layers.LayerNormalization(
                                                epsilon=1e-6)

        self.dropout1 = tf.keras.layers.Dropout(rate)
        self.dropout2 = tf.keras.layers.Dropout(rate)

    def call(self, x, training, mask):
        # (batch_size, input_seq_len, d_model)
        attn_output, _ = self.mha(x, x, x, mask)
        attn_output = self.dropout1(attn_output,
                                    training=training)
        # (batch_size, input_seq_len, d_model)
        out1 = self.layernorm1(x + attn_output) # Residual connection

        # (batch_size, input_seq_len, d_model)
        ffn_output = self.ffn(out1)
        ffn_output = self.dropout2(ffn_output, training=training)
        # (batch_size, input_seq_len, d_model)
        out2 = self.layernorm2(out1 + ffn_output) # Residual conx

        return out2
```

Each layer first computes the output from multi-head attention and passes it through dropout. A residual connection passes the sum of the output and input through LayerNorm. The second part of this block passes the output of the first LayerNorm through the feed-forward layer and another dropout layer.

Again, a residual connection combines the output and input to the feed-forward part before passing it through LayerNorm. Note the use of dropout and residual connections, which were developed for CV in the Transformer architecture.

Layer normalization or LayerNorm

LayerNorm was proposed in 2016 in a paper by the same name as an alternative to BatchNorm for RNNs. BatchNorm, as described in the *CNNs* section, normalizes the outputs across the entire batch. But sequences can be of variable length in the case of RNNs. A different formulation is required for normalization that can handle variable sequence lengths. LayerNorm normalizes across all the hidden units in a given layer. It is independent of the batch size, and the normalization is the same for all the units in a given layer. LayerNorm results in a significant speedup of training and convergence of seq2seq style models.

With `VisualEncoder` in place, we are ready to implement the Decoder before we put this all together into the full Transformer.

Decoder

The Decoder is also composed of blocks, just like the Encoder. Each block of the Decoder, however, contains three sub-blocks, as shown in the diagram in the *The Transformer model* section. There is a masked multi-head attention sub-block, followed by a multi-head attention block, and finally a feed-forward sub-block. The feed-forward sub-block is identical to the Encoder sub-block. We must define a Decoder layer that can be stacked to construct the Decoder. The constructor for this is shown here:

```
class DecoderLayer(tf.keras.layers.Layer):
    def __init__(self, d_model, num_heads, dff, rate=0.1):
        super(DecoderLayer, self).__init__()

        self.mha1 = MultiHeadAttention(d_model, num_heads)
        self.mha2 = MultiHeadAttention(d_model, num_heads)

        self.ffn = point_wise_feed_forward_network(d_model, dff)

        self.layernorm1 = tf.keras.layers.LayerNormalization(
                                                    epsilon=1e-6)
        self.layernorm2 = tf.keras.layers.LayerNormalization(
                                                    epsilon=1e-6)
```

```
self.layernorm3 = tf.keras.layers.LayerNormalization(
                                        epsilon=1e-6)

self.dropout1 = tf.keras.layers.Dropout(rate)
self.dropout2 = tf.keras.layers.Dropout(rate)
self.dropout3 = tf.keras.layers.Dropout(rate)
```

Three sub-blocks should be quite evident based on the preceding variables. Input passes through this layer and is converted into output, as defined by the computations in the `call()` function:

```
def call(self, x, enc_output, training,
        look_ahead_mask, padding_mask):
    # enc_output.shape == (batch_size, input_seq_len, d_model)

    attn1, attn_weights_block1 = self.mha1(
        x, x, x, look_ahead_mask)
    # args ^ => (batch_size, target_seq_len, d_model)

    attn1 = self.dropout1(attn1, training=training)
    out1 = self.layernorm1(attn1 + x) # residual

    attn2, attn_weights_block2 = self.mha2(
        enc_output, enc_output, out1, padding_mask)
    # args ^ =>  (batch_size, target_seq_len, d_model)

    attn2 = self.dropout2(attn2, training=training)
    # (batch_size, target_seq_len, d_model)
    out2 = self.layernorm2(attn2 + out1)

    ffn_output = self.ffn(out2)
    ffn_output = self.dropout3(ffn_output, training=training)
    # (batch_size, target_seq_len, d_model)
    out3 = self.layernorm3(ffn_output + out2)

    return out3, attn_weights_block1, attn_weights_block2
```

The first sub-block, also referred to as the masked multi-head attention block, uses the output tokens, masked to the current position being generated. The outputs, in our case, are the tokens that make up the caption. The look-ahead mask masks tokens that haven't been generated yet.

Note that this sub-block does not use the output of the Encoder. It is trying to predict the relationship of the next token to the previous token that was generated. The second sub-block uses the output of the Encoder, along with the output of the previous sub-block, to generate the outputs. Finally, the feed-forward network generates the final output by operating on the output of the second sub-block. Both the multi-head attention sub-blocks have their own attention weights.

We define the Decoder as a custom layer that is composed of multiple `DecoderLayer` blocks. The structure of the Transformer is symmetrical. The number of Encoder and Decoder blocks is the same. The constructor is defined first:

```
class Decoder(tf.keras.layers.Layer):
    def __init__(self, num_layers, d_model, num_heads,
                dff, target_vocab_size,
                maximum_position_encoding, rate=0.1):
        super(Decoder, self).__init__()

        self.d_model = d_model
        self.num_layers = num_layers

        self.embedding = tf.keras.layers.Embedding(
                                    target_vocab_size, d_model)
        self.pos_encoding = positional_encoding(
                            maximum_position_encoding,
                            d_model)

        self.dec_layers = [DecoderLayer(d_model, num_heads,
                                    dff, rate)
                        for _ in range(num_layers)]
        self.dropout = tf.keras.layers.Dropout(rate)
```

The output of the Decoder is computed by the `call()` function:

```
def call(self, x, enc_output, training,
        look_ahead_mask, padding_mask):

    seq_len = tf.shape(x)[1]
    attention_weights = {}

    x = self.embedding(x)
    x *= tf.math.sqrt(tf.cast(self.d_model, tf.float32))
    x += self.pos_encoding[:, :seq_len, :]
```

```
        x = self.dropout(x, training=training)

        for i in range(self.num_layers):
            x, block1, block2 = self.dec_layers[i](x, enc_output,
                        training, look_ahead_mask, padding_mask)

        attention_weights['decoder_layer{}_block1'.format(i + 1)]  =
    block1
        attention_weights['decoder_layer{}_block2'.format(i + 1)] =
    block2

        # x.shape == (batch_size, target_seq_len, d_model)
        return x, attention_weights
```

Whew, that was a fair amount of code. The structure of the Transformer model is so elegant. The beauty of the model allows us to stack more Encoder and Decoder layers to create more powerful models, as demonstrated by GPT-3 recently. Let's put the Encoder and Decoder together to create a full Transformer.

Transformer

The Transformer is composed of the Encoder, the Decoder, and the final Dense layer for generating output token distributions across the subword vocabulary:

```
class Transformer(tf.keras.Model):
    def __init__(self, num_layers, d_model, num_heads, dff,
                target_vocab_size, pe_input, pe_target, rate=0.1,
                use_pe=True):
        super(Transformer, self).__init__()

        self.encoder = VisualEncoder(num_layers, d_model,
                                num_heads, dff,
                                pe_input, rate, use_pe)

        self.decoder = Decoder(num_layers, d_model, num_heads,
                    dff, target_vocab_size, pe_target, rate)

        self.final_layer = tf.keras.layers.Dense(
                                target_vocab_size)

    def call(self, inp, tar, training, enc_padding_mask,
            look_ahead_mask, dec_padding_mask):
```

```
# (batch_size, inp_seq_len, d_model)
enc_output = self.encoder(inp, training, enc_padding_mask)

# dec_output.shape == (batch_size, tar_seq_len, d_model)
dec_output, attention_weights = self.decoder(
                        tar, enc_output, training,
                        look_ahead_mask, dec_padding_mask)

# (batch_size, tar_seq_len, target_vocab_size)
final_output = self.final_layer(dec_output)

return final_output, attention_weights
```

That was a whirlwind tour of the full Transformer code. Ideally, Keras in TensorFlow will provide a higher-level API for defining a Transformer model without you having to write the code out. If this was too much to absorb, then focus on the masks and VisualEncoder as they are the only deviations from the standard Transformer architecture.

We are now ready to train the model. We'll take a very similar approach to the one we adopted in the previous chapter, by setting up learning rate annealing and checkpointing.

Training the Transformer model with VisualEncoder

Training the Transformer model can take hours as we want to train for around 20 epochs. It is best to put the training code into a file so that it can be run from the command line. Note that the model will be able to show some results even after 4 epochs of training. The training code is in the `caption-training.py` file. At a high level, the following steps need to be performed before starting training. First, the CSV file with captions and image names is loaded in, and the corresponding paths for the files with extracted image features are appended. The Subword Encoder is also loaded in. A `tf.data.Dataset` is created with the encoded captions and image features for easy batching and feeding them into the model for training. A loss function, an optimizer with a learning rate schedule, is created for use in training. A custom training loop is used to train the Transformer model. Let's go over these steps in detail.

Loading training data

The following code loads the CSV file we generated in the pre-processing step:

```
prefix = './data/'
save_prefix = prefix + "features/"  # for storing prefixes
annot = prefix + 'data.csv'

inputs = pd.read_csv(annot, header=None,
                     names=["caption", "image"])
print("Data file loaded")
```

The captions in the data are tokenized using the Subword Encoder we generated and persisted to disk earlier:

```
cap_tokenizer = \
        tfds.features.text.SubwordTextEncoder.load_from_file(
                                          "captions")
print(cap_tokenizer.encode(
                "A man riding a wave on top of a surfboard.".lower())
)
print("Tokenizer hydrated")

# Max Length of captions split by spaces
lens = inputs['caption'].map(lambda x: len(x.split()))

# Max Length of captions after tokenization
# tfds demonstrated in earlier chapters
# This is a quick way if data fits in memory
lens = inputs['caption'].map(
                lambda x: len(cap_tokenizer.encode(x.lower())))
)

# We will set this as the max length of captions
# which cover 99% of the captions without truncation
max_len = int(lens.quantile(0.99) + 1)  # for special tokens
```

The maximum length of the captions is generated to accommodate 99% of the caption lengths. All the captions are truncated or padded to this maximum length:

```
start = '<s>'
end = '</s>'
inputs['tokenized'] = inputs['caption'].map(
```

```
        lambda x: start + x.lower().strip() + end)

def tokenize_pad(x):
    x = cap_tokenizer.encode(x)
    if len(x) < max_len:
        x = x + [0] * int(max_len - len(x))
    return x[:max_len]


inputs['tokens'] = inputs.tokenized.map(lambda x: tokenize_pad(x))
```

Image features are persisted to disk. When training begins, those features need to be read from the disk and fed in, along with the encoded captions. The name of the file containing the image features is then added to the dataset:

```
# now to compute a column with the new name of the saved
# image feature file
inputs['img_features'] = inputs['image'].map(lambda x:
                                        save_prefix +
                                        x.split('/')[-1][:-3]
                                        + 'npy')
```

A `tf.data.Dataset` is created and a map function that reads image features while enumerating batches is set up:

```
captions = inputs.tokens.tolist()
img_names = inputs.img_features.tolist()


# Load the numpy file with extracted ResNet50 feature

def load_image_feature(img_name, cap):
    img_tensor = np.load(img_name.decode('utf-8'))
    return img_tensor, cap


dataset = tf.data.Dataset.from_tensor_slices((img_train,
                                        cap_train))


# Use map to load the numpy files in parallel
dataset = dataset.map(lambda item1, item2: tf.numpy_function(
    load_image_feature, [item1, item2], [tf.float32, tf.int32]),
    num_parallel_calls=tf.data.experimental.AUTOTUNE)
```

Now that the dataset has been prepared, we are ready to instantiate the Transformer model.

Instantiating the Transformer model

We will instantiate a small model in terms of the number of layers, attention heads, embedding dimensions, and feed-forward units:

```
# Small Model
num_layers = 4
d_model = 128
dff = d_model * 4
num_heads = 8
```

For comparison, the BERT base model contains the following parameters:

```
# BERT Base Model
# num_layers = 12
# d_model = 768
# dff = d_model * 4
# num_heads = 12
```

These settings are available in the file but commented out. Using these settings slows down training and requires a large amount of GPU memory. A couple of other parameters need to be set up and the Transformer instantiated:

```
target_vocab_size = cap_tokenizer.vocab_size
# already includes start/end tokens
dropout_rate = 0.1

EPOCHS = 20  # should see results in 4-10 epochs also

transformer = vt.Transformer(num_layers, d_model, num_heads, dff,
                        target_vocab_size,
                        pe_input=49,  # 7x7 pixels
                        pe_target=target_vocab_size,
                        rate=dropout_rate,
                        use_pe=False
                        )
```

This model contains over 4 million trainable parameters. It is a smaller model than we have seen previously:

```
Model: "transformer"
_____
Layer (type)                 Output Shape            Param #
===============================================================
visual_encoder (VisualEncode multiple                1055360

decoder (Decoder)            multiple                2108544

dense_65 (Dense)             multiple                1058445
===============================================================
Total params: 4,222,349
Trainable params: 4,222,349
Non-trainable params: 0
_____
```

However, the model summary is not available since the input dimensions have not yet been supplied. The summary will be available once we've run a training example through the model.

A custom learning rate schedule is created for training the model. A custom learning rate schedule anneals or reduces the learning rate as the model improves its accuracy, resulting in better accuracy. This process is called learning rate decay or learning rate annealing and was discussed in detail in *Chapter 5, Generating Text with RNNs and GPT-2*.

Custom learning rate schedule

This rate schedule is identical to the one proposed in the *Attention Is All You Need* paper:

```python
class CustomSchedule(tf.keras.optimizers.schedules.
LearningRateSchedule):
    def __init__(self, d_model, warmup_steps=4000):
        super(CustomSchedule, self).__init__()

        self.d_model = d_model
        self.d_model = tf.cast(self.d_model, tf.float32)

        self.warmup_steps = warmup_steps
```

```
def __call__(self, step):
    arg1 = tf.math.rsqrt(step)
    arg2 = step * (self.warmup_steps ** -1.5)

    return tf.math.rsqrt(self.d_model) * \
            tf.math.minimum(arg1, arg2)


learning_rate = CustomSchedule(d_model)

optimizer = tf.keras.optimizers.Adam(learning_rate,
                        beta_1=0.9, beta_2=0.98,
                        epsilon=1e-9)
```

The following graph shows the learning schedule:

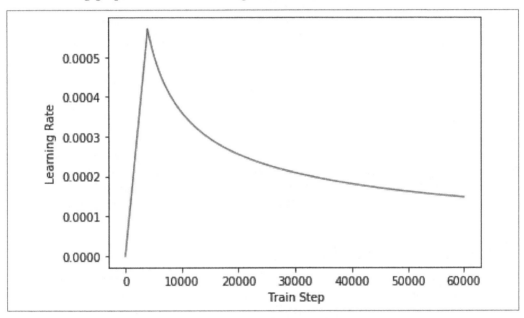

Figure 7.13: Custom learning rate schedule

When training starts, a higher learning rate is used as the loss is high. As the model learns more and more, the loss starts decreasing, which requires a lower learning rate. Using the preceding learning rate schedule significantly speeds up training and convergence. We also need a loss function to optimize.

Loss and metrics

The loss function is based on categorical cross-entropy. It is a common loss function that we have used in previous chapters. In addition to the loss, an accuracy metric is also defined to track how the model is doing on the training set:

```
loss_object = tf.keras.losses.SparseCategoricalCrossentropy(
                            from_logits=True, reduction='none')
```

```
def loss_function(real, pred):
    mask = tf.math.logical_not(tf.math.equal(real, 0))
    loss_ = loss_object(real, pred)

    mask = tf.cast(mask, dtype=loss_.dtype)
    loss_ *= mask

    return tf.reduce_sum(loss_) / tf.reduce_sum(mask)
```

```
train_loss = tf.keras.metrics.Mean(name='train_loss')
train_accuracy = tf.keras.metrics.SparseCategoricalAccuracy(
                        name='train_accuracy')
```

This formulation has been used in previous chapters as well. We are almost ready to start training. There are two more steps we must follow before we get into the custom training function. We need to set up checkpoints to save progress in case of failures, and we also need to mask inputs for the Encoder and Decoder.

Checkpoints and masks

We need to specify a checkpoint directory for TensorFlow to save progress. We will use a CheckpointManager here, which automatically manages the checkpoints and stores a limited number of them. A checkpoint can be quite large. Five checkpoints for the small model would take up approximately 243 MB of space. Larger models would take up more space:

```
checkpoint_path = "./checkpoints/train-small-model-40ep"

ckpt = tf.train.Checkpoint(transformer=transformer,
                            optimizer=optimizer)

ckpt_manager = tf.train.CheckpointManager(ckpt, checkpoint_path,
```

```
                    max_to_keep=5)

# if a checkpoint exists, restore the latest checkpoint.
if ckpt_manager.latest_checkpoint:
    ckpt.restore(ckpt_manager.latest_checkpoint)
    print ('Latest checkpoint restored!!')
```

Next, a method that will create masks for the input images and captions must be defined:

```
def create_masks(inp, tar):
    # Encoder padding mask - This should just be 1's
    # input shape should be (batch_size, 49, 2048)
    inp_seq = tf.ones([inp.shape[0], inp.shape[1]])

    enc_padding_mask = vt.create_padding_mask(inp_seq)

    # Used in the 2nd attention block in the Decoder.
    # This padding mask is used to mask the encoder outputs.
    dec_padding_mask = vt.create_padding_mask(inp_seq)

    # Used in the 1st attention block in the Decoder.
    # It is used to pad and mask future tokens in the input
    # received by the decoder.
    look_ahead_mask = vt.create_look_ahead_mask(tf.shape(tar)[1])
    dec_target_padding_mask = vt.create_padding_mask(tar)
    combined_mask = tf.maximum(dec_target_padding_mask,
                                look_ahead_mask)

    return enc_padding_mask, combined_mask, dec_padding_mask
```

Inputs are always a constant length, so the input sequence is set as ones. Only the captions, which are used by the Decoder, are masked. There are two types of masks for the Decoder. The first mask is the padding mask. Since the captions are set to the maximum length to handle 99% of the captions, which works out at about 22 tokens, any captions that are smaller than this number of tokens have padding appended to the end of them. The padding mask helps separate caption tokens from padding tokens. The second mask is the look-ahead mask. It prevents the Decoder from seeing tokens from the future or tokens it has not generated yet. Now, we are ready to train the model.

Custom training

Similar to the summarization model, teacher forcing will be used for training. Consequently, a custom training function will be used. First, we must define a function that will train on one batch of data:

```
@tf.function
def train_step(inp, tar):
    tar_inp = tar[:, :-1]
    tar_real = tar[:, 1:]

    enc_padding_mask, combined_mask, dec_padding_mask = create_
masks(inp, tar_inp)

    with tf.GradientTape() as tape:
        predictions, _ = transformer(inp, tar_inp,
                                     True,
                                     enc_padding_mask,
                                     combined_mask,
                                     dec_padding_mask)
        loss = loss_function(tar_real, predictions)

    gradients = tape.gradient(loss,
                              transformer.trainable_variables)

    optimizer.apply_gradients(zip(gradients,
                                  transformer.trainable_variables))

    train_loss(loss)
    train_accuracy(tar_real, predictions)
```

This method is very similar to the summarization training code. All we need to do now is define the number of epochs and batch size and start training:

```
# setup training parameters
BUFFER_SIZE = 1000
BATCH_SIZE = 64  # can +/- depending on GPU capacity
# Shuffle and batch
dataset = dataset.shuffle(BUFFER_SIZE).batch(BATCH_SIZE)
dataset = dataset.prefetch(buffer_size=tf.data.experimental.AUTOTUNE)

# Begin Training
for epoch in range(EPOCHS):
```

```
    start_tm = time.time()

    train_loss.reset_states()
    train_accuracy.reset_states()

    # inp -> images, tar -> caption
    for (batch, (inp, tar)) in enumerate(dataset):
        train_step(inp, tar)

        if batch % 100 == 0:
            ts = datetime.datetime.now().strftime(
                            "%d-%b-%Y (%H:%M:%S)")
            print('[{}] Epoch {} Batch {} Loss {:.6f} Accuracy'+\
                    '{:.6f}'.format(ts, epoch + 1, batch,
                                    train_loss.result(),
                                    train_accuracy.result()))

    if (epoch + 1) % 2 == 0:
        ckpt_save_path = ckpt_manager.save()
        print('Saving checkpoint for epoch {} at {}'.format(
                        epoch + 1,
                        ckpt_save_path))

    print('Epoch {} Loss {:.6f} Accuracy {:.6f}'.format(epoch + 1,
                                    train_loss.result(),
                                    train_accuracy.result()))

    print('Time taken for 1 epoch: {} secs\n'.format(
                                    time.time() - start_tm))
```

Training can be started from the command line:

```
(tf24nlp) $ python caption-training.py
```

This training may take some time. An epoch of training takes about 11 minutes on my GPU-enabled machine. If you contrast this to the summarization model, this model is training extremely fast. Compared to the summarization model, which contains 13 million parameters, it is much smaller and trains very fast. This speed boost is due to the lack of recurrence.

The state-of-the-art summarization models use the Transformer architecture along with subword encoding. Given that you have all the pieces of the Transformer, a good exercise to test your understanding would be editing the VisualEncoder to process text and rebuild the summarization model as a Transformer. You will then be able to experience these speedup and accuracy improvements.

A longer training time allows the model to learn better. However, this model can give reasonable results in as few as 5-10 epochs of training. Once training is complete, we can try the model on some images.

Generating captions

First, you need to be congratulated! You made it through a whirlwind implementation of the Transformer. I am sure you must have noticed a number of common building blocks that were used in previous chapters. Since the Transformer model is complex, we left it for this chapter to look at other techniques like Bahdanau attention, custom layers, custom rate schedules, custom training using teacher forcing, and checkpointing so that we could cover a lot of ground quickly in this chapter. You should consider all these building blocks an important part of your toolkit when you try and solve an NLP problem.

Without further ado, let's try and caption some images. Again, we will use a Jupyter notebook for inference so that we can quickly try out different images. All the code for inference is in the `image-captioning-inference.ipynb` file.

The inference code needs to load the Subword Encoder, set up masking, instantiate a ResNet50 model to extract features from test images, and generate captions a token at a time until the end of the sequence or a maximum sequence length is reached. Let's go over these steps one at a time.

Once we've done the appropriate imports and optionally initialized the GPU, we can load the Subword Encoder that was saved when we pre-processed the data:

```
cap_tokenizer = tfds.features.text.SubwordTextEncoder.load_from_
file("captions")
```

We must now instantiate the Transformer model. This is an important step to ensure the parameters are the same as the checkpoint ones:

```
# Small Model
num_layers = 4
```

```
d_model = 128
dff = d_model * 4
num_heads = 8

target_vocab_size = cap_tokenizer.vocab_size  # already includes
                                              # start/end tokens


dropout_rate = 0. # immaterial during inference

transformer = vt.Transformer(num_layers, d_model, num_heads, dff,
                             target_vocab_size,
                             pe_input=49,  # 7x7 pixels
                             pe_target=target_vocab_size,
                             rate=dropout_rate
                             )
```

Restoring the model from the checkpoint requires the optimizer, even though we are not training the model. So, we will reuse the custom scheduler from the training code. As this code was provided previously, it has been omitted here. For the checkpoint, I used a model that was trained for 40 epochs, but without positional encoding in the Encoder:

```
checkpoint_path = "./checkpoints/train-small-model-nope-40ep"

ckpt = tf.train.Checkpoint(transformer=transformer,
                           optimizer=optimizer)

ckpt_manager = tf.train.CheckpointManager(ckpt, checkpoint_path,
                                          max_to_keep=5)

# if a checkpoint exists, restore the latest checkpoint.
if ckpt_manager.latest_checkpoint:
    ckpt.restore(ckpt_manager.latest_checkpoint)
    print ('Latest checkpoint restored!!')
```

Finally, we must set up the masking function for the generated captions. Note that the look ahead masks don't really help during inference as future tokens have not been generated yet:

```
# Helper function for creating masks
def create_masks(inp, tar):
    # Encoder padding mask - This should just be 1's
    # input shape should be (batch_size, 49, 2048)
```

```
inp_seq = tf.ones([inp.shape[0], inp.shape[1]])

enc_padding_mask = vt.create_padding_mask(inp_seq)

# Used in the 2nd attention block in the Decoder.
# This padding mask is used to mask the encoder outputs.
dec_padding_mask = vt.create_padding_mask(inp_seq)

# Used in the 1st attention block in the Decoder.
# It is used to pad and mask future tokens in the input received by
# the decoder.
look_ahead_mask = vt.create_look_ahead_mask(tf.shape(tar)[1])
dec_target_padding_mask = vt.create_padding_mask(tar)
combined_mask = tf.maximum(dec_target_padding_mask,
                           look_ahead_mask)

return enc_padding_mask, combined_mask, dec_padding_mask
```

The main code for inference is in an `evaluate()` function. This method takes in the image features generated by ResNet50 as input and seeds the output caption sequence with the start token. Then, it runs in a loop to generate a token at a time while updating the masks, until an end of sequence token is encountered or the maximum length of the caption is reached:

```
def evaluate(inp_img, max_len=21):
    start_token = cap_tokenizer.encode("<s>")[0]
    end_token = cap_tokenizer.encode("</s>")[0]

    encoder_input = inp_img # batch of 1

    # start token for caption
    decoder_input = [start_token]
    output = tf.expand_dims(decoder_input, 0)
    for i in range(max_len):
        enc_padding_mask, combined_mask, dec_padding_mask = \
                create_masks(encoder_input, output)

        # predictions.shape == (batch_size, seq_len, vocab_size)
        predictions, attention_weights = transformer(
                                            encoder_input,
                                            output,
                                            False,
```

```
                                     enc_padding_mask,
                                     combined_mask,
                                     dec_padding_mask)


        # select the last word from the seq_len dimension
        predictions = predictions[: ,-1:, :]


        predicted_id = tf.cast(tf.argmax(predictions, axis=-1),
                                tf.int32)


        # return the result if predicted_id is equal to end token
        if predicted_id == end_token:
            return tf.squeeze(output, axis=0), attention_weights


        # concatenate the predicted_id to the output which is
        # given to the decoder  as its input.
        output = tf.concat([output, predicted_id], axis=-1)


    return tf.squeeze(output, axis=0), attention_weights
```

A wrapper method is used to call the evaluation method and print out the caption:

```
def caption(image):
    end_token = cap_tokenizer.encode("</s>")[0]
    result, attention_weights = evaluate(image)

    predicted_sentence = cap_tokenizer.decode([i for i in result
                                        if i > end_token])
    print('Predicted Caption: {}'.format(predicted_sentence))
```

The only thing remaining now is instantiating a ResNet50 model to extract features from image files on the fly:

```
rs50 = tf.keras.applications.ResNet50(
    include_top=False,
    weights="imagenet",  # no pooling
    input_shape=(224, 224, 3)
)
new_input = rs50.input
hidden_layer = rs50.layers[-1].output

features_extract = tf.keras.Model(new_input, hidden_layer)
```

It's the moment of truth, finally! Let's try out the model on an image. We will load the image, pre-process it for ResNet50, and extract the features from it:

```
# from keras
image = load_img("./beach-surf.jpg", target_size=(224, 224))
image = img_to_array(image)
image = np.expand_dims(image, axis=0)  # batch of one
image = preprocess_input(image)  # from resnet

eval_img = features_extract.predict(image)

caption(eval_img)
```

The following is the example image and its caption:

Figure 7.14: Generated caption - A man is riding a surfboard on a wave

This looks like an amazing caption for the given image! However, the overall accuracy of the model is in the low 30s. There is a lot of scope for improvement in the model. The next section talks about the state-of-the-art techniques for image captioning and also proposes some simpler ideas that you can try and play around with.

 Note that you may see slightly different results. The reviewer for this book got the result *A man in a black shirt is riding a surfboard* while running this code. This is expected as slight differences in the probabilities and the exact place where the model stops training in the loss surface is not exact. We are operating in the probabilistic realm here, so there may be slight differences. You may have experienced similar differences in the text generation and summarization code in the previous chapters as well.

The following image shows some more examples of images and their captions. The notebook contains several good, as well as some atrocious, examples of the generated labels:

a close up of a vase with flowers in it

a group of people standing around a table with a cake.

a group of people standing on top of a sandy beach.

a group of people walking down a street with luggage.

a man in a suit and tie standing in front of a mirror.

a group of men standing next to each other on a field.

Figure 7.15: Examples of images and their generated captions

None of these images were in the training set. The caption quality goes down from top to bottom. Our model understands close up, cake, groups of people, sandy beaches, streets, and luggage, among other things. However, the bottom two examples are concerning. They hint at some **bias** in the model. In both of the bottom two images, the model is misinterpreting gender.

The images were deliberately chosen to show a woman in a business suit and women playing basketball. In both cases, the model proposes men in the captions. When the model was tried with a female tennis player's image, it guessed the right gender, but it changed genders in an image from a women's soccer game. Bias in models is a very important concern. In cases such as image captioning, this bias is immediately apparent. In fact, over 600,000 images were removed from the ImageNet database (https://bit.ly/3qk4FgN) in 2019 after bias was found in how it classifies and tags people in its pictures. ResNet50 is pre-trained on ImageNet. However, in other models, the bias may be harder to detect. Building fair deep learning models and reducing bias in models are active areas of research in the ML community.

You may have noticed that we skipped running the model on an evaluation set and on the test set. This was done for brevity, and also because those techniques were covered previously.

A quick note on metrics for evaluating the quality of captions. We saw ROUGE metrics in the previous chapters. ROUGE-L is still applicable in the case of image captioning. You can use a mental model of the caption as a summary of an image, as opposed to the summary of a paragraph in text summarization. There can be more than one way to express the summary, and ROUGE-L tries to capture the intent. There are two other commonly reported metrics:

- **BLEU**: This stands for **Bilingual Evaluation Understudy** and is the most popular metric in machine translation. We can cast the image captioning problem as a machine translation problem as well. It relies on n-grams for computing the overlap of the predicted text with a number of reference texts and combines the results into one score.

- **CIDEr**: This stands for **Consensus-Based Image Description Evaluation** and was proposed in a paper by the same name in 2015. It tries to deal with the difficulty of automatic evaluation when multiple captions could be reasonable by combining TF-IDF and n-grams. The metric tries to compare the captions generated by the model against multiple captions by human annotators and tries to score them based on consensus.

Before wrapping up this chapter, let's spend a little time discussing ways to improve performance and state-of-the-art models.

Improving performance and state-of-the-art models

Let's first talk through some simple experiments you can try to improve performance before talking about the latest models. Recall our discussion on positional encodings for inputs in the Encoder. Adding or removing positional encodings helps or hinders performance. In the previous chapter, we implemented the beam search algorithm for generating summaries. You can adapt the beam search code and see an improvement in the results with beam search. Another avenue of exploration is the ResNet50. We used a pre-trained network and did not fine-tune it further. It is possible to build an architecture where ResNet is part of the architecture and not a pre-processing step. Image files are loaded in, and features are extracted from ResNet50 as part of the VisualEncoder. ResNet50 layers can be trained from the get-go, or only in the last few iterations. This idea is implemented in the `resnet-finetuning.py` file for you to try. Another line of thinking is using a different object detection model than ResNet50 or using the output from a different layer. You can try a more complex version of ResNet like ResNet152, or a different object detection model like Detectron from Facebook or other models. It should be quite easy to use a different model in our code as it is quite modular.

When you use a different model for extracting image features, the key will be to make sure tensor dimensions are flowing properly through the Encoder. The Decoder should not require any changes. Depending on the complexity of the model, you can either pre-process and store the image features or compute them on the fly.

Recall that we just used the pixels from the image directly. This was based on a paper published recently at CVPR titled *Pixel-BERT*. Most models use region proposals extracted from images instead of the pixels directly. Object detection in an image involves drawing a boundary around that object in the image. Another way to perform the same task is to classify each pixel into an object or background. These region proposals can be in the form of bounding boxes in an image. State-of-the-art models use bounding boxes or region proposals as input.

The second-biggest gain in image captioning comes from pre-training. Recall that BERT and GPT are pre-trained on specific pre-training objectives. Models differ based on whether the Encoder is pre-trained or both the Encoder and Decoder are pre-trained. A common pre-training objective is a version of the BERT MLM task. Recall that BERT inputs are structured as [CLS] I1 I2 … In [SEP] J1 J2 … Jk [SEP], where some of the tokens from the input sequence are masked. This is adapted for image captioning, where the image features and caption tokens in the input are concatenated. Caption tokens are masked similar to how they are in the BERT model, and the pre-training objective is for the model to predict the masked token. After pre-training, the output of the CLS token can be used for classification or fed to the Decoder to generate the caption. Care must be exercised to not pre-train on the same dataset, like that for evaluation. An example of the setup could be using the Visual Genome and Flickr30k datasets for pre-training and COCO for fine-tuning.

Image captioning is an active area of research. The research is just getting started on multi-modal networks in general. Now, let's recap everything we've learned in this chapter.

Summary

In the world of deep learning, specific architectures have been developed to handle specific modalities. **Convolutional Neural Networks (CNNs)** have been incredibly effective in processing images and is the standard architecture for CV tasks. However, the world of research is moving toward the world of multi-modal networks, which can take multiple types of inputs, like sounds, images, text, and so on and perform cognition like humans. After reviewing multi-modal networks, we dived into vision and language tasks as a specific focus. There are a number of problems in this particular area, including image captioning, visual question answering, VCR, and text-to-image, among others.

Building on our learnings from previous chapters on seq2seq architectures, custom TensorFlow layers and models, custom learning schedules, and custom training loops, we implemented a Transformer model from scratch. Transformers are state of the art at the time of writing. We took a quick look at the basic concepts of CNNs to help with the image side of things. We were able to build a model that may not be able to generate a thousand words for a picture but is definitely able to generate a human-readable caption. Its performance still needs improvement, and we discussed a number of possibilities so that we can try to do so, including the latest techniques.

It is apparent that deep models perform very well when they contain a lot of data. The BERT and GPT models have shown the value of pre-training on massive amounts of data. It is still very hard to get good quality labeled data for use in pre-training or fine-tuning. In the world of NLP, we have a lot of text data, but not enough labeled data. The next chapter focuses on weak supervision to build classification models that can label data for pre-training or even fine-tuning tasks.

8
Weakly Supervised Learning for Classification with Snorkel

Models such as BERT and GPT use massive amounts of unlabeled data along with an unsupervised training objective, such as a **masked language model (MLM)** for BERT or a next word prediction model for GPT, to learn the underlying structure of text. A small amount of task-specific data is used for fine-tuning the pre-trained model using transfer learning. Such models are quite large, with hundreds of millions of parameters, and require massive datasets for pre-training and lots of computation capacity for training and pre-training. Note that the critical problem being solved is the lack of adequate training data. If there were enough domain-specific training data, the gains from BERT-like pre-trained models would not be that big. In certain domains such as medicine, the vocabulary used in task-specific data is typical for the domain. Modest increases in training data can improve the quality of the model to a large extent. However, hand labeling data is a tedious, resource-intensive, and unscalable task for the amounts required for deep learning to be successful.

We discuss an alternative approach in this chapter, based on the concept of weak supervision. Using the Snorkel library, we label tens of thousands of records in a couple of hours and exceed the accuracy of the model developed in *Chapter 3, Named Entity Recognition (NER) with BiLSTMs, CRFs, and Viterbi Decoding* using, BERT. This chapter covers:

- An overview of weakly supervised learning
- An overview of the differences between generative and discriminative models

- Building a baseline model with handcrafted features for labeling data
- Snorkel library basics
- Augmenting training data using Snorkel labeling functions at scale
- Training models using noisy machine-labeled data

It is essential to understand the concept of weakly supervised learning, so let's cover that first.

Weak supervision

Deep learning models have delivered incredible results in the recent past. Deep learning architectures obviated the need for feature engineering, given enough training data. However, enormous amounts of data are needed for a deep learning model to learn the underlying structure of the data. On the one hand, deep learning reduced the manual effort required to handcraft features, but on the other, it significantly increased the need for labeled data for a specific task. In most domains, gathering a sizable set of high-quality, labeled data is an expensive and resource-intensive task.

This problem can be solved in several different ways. In previous chapters, we have seen the use of transfer learning to train a model on a large dataset before fine-tuning the model for a specific task. *Figure 8.1* shows this and other approaches to acquiring labels:

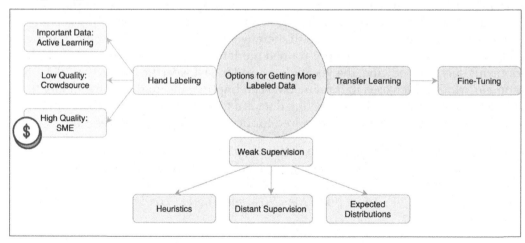

Figure 8.1: Options for getting more labeled data

Hand labeling the data is a common approach. Ideally, we have enough time and money to hire **subject matter experts** (**SMEs**) to hand label every piece of data, which is not practical. Consider labeling a tumor detection dataset and hiring oncologists for the labeling task. Labeling data is probably way lower in priority for an oncologist than treating tumor patients. In a previous company, we organized pizza parties where we would feed people lunch for labels. In an hour, a person could label about 100 records. Feeding 10 people monthly for a year resulted in 12,000 labeled records! This scheme was useful for ongoing maintenance of models, where we would sample the records that were out of distribution, or that the model had shallow confidence in. Thus, we adopted active learning, which determines the records upon labeling, which would have the highest impact on the performance of a classifier.

Another option is to hire labelers that are not experts but are more abundant and cheaper. This is the approach taken by the Amazon Mechanical Turk service. There are a large number of companies that provide labeling services. Since the labelers are not experts, the same record is labeled by multiple people, and some mechanism, like majority vote, is used to decide on the final label of the record. The charge for labeling one record by one labeler may vary from a few cents to a few dollars depending on the complexity of the steps needed for associating a label. The output of such a process is a set of noisy labels that have high coverage, as long as your budget allows for it. We still need to figure out the quality of the labels acquired to see how these labels can be used in the eventual model.

Weak supervision tries to address the problem differently. What if, using heuristics, an SME could hand label thousands of records in a fraction of the time? We will work on the IMDb movie review dataset and try to predict the sentiment of the review. We used the IMDb dataset in *Chapter 4* , *Transfer Learning with BERT*, where we explored transfer learning. It is appropriate to use the same example to show an alternate technique to transfer learning.

Weak supervision techniques don't have to be used as substitutes for transfer learning. Weak supervision techniques help create larger domain-specific labeled datasets. In the absence of transfer learning, a larger labeled dataset improves model performance even with noisy labels coming from weak supervision. However, the gain in model performance will be even more significant if transfer learning and weak supervision are both used together.

An example of a simple heuristic function for labeling a review as having a positive sentiment can be shown with the following pseudocode:

```
if movie.review has "amazing acting" in it:
then sentiment is positive
```

While this may seem like a trivial example for our use case, you will be surprised how effective it can be. In a more complicated setting, an oncologist can provide some of these heuristics and define a few of these functions, which can be called labeling functions, to label some records. These functions may conflict or overlap with each other, similar to crowdsourced labels. Another approach for getting labels is through *distant supervision*. An external knowledge base, like Wikipedia, can be used to label data records heuristically. In a **Named-Entity Recognition (NER)** use case, a gazetteer is used to match entities to a list of known entities, as discussed in *Chapter 2, Understanding Sentiment in Natural Language with BiLSTMs*. In relation extraction between entities, for example, *employee of* or *spouse of*, the Wikipedia page of an entity can be mined to extract the relation, and the data record can be labeled. There are other methods of obtaining these labels, such as using thorough knowledge of the underlying distributions generating the data.

For a given data set, there can be several sources for labels. Each crowdsourced labeler is a source. Each heuristic function, like the "amazing acting" one shown above, is also a source. The core problem in weak supervision is combining these multiple sources to yield labels of sufficient quality for the final classifier. The key points of the model are described in the next section.

 The domain-specific model is being referred to as the classifier in this chapter as the example we are taking is the binary classification of movie review sentiment. However, the labels generated can be used for a variety of domain-specific models.

Inner workings of weak supervision with labeling functions

The idea that a few heuristic labeling functions with low coverage and less than perfect accuracy can help improve the accuracy of a discriminative model sounds fantastic. This section provides a high-level overview of how this works, before we see it in practice on the IMDb sentiment analysis dataset.

We assume a binary classification problem for the sake of explanation though the scheme works for any number of labels. The set of labels for binary classification is {NEG, POS}. We have a set of unlabeled data points, X, with m samples.

Note that we do not have access to the actual labels for these data points, but we represent the generated labels using Y. Let's assume we have n labeling functions LF_1 to LF_n, each of which produces a label. However, we add another label for weak supervision – an abstain label. Each labeling function has the ability to choose whether it wants to apply a label or abstain from labeling. This is a vital aspect of the weak supervision approach. Hence, the set of labels produced by labeling functions is expanded to {NEG, ABSTAIN, POS}.

In this setting, the objective is to train a generative model which models two things:

- The probability of a given labeling function abstaining for a given data point
- The probability of a given labeling function correctly assigning a label to a data point

By applying all the labeling functions on all the data points, we generate an $m \times n$ matrix of data points and their labels. The label generated by the heuristic LF_j on the data point X_i can be represented by:

$$HL_{i,j} = LF_j(X_m)$$

The generative model is trying to learn from the agreements and disagreements between the labeling functions to learn the parameters.

Generative versus Discriminative models

If we have a set of data, X, and labels, Y corresponding to the data, then we can say that the discriminative model tries to capture the *conditional probability $p(Y \mid X)$*. A generative model captures the *joint probability $p(X, Y)$*. Generative models, as their name implies, can generate new data points. We saw examples of generative models in *Chapter 5, Generating Text with RNNs and GPT-2*, where we generated news headlines. **GANs (Generative Adversarial Networks)** and AutoEncoders are well-known generative models. Discriminative models label data points in a given data set. It does so by drawing a plane in the space of features that separates the data points into different classes. Classifiers, like the IMDb sentiment review prediction model, are typically discriminative models.

As can be imagined, generative models have a much more challenging task of learning the whole underlying structure of the data.

The parameter weights, w, of the generative model P_w can be estimated via:

$$\hat{w} = \underset{w}{\operatorname{argmax}} \log \sum_{Y \in \{NEG,POS\}^m} P_w(HL,Y)$$

Not that the log marginal likelihood of the observed labels factors out the predicted labels Y. Hence, this generative model works in an unsupervised fashion. Once the parameters of the generative model are computed, we can predict the labels for the data points as:

$$\hat{Y}_i = P_{\hat{w}}(Y_i \mid LF)$$

Where Y_i represents labels based on labeling functions and $\hat{Y}_i$ represents the predicted label from the generative model. These predicted labels can be fed to a downstream discriminative model for classification.

These concepts were implemented in the Snorkel library. The authors of the Snorkel library were the key contributors to introducing the *Data Programming* approach, in a paper of the same name presented at the Neural Information Process Systems conference in 2016. The Snorkel library was introduced formally in a paper titled *Snorkel: rapid training data creation with weak supervision* by Ratner et al. in 2019. Apple and Google have published papers using the Snorkel library, with papers on *Overton* and *Snorkel Drybell*, respectively. These papers can provide an in-depth discussion of the mathematical proof underlying the creation of training data with weak supervision.

As complex as the underlying principles may be, using Snorkel for labeling data is not difficult in practice. Let us get started by preparing the data set.

Using weakly supervised labels to improve IMDb sentiment analysis

Sentiment analysis of movie reviews on the IMDb website is a standard task for classification-type **Natural Language Processing (NLP)** models. We used this data in Chapter 4 to demonstrate transfer learning with GloVe and VERT embeddings. The IMDb data set has 25,000 training examples and 25,000 testing examples. The dataset also includes 50,000 unlabeled reviews. In previous attempts, we ignored these unsupervised data points. Adding more training data will improve the accuracy of the model. However, hand labeling would be a time-consuming and expensive exercise. We'll use Snorkel-powered labeling functions to see if the accuracy of the predictions can be improved on the testing set.

Pre-processing the IMDb dataset

Previously, we used the `tensorflow_datasets` package to download and manage the dataset. However, we need lower-level access to the data to enable writing the labeling functions. Hence, the first step is to download the dataset from the web.

The code for this chapter is split across two files. The `snorkel-labeling.ipynb` file contains the code for downloading data and generating labels using Snorkel. The second file, `imdb-with-snorkel-labels.ipynb`, contains the code that trains models with and without the additional labeled data. If running the code, then it is best to run all the code in the `snorkel-labeling.ipynb` file first so that all the labeled data files are generated.

The dataset is available in one compressed archive and can be downloaded and expanded like so, as shown in `snorkel-labeling.ipynb`:

```
(tf24nlp) $ wget https://ai.stanford.edu/~amaas/data/sentiment/aclImdb_
v1.tar.gz
(tf24nlp) $ tar xvzf aclImdb_v1.tar.gz
```

This expands the archive in the `aclImdb` directory. The training and unsupervised data is in the `train/` subdirectory while the testing data is in the `test/` subdirectory. There are additional files, but they can be ignored. *Figure 8.2* below shows the directory structure:

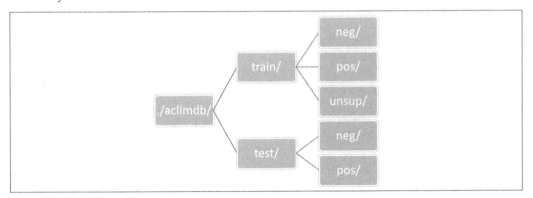

Figure 8.2: Directory structure for the IMDb data

Reviews are stored as individual text files inside the leaf directories. Each file is named using the format `<review_id>_<rating>.txt`. Review identifiers are sequentially numbered from 0 to 24999 for training and testing examples. For the unsupervised data, the highest review number is 49999.

The rating is a number between 0 and 9 and has meaning only in the test and training data. This number reflects the actual rating given to a certain review. The sentiment of all reviews in the pos/ subdirectory is positive. The sentiment of reviews in the neg/ subdirectory is negative. Ratings of 0 to 4 are considered negative, while ratings between 5 and 9 inclusive are considered positive. In this particular example, we do not use the actual rating and only consider the overall sentiment.

We load the data into pandas DataFrames for ease of processing. A convenience function is defined to load reviews from a subdirectory into a DataFrame:

```
def load_reviews(path, columns=["filename", 'review']):
    assert len(columns) == 2
    l = list()
    for filename in glob.glob(path):
        # print(filename)
        with open(filename, 'r') as f:
            review = f.read()
            l.append((filename, review))
    return pd.DataFrame(l, columns=columns)
```

The method above loads the data into two columns – one for the name of the file and one for the text of the file. Using this method, the unsupervised dataset is loaded:

```
unsup_df = load_reviews("./aclImdb/train/unsup/*.txt")
unsup_df.describe()
```

	filename	review
count	50000	50000
unique	50000	49507
top	./aclImdb/train/unsup/24211_0.txt	Am not from America, I usually watch this show...
freq	1	5

A slightly different method is used for the training and testing datasets:

```
def load_labelled_data(path, neg='/neg/',
                       pos='/pos/', shuffle=True):
    neg_df = load_reviews(path + neg + "*.txt")
    pos_df = load_reviews(path + pos + "*.txt")
    neg_df['sentiment'] = 0
    pos_df['sentiment'] = 1
    df = pd.concat([neg_df, pos_df], axis=0)
    if shuffle:
        df = df.sample(frac=1, random_state=42)
    return df
```

This method returns three columns – the file name, the text of the review, and a sentiment label. The sentiment label is 0 if the sentiment is negative and 1 if the sentiment is positive, as determined by the directory the review is found in.

The training dataset can now be loaded in like so:

```
train_df = load_labelled_data("./aclImdb/train/")
train_df.head()
```

	filename	review	sentiment
6868	./aclImdb/ train// neg/6326_4.txt	If you're in the mood for some dopey light ent...	0
11516	./aclImdb/ train// pos/11177_8.txt	*****Spoilers herein***** What real...	1
9668	./aclImdb/ train// neg/2172_2.txt	Bottom of the barrel, unimaginative, and pract...	0
1140	./aclImdb/ train// pos/2065_7.txt	Fearful Symmetry is a pleasant episode with a ...	1
1518	./aclImdb/ train// pos/7147_10.txt	I found the storyline in this movie to be very...	1

While we don't use the raw scores for the sentiment analysis, it is a good exercise for you to try predicting the score instead of the sentiment on your own. To help with processing the score from the raw files, the following code can be used, which extracts the scores from the file names:

```
def fn_to_score(f):
    scr = f.split("/")[-1]  # get file name
    scr = scr.split(".")[0] # remove extension
    scr = int (scr.split("_")[-1]) #the score
    return scr
train_df['score'] = train_df.filename.apply(fn_to_
score)
```

This adds a new *score* column to the DataFrame, which can be used as a starting point.

The testing data can be loaded using the same convenience function by passing a different starting data directory.

```
test_df = load_labelled_data("./aclImdb/test/")
```

Once the reviews are loaded in, the next step is to create a tokenizer.

Learning a subword tokenizer

A subword tokenizer can be learned using the `tensorflow_datasets` package. Note that we want to pass all the training and unsupervised reviews while learning this tokenizer.

```
text = unsup_df.review.to_list() + train_df.review.to_list()
```

This step creates a list of 75,000 items. If the text of the reviews is inspected, there are some HTML tags in the reviews as they were scraped from the IMDb website. We use the Beautiful Soup package to clean these tags.

```
txt = [ BeautifulSoup(x).text for x in text ]
```

Then, we learn the vocabulary with 8,266 entries.

```
encoder = tfds.features.text.SubwordTextEncoder.\
            build_from_corpus(txt, target_vocab_size=2**13)
encoder.save_to_file("imdb")
```

This encoder is saved to disk. Learning the vocabulary can be a time-consuming task and needs to be done only once. Saving it to disk saves effort on subsequent runs of the code.

 A pre-trained subword encoder is supplied. It can be found in the GitHub folder corresponding to this chapter and is titled `imdb.subwords` in case you want to skip these steps.

Before we jump into a model using data labeled with Snorkel, let us define a baseline model so that we can compare the performance of the models before and after the addition of weakly supervised labels.

A BiLSTM baseline model

To understand the impact of additional labeled data on model performance, we need a point of comparison. So, we set up a BiLSTM model that we have seen previously as the baseline. There are a few steps of data processing, like tokenizing, vectorization, and padding/truncating the lengths of the data. Since this is code we have seen before in Chapter 3 and 4, it is replicated here for completeness with concise descriptions.

Snorkel is effective when the training data size is 10x to 50x the original. IMDb provides 50,000 unlabeled examples. If all these were labeled, then the training data would be 3x the original, which is not enough to show the value of Snorkel. Consequently, we simulate an ~18x ratio by limiting the training data to only 2,000 records. The rest of the training records are treated as unlabeled data, and Snorkel is used to supply noisy labels. To prevent the leakage of labels, we split the training data and store two separate DataFrames. The code for this split can be found in the `snorkel-labeling.ipynb` notebook. The code fragment used to generate the split is shown below:

```
from sklearn.model_selection import train_test_split

# Randomly split training into 2k / 23k sets
train_2k, train_23k = train_test_split(train_df, test_size=23000,
                                       random_state=42,
                                       stratify=train_df.sentiment)
train_2k.to_pickle("train_2k.df")
```

A stratified split is used to ensure an equal number of positive and negative labels are sampled. A DataFrame with 2,000 records is saved. This DataFrame is used for training the baseline. Note that this may look like a contrived example but remember that the key feature of text data is that there is a lot of it; however, labels are scarce. Often the main barrier to labeling is the amount of effort required to label more data. Before we see how to label large amounts of data, let's complete training the baseline model for comparison.

Tokenization and vectorizing data

We tokenize all reviews in the training set and truncate/pad to a maximum of 150 tokens. Reviews are passed through Beautiful Soup to remove any HTML markup. All the code for this section can be found in the section titled *Training Data Vectorization* in the `imdb-with-snorkel-labels.ipynb` file. Only the specific pieces of code are shown here for brevity:

```
# we need a sample of 2000 reviews for training
num_recs = 2000
train_small = pd.read_pickle("train_2k.df")
# we dont need the snorkel column
train_small = train_small.drop(columns=['snorkel'])


# remove markup
cleaned_reviews = train_small.review.apply(lambda x: BeautifulSoup(x).
text)
# convert pandas DF in to tf.Dataset
train = tf.data.Dataset.from_tensor_slices(
                        (cleaned_reviews.values,
                         train_small.sentiment.values))
```

Tokenization and vectorization are done through helper functions and applied over the dataset:

```
# transformation functions to be used with the dataset
from tensorflow.keras. pre-processing import sequence

def encode_pad_transform(sample):
    encoded = imdb_encoder.encode(sample.numpy())
    pad = sequence.pad_sequences([encoded], padding='post', maxlen=150)
    return np.array(pad[0], dtype=np.int64)


def encode_tf_fn(sample, label):
```

```
    encoded = tf.py_function(encode_pad_transform,
                                  inp=[sample],
                                  Tout=(tf.int64))
    encoded.set_shape([None])
    label.set_shape([])
    return encoded, label

encoded_train = train.map(encode_tf_fn,
                num_parallel_calls=tf.data.experimental.AUTOTUNE)
```

The test data is also processed similarly:

```
# remove markup
cleaned_reviews = test_df.review.apply(
lambda x: BeautifulSoup(x).text)
# convert pandas DF in to tf.Dataset
test = tf.data.Dataset.from_tensor_slices((cleaned_reviews.values,
                                  test_df.sentiment.values))
encoded_test = test.map(encode_tf_fn,
                num_parallel_calls=tf.data.experimental.AUTOTUNE)
```

Once the data is ready, the next step is setting up the model.

Training using a BiLSTM model

The code for creating and training the baseline is in the *Baseline Model* section of the notebook. A modestly sized model is created as the focus is on showing the gains from unsupervised labeling as opposed to model complexity. Plus, a smaller model trains faster and allows more iteration:

```
# Length of the vocabulary
vocab_size = imdb_encoder.vocab_size

# Number of RNN units
rnn_units = 64

# Embedding size
embedding_dim = 64

#batch size
BATCH_SIZE=100
```

The model uses a small 64-dimensional embedding and RNN units. The function for creating the model is below:

```
from tensorflow.keras.layers import Embedding, LSTM, \
                                     Bidirectional, Dense,\
                                     Dropout


dropout=0.5

def build_model_bilstm(vocab_size, embedding_dim, rnn_units, batch_
size, dropout=0.):
    model = tf.keras.Sequential([
        Embedding(vocab_size, embedding_dim, mask_zero=True,
                batch_input_shape=[batch_size, None]),
        Bidirectional(LSTM(rnn_units, return_sequences=True)),
        Bidirectional(tf.keras.layers.LSTM(rnn_units)),
        Dense(rnn_units, activation='relu'),
        Dropout(dropout),
        Dense(1, activation='sigmoid')
      ])
    return model
```

A modest amount of dropout is added to have the model generalize better. This model has about 700K parameters.

```
bilstm = build_model_bilstm(
  vocab_size = vocab_size,
  embedding_dim=embedding_dim,
  rnn_units=rnn_units,
  batch_size=BATCH_SIZE)


bilstm.summary()
```

```
Model: "sequential"

Layer (type)                 Output Shape              Param #
=================================================================
embedding_4 (Embedding)      (100, None, 64)           529024

bidirectional_8 (Bidirection (100, None, 128)          66048

bidirectional_9 (Bidirection (100, 128)                98816
```

dense_6 (Dense)	(100, 64)	8256
dropout_6 (Dropout)	(100, 64)	0
dense_7 (Dense)	(100, 1)	65

```
Total params: 702,209
Trainable params: 702,209
Non-trainable params: 0
```

The model is compiled with a binary cross-entropy loss function and the ADAM optimizer. Accuracy, precision, and recall metrics are tracked. This model is trained for 15 epochs and it can be seen that the model is saturated:

```
bilstm.compile(loss='binary_crossentropy',
            optimizer='adam',
            metrics=['accuracy', 'Precision', 'Recall'])

encoded_train_batched = encoded_train.shuffle(num_recs, seed=42).\
                                batch(BATCH_SIZE)

bilstm.fit(encoded_train_batched, epochs=15)
```

```
Train for 15 steps
Epoch 1/15
20/20 [==============================] - 16s 793ms/step - loss: 0.6943
- accuracy: 0.4795 - Precision: 0.4833 - Recall: 0.5940
...
Epoch 15/15
20/20 [==============================] - 4s 206ms/step - loss: 0.0044 -
accuracy: 0.9995 - Precision: 0.9990 - Recall: 1.0000
```

As we can see, the model is overfitting to the small training set even after dropout regularization.

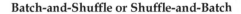

> **Batch-and-Shuffle or Shuffle-and-Batch**
>
>
>
> Note the second line of code in the fragment above, which shuffles and batches the data. The data is shuffled and then batched. Shuffling data between epochs is a form of regularization and enables the model to learn better. Shuffling before batching is a key point to remember in TensorFlow. If data is batched before shuffling, then only the order of the batches will be moved around when being fed to the model. However, the composition of each batch remains the same across epochs. By shuffling before batching, we ensure each batch looks different in each epoch. You are encouraged to train with and without shuffled data. While shuffling increases training time slightly, it gives better performance on the test set.

Let us see how this model does on the test data:

```
bilstm.evaluate(encoded_test.batch(BATCH_SIZE))
```

```
250/250 [==============================] - 33s 134ms/step - loss:
2.1440 - accuracy: 0.7591 - precision: 0.7455 - recall: 0.7866
```

The model has 75.9% accuracy. The precision of the model is higher than the recall. Now that we have a baseline, we can see if weakly supervised labeling helps improve model performance. That is the focus of the next section.

Weakly supervised labeling with Snorkel

The IMDb dataset has 50,000 unlabeled reviews. This is double the size of the training set, which has 25,000 labeled reviews. As explained in the previous section, we have reserved 23,000 records from the training data in addition to the unsupervised set for weakly supervised labeling. Labeling records in Snorkel is performed via labeling functions. Each labeling function can return one of the possible labels of abstain from labeling. Since this is a binary classification problem, corresponding constants are defined. A sample labeling function is also shown. All the code for this section can be found in the notebook titled snorkel-labeling.ipynb:

```
POSITIVE = 1
NEGATIVE = 0
ABSTAIN = -1

from snorkel.labeling.lf import labeling_function
```

```
@labeling_function()
def time_waste(x):
    if not isinstance(x.review, str):
        return ABSTAIN
    ex1 = "time waste"
    ex2 = "waste of time"
    if ex1 in x.review.lower() or ex2 in x.review.lower():
        return NEGATIVE
    return ABSTAIN
```

Labeling functions are annotated with a `labeling_function()` provided Snorkel. Note that the Snorkel library needs to be installed. Detailed instructions can be found on GitHub in this chapter's subdirectory. In short, Snorkel can be installed by:

```
(tf24nlp) $ pip install snorkel==0.9.5
```

Any warnings you see can be safely ignored as the library uses different versions of components such as TensorBoard. To be doubly sure, you can create a separate conda/virtual environment for Snorkel and its dependencies.

 This chapter would not have been possible without the support of the Snorkel.ai team. Frederic Sala and Alexander Ratner from Snorkel.ai were instrumental in providing guidance and the script for hyperparameter tuning to get the most out of Snorkel.

Coming back to the labeling function, the function above is expecting a row from a DataFrame. It is expecting that the row has a text "review" column. This function tries to see if the review states that the movie or show was a waste of time. If so, it returns a negative label; else, it abstains from labeling the row of data. Note that we are trying to label thousands of rows of data in a short time using these labeling functions. The best way to do this is to print some random samples of positive and negative reviews and use some words from the text as labeling functions. The central idea here is to create a number of functions that have good accuracy for a subset of the rows. Let's examine some negative reviews in the training set to see what labeling functions can be created:

```
neg = train_df[train_df.sentiment==0].sample(n=5, random_state=42)
for x in neg.review.tolist():
    print(x)
```

One of the reviews starts off as "A very cheesy and dull road movie," which gives an idea for a labeling function:

```python
@labeling_function()
def cheesy_dull(x):
    if not isinstance(x.review, str):
        return ABSTAIN
    ex1 = "cheesy"
    ex2 = "dull"
    if ex1 in x.review.lower() or ex2 in x.review.lower():
        return NEGATIVE
    return ABSTAIN
```

There are a number of different words that occur in negative reviews. Here is a subset of negative labeling functions. The full list is in the notebook:

```python
@labeling_function()
def garbage(x):
    if not isinstance(x.review, str):
        return ABSTAIN
    ex1 = "garbage"
    if ex1 in x.review.lower():
        return NEGATIVE
    return ABSTAIN


@labeling_function()
def terrible(x):
    if not isinstance(x.review, str):
        return ABSTAIN
    ex1 = "terrible"
    if ex1 in x.review.lower():
        return NEGATIVE
    return ABSTAIN


@labeling_function()
def unsatisfied(x):
    if not isinstance(x.review, str):
        return ABSTAIN
    ex1 = "unsatisf"  # unsatisfactory, unsatisfied
    if ex1 in x.review.lower():
        return NEGATIVE
    return ABSTAIN
```

All the negative labeling functions are added to a list:

```
neg_lfs = [atrocious, terrible, piece_of, woefully_miscast,
           bad_acting, cheesy_dull, disappoint, crap, garbage,
           unsatisfied, ridiculous]
```

Examining a sample of negative reviews can give us many ideas. Typically, a small amount of effort from a domain expert can yield multiple labeling functions that can be implemented easily. If you have ever watched a movie, you are an expert as far as this dataset is concerned. Examining a sample of positive reviews results in more labeling functions. Here is a sample of labeling functions that identify positive sentiment in reviews:

```
import re

@labeling_function()
def classic(x):
    if not isinstance(x.review, str):
        return ABSTAIN
    ex1 = "a classic"
    if ex1 in x.review.lower():
        return POSITIVE
    return ABSTAIN

@labeling_function()
def great_direction(x):
    if not isinstance(x.review, str):
        return ABSTAIN
    ex1 = "(great|awesome|amazing|fantastic|excellent) direction"
    if re.search(ex1, x.review.lower()):
        return POSITIVE
    return ABSTAIN

@labeling_function()
def great_story(x):
    if not isinstance(x.review, str):
        return ABSTAIN
    ex1 = "(great|awesome|amazing|fantastic|excellent|dramatic)
(script|story)"
    if re.search(ex1, x.review.lower()):
        return POSITIVE
    return ABSTAIN
```

All of the positive labeling functions can be seen in the notebook. Similar to the negative functions, a list of the positive labeling functions is defined:

```
pos_lfs = [classic, must_watch, oscar, love, great_entertainment,
           very_entertaining, amazing, brilliant, fantastic,
           awesome, great_acting, great_direction, great_story,
           favourite]

# set of labeling functions
lfs = neg_lfs + pos_lfs
```

The development of labeling is an iterative process. Don't be intimidated by the number of labeling functions shown here. You can see that they are quite simple, for the most part. To help you understand the amount of effort, I spent a total of 3 hours on creating and testing labeling functions:

Note that the notebook contains a large number of simple labeling functions, of which only a subset are shown here. Please refer to the actual code for all the labeling functions.

The process involved looking at some samples and creating the labeling functions, followed by evaluating the results on a subset of the data. Checking out examples of where the labeling functions disagreed with the labeled examples was very useful in making functions narrower or adding compensating functions. So, let's see how we can evaluate these functions so we can iterate on them.

Iterating on labeling functions

Once a set of labeling functions are defined, they can be applied to a pandas DataFrame, and a model can be trained to compute the weights assigned to various labeling functions while computing the labels. Snorkel provides functions that help with these tasks. First, let us apply these labeling functions to compute a matrix. This matrix has as many columns as there are labeling functions for every row of data:

```
# Let's take a sample of 100 records from training set
lf_train = train_df.sample(n=1000, random_state=42)

from snorkel.labeling.model import LabelModel
from snorkel.labeling import PandasLFApplier
```

```
# Apply the LFs to the unlabeled training data
applier = PandasLFApplier(lfs)
L_train = applier.apply(lf_train)
```

In the code above, a sample of 1000 rows of data from the training data is extracted. Then, the list of all labeling functions created previously is passed to Snorkel and applied to this sample of training data. If we created 25 labeling functions, the shape of L_train would be (1000, 25). Each column represents the output of a labeling function. A generative model can now be trained on this label matrix:

```
# Train the Label model and compute the training labels
label_model = LabelModel(cardinality=2, verbose=True)
label_model.fit(L_train, n_epochs=500, log_freq=50, seed=123)
lf_train["snorkel"] = label_model.predict(L=L_train,
                                  tie_break_policy="abstain")
```

A LabelModel instance is created with a parameter specifying how many labels are in the actual model. This model is then trained, and labels are predicted for the subset of data. These predicted labels are added as a new column to the DataFrame. Note the tie_break_policy parameter being passed into the predict() method. In case the model has conflicting outputs from labeling functions, and they have the same scores from the model, this parameter specifies how the conflict should be resolved. Here, we instruct the model to abstain from labeling the records in case of a conflict. Another possible setting is "random," where the model will randomly assign the output from one of the tied labeling functions. The main difference between these two options, in the context of the problem at hand, is precision. By asking the model to abstain from labeling, we get higher precision results, but fewer records will be labeled. Randomly choosing one of the functions that were tied results in higher coverage, but presumably at lower quality. This hypothesis can be tested by training the same model with the outputs of the two options separately. You are encouraged to try these options and see the results for yourself.

Since the abstain policy was chosen, all of the 1000 rows may not have been labeled:

```
pred_lfs = lf_train[lf_train.snorkel > -1]
pred_lfs.describe()
```

	sentiment	score	snorkel
count	598.000000	598.000000	598.000000

Out of 1000 records, only 458 were labeled. Let's check how many of these were labeled incorrectly:

```
pred_mistake = pred_lfs[pred_lfs.sentiment != pred_lfs.snorkel]
pred_mistake.describe()
```

	sentiment	score	snorkel
count	164.000000	164.000000	164.000000

Snorkel, armed with our labeling functions, labeled 598 records, out of which 434 labels were correct and 164 records were incorrectly labeled. The label model has an accuracy of ~72.6%. To get inspiration for more labeling functions, you should inspect a few of the rows where the label model produced the wrong results and update or add labeling functions. As mentioned above, a total of approximately 3 hours was spent on iterating and creating labeling functions to get a total of 25 functions. To get more out of Snorkel, we need to increase the amount of training data. The objective is to develop a method that gets us many labels quickly, without a lot of manual effort. One technique that can be used in this specific case is training a simple Naïve-Bayes model to get words that are highly correlated with positive or negative labels. This is the focus of the next section. **Naïve-Bayes (NB)** is a basic technique covered in many basic NLP books.

Naïve-Bayes model for finding keywords

Building an NB model on this dataset takes under an hour and has the potential to significantly increase the quality and coverage of the labeling functions. The core model code for the NB model can be found in the spam-inspired-technique-naive-bayes.ipynb notebook. Note that these explorations are aside from the main labeling code, and this section can be skipped if desired, as the learnings from this section are applied to construct better labeling functions outlined in the snorkel-labeling.ipynb notebook.

The main flow of the NB-based exploration is to load the reviews, remove stop words, take the top 2,000 words to construct a simple vectorization scheme, and train an NB model. Since data loading is the same as covered in previous sections, the details are skipped in this section.

This section uses the NLTK and `wordcloud` Python packages. NLTK should already be installed as we have used it in *Chapter 1, Essentials of NLP*. `wordcloud` can be installed with:

```
(tf24nlp) $ pip install wordcloud==1.8
```

Word clouds help get an aggregate understanding of the positive and negative review text. Note that counters are required for the top-2000 word vectorization scheme. A convenience function that cleans HTML text along with removing stop words and tokenizing the rest into a list is defined as follows:

```
en_stopw = set(stopwords.words("english"))

def get_words(review, words, stopw=en_stopw):
    review = BeautifulSoup(review).text       # remove HTML tags
    review = re.sub('[^A-Za-z]', ' ', review)  # remove non letters
    review = review.lower()

    tok_rev = wt(review)
    rev_word = [word for word in tok_rev if word not in stopw]
    words += rev_word
```

Then, the positive reviews are separated and a word cloud is generated for visualization purposes:

```
pos_rev = train_df[train_df.sentiment == 1]
pos_words = []
pos_rev.review.apply(get_words, args=(pos_words,))
from wordcloud import WordCloud
import matplotlib.pyplot as plt

pos_words_sen = " ".join(pos_words)
pos_wc = WordCloud(width = 600,height = 512).generate(pos_words_sen)
plt.figure(figsize = (12, 8), facecolor = 'k')
plt.imshow(pos_wc)
plt.axis('off')
plt.tight_layout(pad = 0)
plt.show()
```

The output of the preceding code is shown in *Figure 8.3*:

Figure 8.3: Positive reviews word cloud

It is not surprising that *movie* and *film* are the biggest words. However, there are a number of other suggestions for keywords that can be seen here. Similarly, a word cloud for the negative reviews can be generated, as shown in *Figure 8.4*:

Figure 8.4: Negative reviews word cloud

These visualizations are interesting; however, a clearer picture will emerge after training the model. Only the top 2,000 words are needed for training the model:

```
from collections import Counter
pos = Counter(pos_words)
neg = Counter(neg_words)
# Let's try to build a naive bayes model for sentiment classification
tot_words = pos + neg
tot_words.most_common(10)
```

```
[('movie', 44031),
 ('film', 40147),
 ('one', 26788),
 ('like', 20274),
 ('good', 15140),
 ('time', 12724),
 ('even', 12646),
 ('would', 12436),
 ('story', 11983),
 ('really', 11736)]
```

Combined counters show the top 10 most frequently appearing words in all reviews. These are extracted into a list:

```
top2k = [x for (x, y) in tot_words.most_common(2000)]
```

The vectorization of each review is fairly simple – each of the 2000 words becomes a column for a given review. If the word represented by the column is present in the review, the value of the column is marked as 1 for that review, or 0 otherwise. So, each review is represented by a sequence of 0s and 1s representing which of the top 2000 words the review contained. The code below shows this transformation:

```
def featurize(review, topk=top2k, stopw=en_stopw):
    review = BeautifulSoup(review).text       # remove HTML tags
    review = re.sub('[^A-Za-z]', ' ', review)  # remove nonletters
    review = review.lower()

    tok_rev = wt(review)
    rev_word = [word for word in tok_rev if word not in stopw]
    features = {}
    for word in top2k:
        features['contains({})'.format(word)] = (word in rev_word)
    return features
```

```
train = [(featurize(rev), senti) for (rev, senti) in
                    zip(train_df.review, train_df.sentiment)]
```

Training the model is quite trivial. Note that the Bernoulli NB model is used here as each word is represented according to its presence or absence in the review. Alternatively, the frequency of the word in the review could also be used. If the frequency of the word is used while vectorizing the review above, then the multinomial form of NB should be used.

NLTK also provides a way to inspect the most informative features:

```
classifier = nltk.NaiveBayesClassifier.train(train)
# 0: negative sentiment, 1: positive sentiment
classifier.show_most_informative_features(20)
```

```
Most Informative Features
         contains(unfunny) = True         0 : 1        =      14.1 : 1.0
           contains(waste) = True         0 : 1        =      12.7 : 1.0
        contains(pointless) = True        0 : 1        =      10.4 : 1.0
        contains(redeeming) = True        0 : 1        =      10.1 : 1.0
        contains(laughable) = True        0 : 1        =       9.3 : 1.0
           contains(worst) = True         0 : 1        =       9.0 : 1.0
            contains(awful) = True        0 : 1        =       8.4 : 1.0
           contains(poorly) = True        0 : 1        =       8.2 : 1.0
      contains(wonderfully) = True        1 : 0        =       7.6 : 1.0
            contains(sucks) = True        0 : 1        =       7.0 : 1.0
             contains(lame) = True        0 : 1        =       6.9 : 1.0
         contains(pathetic) = True        0 : 1        =       6.4 : 1.0
       contains(delightful) = True        1 : 0        =       6.0 : 1.0
           contains(wasted) = True        0 : 1        =       6.0 : 1.0
             contains(crap) = True        0 : 1        =       5.9 : 1.0
      contains(beautifully) = True        1 : 0        =       5.8 : 1.0
         contains(dreadful) = True        0 : 1        =       5.7 : 1.0
             contains(mess) = True        0 : 1        =       5.6 : 1.0
         contains(horrible) = True        0 : 1        =       5.5 : 1.0
           contains(superb) = True        1 : 0        =       5.4 : 1.0
          contains(garbage) = True        0 : 1        =       5.3 : 1.0
            contains(badly) = True        0 : 1        =       5.3 : 1.0
           contains(wooden) = True        0 : 1        =       5.2 : 1.0
         contains(touching) = True        1 : 0        =       5.1 : 1.0
         contains(terrible) = True        0 : 1        =       5.1 : 1.0
```

This whole exercise was done to find which words are most useful in predicting negative and positive reviews. The table above shows the words and the likelihood ratios. Taking the first row of the output for the word *unfunny* as an example, the model is saying that reviews containing *unfunny* are negative 14.1 times more often than they are positive. The labeling functions are updated using a number of these keywords.

Upon analyzing the labels assigned by the labeling functions in snorkel-labeling. ipynb, it can be seen that more negative reviews are being labeled as compared to positive reviews. Consequently, the labeling functions use a larger list of words for positive labels as compared to negative labels. Note that imbalanced datasets have issues with overall training accuracy and specifically with recall. The following code fragment shows augmented labeling functions using the keywords discovered through NB above:

```
# Some positive high prob words - arbitrary cutoff of 4.5x
'''
        contains(wonderfully) = True       1 : 0      =       7.6 : 1.0
         contains(delightful) = True       1 : 0      =       6.0 : 1.0
        contains(beautifully) = True       1 : 0      =       5.8 : 1.0
             contains(superb) = True       1 : 0      =       5.4 : 1.0
           contains(touching) = True       1 : 0      =       5.1 : 1.0
        contains(brilliantly) = True       1 : 0      =       4.7 : 1.0
         contains(friendship) = True       1 : 0      =       4.6 : 1.0
             contains(finest) = True       1 : 0      =       4.5 : 1.0
            contains(terrific) = True       1 : 0      =       4.5 : 1.0
                contains(gem) = True       1 : 0      =       4.5 : 1.0
         contains(magnificent) = True       1 : 0      =       4.5 : 1.0
'''
```

```
wonderfully_kw = make_keyword_lf(keywords=["wonderfully"],
label=POSITIVE)
delightful_kw = make_keyword_lf(keywords=["delightful"],
label=POSITIVE)
superb_kw = make_keyword_lf(keywords=["superb"], label=POSITIVE)

pos_words = ["beautifully", "touching", "brilliantly",
"friendship", "finest", "terrific", "magnificent"]
pos_nb_kw = make_keyword_lf(keywords=pos_words, label=POSITIVE)

@labeling_function()
def superlatives(x):
    if not isinstance(x.review, str):
```

```
        return ABSTAIN
ex1 = ["best", "super", "great","awesome","amaz", "fantastic",
        "excellent", "favorite"]
pos_words = ["beautifully", "touching", "brilliantly",
            "friendship", "finest", "terrific", "magnificent",
            "wonderfully", "delightful"]
ex1 += pos_words
rv = x.review.lower()
counts = [rv.count(x) for x in ex1]
if sum(counts) >= 3:
    return POSITIVE
return ABSTAIN
```

Since keyword-based labeling functions are quite common, Snorkel provides an easy way to define such functions. The following code fragment uses two programmatic ways of converting a list of words into a set of labeling functions:

```
# Utilities for defining keywords based functions
def keyword_lookup(x, keywords, label):
    if any(word in x.review.lower() for word in keywords):
        return label
    return ABSTAIN


def make_keyword_lf(keywords, label):
    return LabelingFunction(
        name=f"keyword_{keywords[0]}",
        f=keyword_lookup,
        resources=dict(keywords=keywords, label=label),
    )
```

The first function does the simple matching and returns the specific label, or it abstains. Check out the snorkel-labeling.ipynb file for the full list of labeling functions that were iteratively developed. All in all, I spent approximately 12-14 hours on labeling functions and investigations.

Before we try to train the model using this data, let us evaluate the accuracy of this model on the entire training data set.

Evaluating weakly supervised labels on the training set

We apply the labeling functions and train a model on the entire training dataset just to evaluate the quality of this model:

```
L_train_full = applier.apply(train_df)
label_model = LabelModel(cardinality=2, verbose=True)
label_model.fit(L_train_full, n_epochs=500, log_freq=50, seed=123)

metrics = label_model.score(L=L_train_full, Y=train_df.sentiment,
                            tie_break_policy="abstain",
                            metrics=["accuracy", "coverage",
                                    "precision",
                                    "recall", "f1"])
print("All Metrics: ", metrics)
```

```
Label Model Accuracy:      78.5%
All Metrics:  {'accuracy': 0.7854110013835218, 'coverage': 0.83844,
 'precision': 0.8564883605745418, 'recall': 0.6744344773790951, 'f1':
 0.7546367008509709}
```

Our set of labeling functions covers 83.4% of the 25,000 training records, with 85.6% correct labels. Snorkel provides the ability to analyze the performance of each labeling function:

```
from snorkel.labeling import LFAnalysis

LFAnalysis(L=L_train_full, lfs=lfs).lf_summary()
```

	j	Polarity	Coverage	Overlaps	Conflicts
atrocious	0	[0]	0.00816	0.00768	0.00328
terrible	1	[0]	0.05356	0.05356	0.02696
piece_of	2	[0]	0.00084	0.00080	0.00048
woefully_miscast	3	[0]	0.00848	0.00764	0.00504
bad_acting	4	[0]	0.08748	0.08348	0.04304
cheesy_dull	5	[0]	0.05136	0.04932	0.02760
bad	11	[0]	0.03624	0.03624	0.01744
keyword_waste	12	[0]	0.07336	0.06848	0.03232
keyword_pointless	13	[0]	0.01956	0.01836	0.00972
keyword_redeeming	14	[0]	0.01264	0.01192	0.00556
keyword_laughable	15	[0]	0.41036	0.37368	0.20884
negatives	16	[0]	0.35300	0.34720	0.17396

classic	17	[1]	0.01684	0.01476	0.00856
must_watch	18	[1]	0.00176	0.00140	0.00060
oscar	19	[1]	0.00064	0.00060	0.00016
love	20	[1]	0.08660	0.07536	0.04568
great_entertainment	21	[1]	0.00488	0.00488	0.00292
very_entertaining	22	[1]	0.00544	0.00460	0.00244
amazing	23	[1]	0.05028	0.04516	0.02340
great	31	[1]	0.27728	0.23568	0.13800
keyword_wonderfully	32	[1]	0.01248	0.01248	0.00564
keyword_delightful	33	[1]	0.01188	0.01100	0.00500
keyword_superb	34	[1]	0.02948	0.02636	0.01220
keyword_beautifully	35	[1]	0.08284	0.07428	0.03528
superlatives	36	[1]	0.14656	0.14464	0.07064
keyword_remarkable	37	[1]	0.32052	0.26004	0.14748

Note that a snipped version of the output has been presented here. The full output is available in the notebook. For each labeling function, the table presents what labels are produced and the coverage of the function – that is, the fraction of records it provides a label for, the fraction where it overlaps with another function producing the same label, and the fraction where it conflicts with another function producing a different label. A positive and a negative label function are highlighted. The bad_acting() function covers 8.7% of the records but overlaps with other functions about 8.3% of the time. However, it conflicts with a function producing a positive label about 4.3% of the time. The amazing() function covers about 5% of the dataset. It conflicts about 2.3% of the time. This data can be used to fine-tune specific functions further and examine how we've separated the data. *Figure 8.5* shows the balance between positive, negative, and abstain labels:

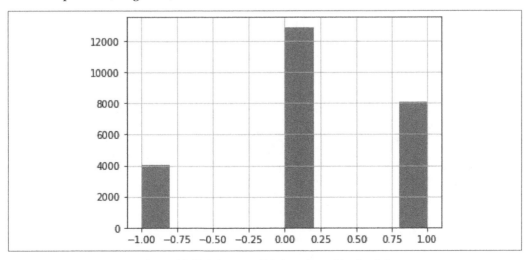

Figure 8.5: Distribution of labels generated by Snorkel

Snorkel has several options for hyperparameter tuning to improve the quality of labeling even further. We execute a grid search over the parameters to find the best training parameters, while we exclude the labeling functions that are adding noise in the final output.

Hyperparameter tuning is done via choosing different learning rates, L2 regularizations, numbers of epochs to run training on, and optimizers to use. Finally, a threshold is used to determine which labeling functions should be kept for the actual labeling task:

```
# Grid Search
from itertools import product

lrs = [1e-1, 1e-2, 1e-3]
l2s = [0, 1e-1, 1e-2]
n_epochs = [100, 200, 500]
optimizer = ["sgd", "adam"]
thresh = [0.8, 0.9]
lma_best = 0
params_best = []


for params in product(lrs, l2s, n_epochs, optimizer, thresh):
    # do the initial pass to access the accuracies
    label_model.fit(L_train_full, n_epochs=params[2], log_freq=50,
                    seed=123, optimizer=params[3], lr=params[0],
                    l2=params[1])

    # accuracies
    weights = label_model.get_weights()

    # LFs above our threshold
    vals = weights > params[4]

    # the LM requires at least 3 LFs to train
    if sum(vals) >= 3:
        L_filtered = L_train_full[:, vals]

        label_model.fit(L_filtered, n_epochs=params[2],
                        log_freq=50, seed=123,
                        optimizer=params[3], lr=params[0],
                        l2=params[1])

        label_model_acc = label_model.score(L=L_filtered,
```

```
                              Y=train_df.sentiment,
                     tie_break_policy="abstain")["accuracy"]


        if label_model_acc > lma_best:
            lma_best = label_model_acc
            params_best = params


  print("best = ", lma_best, " params ", params_best)
```

Snorkel may print a warning that metrics are being calculated over non-abstain labels only. This is by design, as we are interested in high-confidence labels. If there is a conflict between labeling functions, then our model abstains from giving it a label. The best parameters printed out are:

```
  best = 0.8399649430324277  params (0.001, 0.1, 200, 'adam', 0.9)
```

Through this tuning, the accuracy of the model improved from 78.5% to 84%!

Using these parameters, we label the 23k records from the training set and 50k records from the unsupervised set. For the first part, we label all the 25k training records and then split them into two sets. This particular part of splitting was referenced in the baseline model section above:

```
  train_df["snorkel"] = label_model.predict(L=L_filtered,
                                  tie_break_policy="abstain")
  from sklearn.model_selection import train_test_split

  # Randomly split training into 2k / 23k sets
  train_2k, train_23k = train_test_split(train_df, test_size=23000,
                                          random_state=42,
                                          stratify=train_df.sentiment)

  train_23k.snorkel.hist()
  train_23k.sentiment.hist()
```

The last two lines of code inspect the state of the labels and contrasts with actual labels and generate the graph shown in *Figure 8.6*:

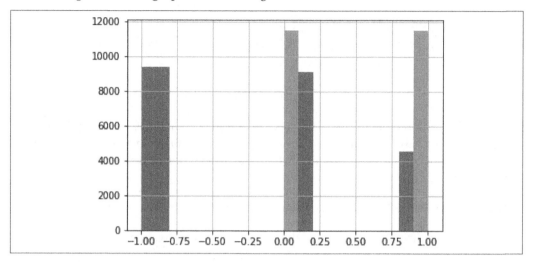

Figure 8.6: Comparison of labels in the training set versus labels generated using Snorkel

When the Snorkel model abstains from labeling, it assigns -1 for the label. We see that the model is able to label a lot more negative reviews than positive labels. We filter out the rows where Snorkel abstained from labeling and saved the records:

```
lbl_train = train_23k[train_23k.snorkel > -1]
lbl_train = lbl_train.drop(columns=["sentiment"])
p_sup = lbl_train.rename(columns={"snorkel": "sentiment"})
p_sup.to_pickle("snorkel_train_labeled.df")
```

However, the key question that we face is that if we augmented the training data with these noisy labels, which are 84% accurate, would it make our model perform better or worse? Note that the baseline model had an accuracy of ~74%.

To answer this question, we label the unsupervised set and then train the same model architecture as the baseline.

Generating unsupervised labels for unlabeled data

As we saw in the previous section, where we labeled the training data set, it is quite simple to run the model on the unlabeled reviews of the dataset:

```
# Now apply this to all the unsupervised reviews
# Apply the LFs to the unlabeled training data
applier = PandasLFApplier(lfs)

# now let's apply on the unsupervised dataset
L_train_unsup = applier.apply(unsup_df)
label_model = LabelModel(cardinality=2, verbose=True)
label_model.fit(L_train_unsup[:, vals], n_epochs=params_best[2],
                optimizer=params_best[3],
                lr=params_best[0], l2=params_best[1],
                log_freq=100, seed=42)

unsup_df["snorkel"] = label_model.predict(L=L_train_unsup[:, vals],
                                   tie_break_policy="abstain")
# rename snorkel to sentiment & concat to the training dataset
pred_unsup_lfs = unsup_df[unsup_df.snorkel > -1]
p2 = pred_unsup_lfs.rename(columns={"snorkel": "sentiment"})
print(p2.info())
p2.to_pickle("snorkel-unsup-nbs.df")
```

Now the label model is trained, and predictions are added to an additional column of the unsupervised dataset. The model labels 29,583 records out of 50,000. This is almost equal to the size of the training dataset. Assuming that the error rate on the unsupervised set is similar to that observed on the training set, we just added ~24,850 records with correct labels and ~4,733 records with incorrect labels into the training set. However, the balance of this dataset is very tilted, as positive label coverage is still poor. There are approximately 9,000 positive labels for over 20,000 negative labels. The *Increase Positive Label Coverage* section of the notebook tries to further improve the coverage of the positive labels by adding more keyword functions.

This results in a slightly more balanced set, as shown in the following chart:

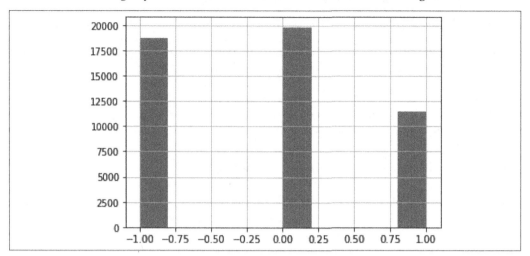

Figure 8.7: Further improvements in labeling functions applied to the
unsupervised dataset improves the positive labels

This dataset is saved to disk for use during training:

```
p3 = pred_unsup_lfs2.rename(columns={"snorkel2": "sentiment"})
print(p3.info())
p3.to_pickle("snorkel-unsup-nbs-v2.df")
```

 Labeled datasets are saved to disk and reloaded in the training
code for better modularity and ease of readability. In a production
pipeline, intermediate outputs may not be persisted and fed
directly into the training steps. Another small consideration here is
the separation of virtual/conda environments for running Snorkel.
Having a separate script for weakly supervised labeling allows the
use of a different Python environment as well.

We switch our focus back to the `imdb-with-snorkel-labels.ipynb` notebook,
which has the models for training. The code for this part begins from the section
With Snorkel Labeled Data. The newly labeled records need to be loaded from disk,
cleansed, vectorized, and padded before training can be run. We extract the labeled
records and remove HTML markup, as shown below:

```
# labelled version of training data split
p1 = pd.read_pickle("snorkel_train_labeled.df")

p2 = pd.read_pickle("snorkel-unsup-nbs-v2.df")
```

```
p2 = p2.drop(columns=['snorkel']) # so that everything aligns

# now concatenate the three DFs
p2 = pd.concat([train_small, p1, p2]) # training plus snorkel
                                      # labelled data
print("showing hist of additional data")

# now balance the labels
pos = p2[p2.sentiment == 1]
neg = p2[p2.sentiment == 0]
recs = min(pos.shape[0], neg.shape[0])
pos = pos.sample(n=recs, random_state=42)
neg = neg.sample(n=recs, random_state=42)

p3 = pd.concat((pos,neg))
p3.sentiment.hist()
```

The original training dataset was balanced across positive and negative labels. However, there is an imbalance in the data labeled using Snorkel. We balance the dataset and ignore the excess rows with negative labels. Note that the 2,000 training records used in the baseline model also need to be added, resulting in a total of 33,914 training records. As mentioned before, it really shines when the amount of data is 10x to 50x the original dataset. Here, we achieve a ratio closer to 17x, or 18x if the 2,000 training records are also included.

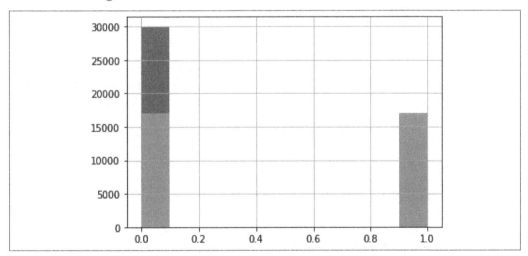

Figure 8.8: Distribution of records after using Snorkel and weak supervision

As shown in *Figure 8.8* above, the records in blue are dropped to balance the dataset. Next, the data needs to be cleansed and vectorized using the subword vocabulary:

```
# remove markup
cleaned_unsup_reviews = p3.review.apply(
                            lambda x: BeautifulSoup(x).text)
snorkel_reviews = pd.concat((cleaned_reviews, cleaned_unsup_reviews))
snorkel_labels = pd.concat((train_small.sentiment, p3.sentiment))
```

Finally, we convert the pandas DataFrames into TensorFlow data sets and vectorize and pad them:

```
# convert pandas DF in to tf.Dataset
snorkel_train = tf.data.Dataset.from_tensor_slices((
                            snorkel_reviews.values,
                            snorkel_labels.values))
encoded_snorkel_train = snorkel_train.map(encode_tf_fn,
                num_parallel_calls=tf.data.experimental.AUTOTUNE)
```

We are ready to try training our BiLSTM model to see if the performance improves on this task.

Training BiLSTM on weakly supervised data from Snorkel

To ensure we are comparing apples to apples, we use the same BiLSTM as the baseline model. We instantiate a model with 64-dimensional embeddings, 64 RNN units, and a batch size of 100. The model uses the binary cross-entropy loss and the Adam optimizer. Accuracy, precision, and recall are tracked as the model is trained. An important step is to shuffle the datasets every epoch to help the model keep errors to a minimum.

This is an important concept. Deep models work on the assumption that the loss is a convex surface, and the gradient is descending to the bottom of this surface. The surface has many local minima or saddle points in reality. If the model gets stuck in local minima during a mini-batch, it will be hard for the model to come out of it as across epochs, it receives the same data points again and again. Shuffling the data changes the data set and the order in which the model receives it. This enables the model to learn better by getting out of these local minima faster. The code for this section is in the imdb-with-snorkel-labels.ipynb file:

```
shuffle_size = snorkel_reviews.shape[0] // BATCH_SIZE * BATCH_SIZE
encoded_snorkel_batched = encoded_snorkel_train.shuffle(
                                    buffer_size=shuffle_size,
                                    seed=42).batch(BATCH_SIZE,
                                    drop_remainder=True)
```

Note that we cache all the records that will be part of the batch so that we can get perfect buffering. This comes at the cost of slightly slower training and higher memory use. Also, since our batch size is 100 and the dataset has 35,914 records, we drop the remainder of the records. We train the model for 20 epochs, a little more than the baseline model. The baseline model was overfitting at 15 epochs. So, it was not useful to train it longer. This model has a lot more data to train on. Consequently, it needs more epochs to learn:

```
bilstm2.fit(encoded_snorkel_batched, epochs=20)
```

```
Train for 359 steps
Epoch 1/20
359/359 [==============================] - 92s 257ms/step - loss:
0.4399 - accuracy: 0.7860 - Precision: 0.7900 - Recall: 0.7793
...
Epoch 20/20
359/359 [==============================] - 82s 227ms/step - loss:
0.0339 - accuracy: 0.9886 - Precision: 0.9879 - Recall: 0.9893
```

The model achieves an accuracy of 98.9%. The precision and recall numbers are quite close to each other. Evaluating the baseline model on the test data gave an accuracy score of 76.23%, which clearly proved that it was overfitting to the training data. Upon evaluating the model trained with weakly supervised labeling, the following results are obtained:

```
bilstm2.evaluate(encoded_test.batch(BATCH_SIZE))
```

```
250/250 [==============================] - 35s 139ms/step - loss:
1.9134 - accuracy: 0.7658 - precision: 0.7812 - recall: 0.7386
```

This model trained on weakly supervised noisy labels achieves 76.6% accuracy, which is 0.7%% higher than baseline mode. Also note that the precision went from 74.5% to 78.1% but recall decreased. In this toy setting, we kept a lot of the variables constant, such as model type, dropout ratio, etc. In a realistic setting, we can drive the accuracy even higher by optimizing the model architecture and hyperparameter tuning. There are other options to try. Recall that we instruct Snorkel to abstain from labeling if it is unsure.

By changing that to a majority vote or some other policy, the amount of training data could be increased even further. You could also try and train on unbalanced datasets and see the impact. The focus here was on showing the value of weak supervision for massively increasing the amount of training data rather than building the best model. However, you should be able to take these lessons and apply them to your projects.

It is important to take a moment and think about the causes of this result. There are a few important deep learning lessons hidden in this story. First, more labeled data is always good, given a model of sufficient complexity. There is a correlation between the amount of data and model capacity. Models with higher capacities can handle more complex relationships in the data. They also need much larger datasets to learn the complexities. However, if the model is kept a constant and with sufficient capacity, the quantity of labeled data makes a huge difference, as evidenced here. There are some limits to how much of an improvement we can achieve by increasing labeled data scale. In a paper titled *Revisiting Unreasonable Effectiveness of Data in Deep Learning Era* by Chen Sun et al., published at ICCV 2017, the authors examine the role of data in the computer vision domain. They report that the performance of models increases logarithmically with an increase in training data. The second result they report is that learning representations through pretraining helps downstream tasks quite a bit. Techniques in this chapter can be applied to generate more data for the fine-tuning step, which will significantly boost the performance of the fine-tuned model.

The second lesson is one about the basics of machine learning – shuffling the training data set has a disproportionate impact on the performance of the model. In the book, we have not always done this in order to manage training times. For training production models, it is important to focus on basics such as shuffling data sets before each epoch.

Let's review everything we learned in this chapter.

Summary

It is apparent that deep models perform very well when they have a lot of data. BERT and GPT models have shown the value of pre-training on massive amounts of data. It is still very hard to get good-quality labeled data for use in pretraining or fine-tuning. We used the concepts of weak supervision combined with generative models to cheaply label data. With relatively small amounts of effort, we were able to multiply the amount of training data by 18x. Even though the additional training data was noisy, the BiLSTM model was able to learn effectively and beat the baseline model by 0.6%.

Representation learning or pre-training leads to transfer learning and fine-tuning models performing well on their downstream tasks. However, in many domains like medicine, the amount of labeled data may be small or quite expensive to acquire. Using the techniques learned in this chapter, the amount of training data can be expanded rapidly with little effort. Building a state-of-the-art- beating model helped recall some basic lessons in deep learning, such as how larger data boosts performance quite a bit, and that larger models are not always better.

Now, we turn our focus to conversational AI. Building a conversational AI system is a very challenging task with many layers. The material covered so far in the book can help in building various parts of chatbots. The next chapter goes over the key parts of conversational AI or chatbot systems and outlines effective ways to build them.

9

Building Conversational AI Applications with Deep Learning

The art of conversation is considered a uniquely human trait. The ability of machines to have a dialog with humans has been a research topic for many years. Alan Turing proposed the now-famous Turing Test to see if a human could converse with another human and a machine through written messages, and identify each participant as machine or human correctly. In recent times, digital assistants such as Alexa by Amazon and Siri by Apple have made considerable strides in conversational AI. This chapter discusses different conversational agents and puts the techniques learned in the previous chapters into context. While there are several approaches to building conversational agents, we'll focus on the more recent deep learning approaches and cover the following topics:

- Overview of conversational agents and their general architecture
- An end-to-end pipeline for building a conversational agent
- The architecture of different types of conversational agents, such as

    - Question-answering bots
    - Slot-filling or task-oriented bots
    - General conversation bots

We'll start with an overview of the general architecture of conversational agents.

Overview of conversational agents

A conversational agent interacts with people using speech or text. Facebook Messenger would be an example of a text-based agent while Alexa and Siri are examples of agents that interact through speech. In either case, the agent needs to understand the user's intent and respond accordingly. Hence, the core part of the agent would be a **natural language understanding (NLU)** module. This module would interface with a **natural language generation (NLG)** module to supply a response back to the user. Voice agents differ from text-based agents in having an additional module that converts voice to text and vice versa. We can imagine the system having the following logical structure for a voice-activated agent:

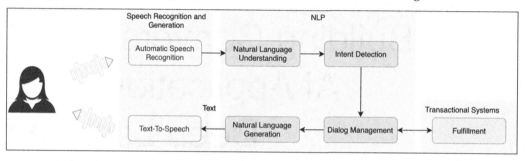

Figure 9.1: Conceptual architecture of a conversational AI system

The main difference between a speech-based system and a text-based system is how the users communicate with the system. All the other parts to the right of the Speech Recognition and Generation section shown in *Figure 9.1* above are identical in both types of conversational AI systems.

The user communicates with the agent using speech. The agent first converts speech to text. Many advancements have been made in the past few years in this area, and it is generally considered a solved problem for major languages like English.

English is spoken in many countries across the globe, resulting in many different pronunciations and dialects. Consequently, companies like Apple develop various models for different accents, such as British English, Indian English, and Australian English. *Figure 9.2* below shows some English and French accents from the Siri control panel on an iPhone 11 running iOS 13.6. French, German, and some other languages also have multiple variants. Another way to do this could be by putting an accent and language classification model as the first step and then processing the input through the appropriate speech recognition model:

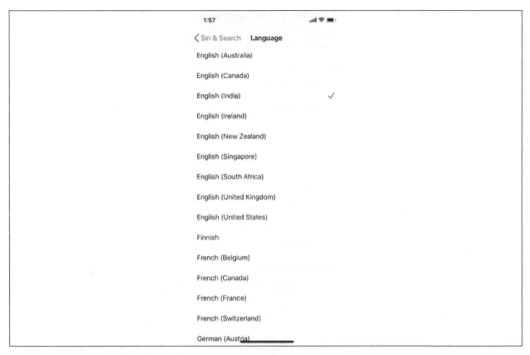

Figure 9.2: Language variants in Siri for speech recognition

For virtual assistants, there are specific models for wake word detection. The model's objective is to start the bot once it detects a wake word or phrase such as "OK Google." The wake word triggers the bot to listen to the utterances until the conversation is completed. Once the user's speech has been converted into words, it is easy to apply to various NLP techniques that we have seen in multiple chapters in this book. The breakdown of the elements shown inside the NLP box in *Figure 9.1* can be considered conceptual. Depending on the system and the task, these components may be different models or one end-to-end model. However, it is useful to think of the logical breakdown, as shown in the figure.

Understanding the user's commands and the intent is a crucial part. Intent identification is essential for general-purpose systems like Amazon's Alexa or Apple's Siri, which serve multiple purposes. Specific dialogue management systems may be invoked based on the intent identified. The dialog management may invoke APIs provided by a fulfillment system. In a banking bot, the command may be to get the latest balances, and the fulfillment may be a banking system that retrieves the latest balance. The dialogue manager would process the balance and use an NLG system to convert the balance into a proper sentence. Note that some of these systems are built on rules-based systems and others use end-to-end deep learning. A question-answering system is an example of an end-to-end deep learning system where dialog management, and NLU are a single unit.

There are different types of conversational AI applications. The most common ones are:

- Task-oriented or slot-filling systems
- Question-answering
- Machine reading comprehension
- Social or chit-chat bots

Each of these types is described in the following sections.

Task-oriented or slot-filling systems

Task-oriented systems are purpose-built to satisfy a specific task. Some examples of tasks are ordering a pizza, getting the latest balance of a bank account, calling a person, sending a text message, turning a light on, and so on. Most of the capabilities exposed by virtual assistants can be classified into this category. Once the user's intent has been identified, control is transferred to the model managing a specific intent to gather all the information to perform the task and manage the dialog with the user. NER and POS detection models form a crucial part of such systems. Imagine that the user needs to fill a form with some information, and the bot interacts with the user to find the required information to fulfill the task. Let's take the example of ordering a pizza. The table below shows a simplified example of the choices in this process:

Size	Crust	Toppings	Delivery	Quantity
Small	Thin	Cheese		1
Medium	Regular	Jalapeno	Take-out	2
Large	Deep dish	Pineapple	Delivery	...
XL	Gluten-free	Pepperoni		

Here is a made-up example of a conversation with a bot:

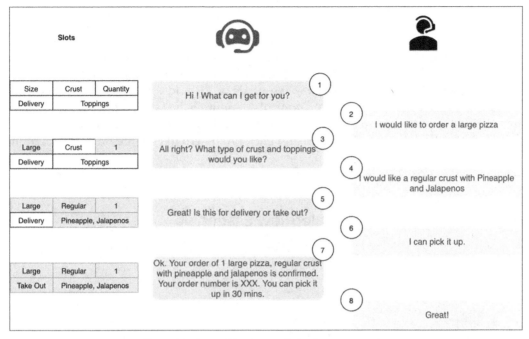

Figure 9.3: A possible pizza-ordering bot conversation

The bot tracks the information needed and keeps marking the information it has received from the person as the conversation progresses. Once the bot has all the information needed to complete the task, it can execute the task. Note that some steps, such as confirming the order or the customer asking for options for toppings, have been excluded for brevity.

In today's world, solutions like Dialogflow, part of Google Cloud, and LUIS, part of Azure, simplify building such conversational agents to just the configuration. Let's see how a simple bot that implements a portion of the pizza-ordering task above can be implemented with Dialogflow. Note that this example has been kept small to simplify configuration and use the free tier of Dialogflow. The first step is to navigate to `https://cloud.google.com/dialogflow`, which is the home page for this service. There are two version of Dialogflow – Essentials or ES, and CX. CX is the advanced version with a lot more features and controls. Essentials is a simplified version with a free tier that is perfect for a bot's trial build. Scroll down on the page so that you can see the Dialogflow Essentials section and click on the **Go to console** link, as shown in *Figure 9.4* below:

Dialogflow Essentials

Go to console

View documentation

Advanced natural language and speech

Natural language understanding in Dialogflow Essentials lets developers take advantage of 40+ prebuilt agents as templates. Powered by Speech-to-Text and Text-to-Speech, Dialogflow Essentials supports real-time streaming and synchronous modes.

Quick to build and deploy

Fast and easy builder for small bots with single topic conversations. Perfect for simple interactions with growing customer needs.

Cross channel

Deploy across popular digital channels, including Google Assistant, Facebook Messenger, Slack, and more.

Figure 9.4: Dialogflow console access

Clicking on the console may require the authorization of the service, and you may need to log in with your Google Cloud account. Alternatively, you may navigate to `dialogflow.cloud.google.com/#/agents` to see a list of configured agents. This screen is shown in *Figure 9.5*:

Figure 9.5: Agents configuration in Dialogflow

A new agent can be created by clicking on the blue **CREATE AGENT** button on the top right. If you see a different interface, please check that you are using Dialogflow Essentials. You can also use this URL to get to the agents section: `https://dialogflow.cloud.google.com/#/agents`. This brings up the new agent configuration screen, shown in *Figure 9.6*:

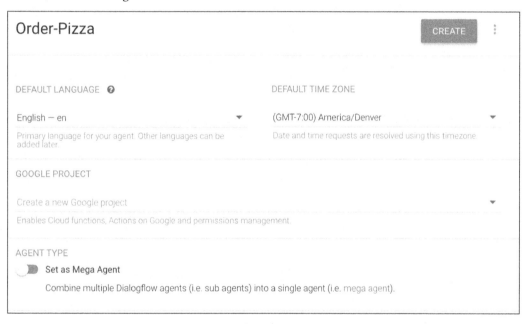

Figure 9.6: Creating a new agent

Please note that this is not a comprehensive tutorial of Dialogflow, so we will be using several default values to illustrate the concept of building slot-filling bots. Hitting **CREATE** will build a new bot and load a screen, as shown in *Figure 9.7*. The main part of building the bot is to define intent. The main intent of our bot is to order pizza. Before we create an intent, we will configure a few entities:

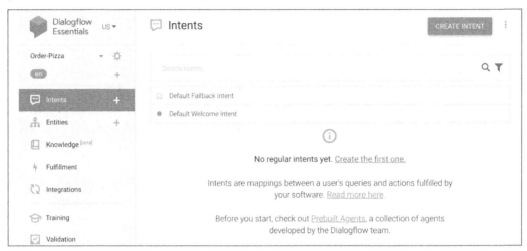

Figure 9.7: A barebones agent ready for configuration

These entities are the slots that the bot will fill out in conversation with the user. In this case, we will define two entities – the crust of the pizza and the size of the pizza. Click on the **+** sign next to Entities on the left in the previous screenshot, and you'll see the following screen:

Figure 9.8: Configuring options for the crust entity in Dialogflow

The values on the left represent the values for the crust entity, and the multiple options or synonyms on the right are the terms the user can input or speak corresponding to each choice. We will configure four options corresponding to the table above. Another entity will be created for the size of the pizza. The configured entity looks like *Figure 9.9*:

Figure 9.9: Configuration of the size entity

Now we are ready to build the intent. Click on the **+** sign next to the **Intents** section on the left navigation bar. We will name this intent order, as this intent will get the options for crust and size from the user. First, we need to specify a set of training phrases that will trigger this intent. Some examples of such training phrases can be "I would like to order pizza" or "Can I get a pizza?". *Figure 9.10* shows some of the configured training phrases for the intent:

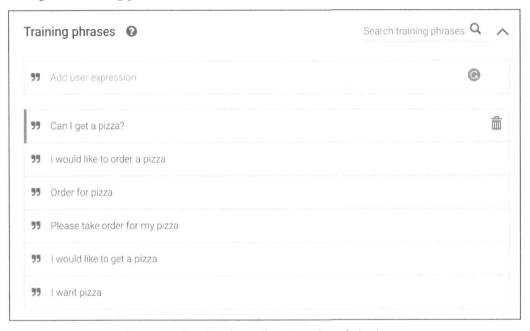

Figure 9.10: Training phrases that trigger the ordering intent

There is a lot of hidden machine learning and deep learning happening in this picture, simplified by Dialogflow. For example, the platform can process text input as well as speech. These training examples are indicative, and the actual phrasing does not need to match any of these expressions directly.

The next step is to define the parameters we need from the user. We add an action with two parameters – size and crust. Note that the **ENTITY** column links the parameter with the defined entities and their values. The **VALUE** column defines a variable name that can be used in future dialogue or for integration with APIs:

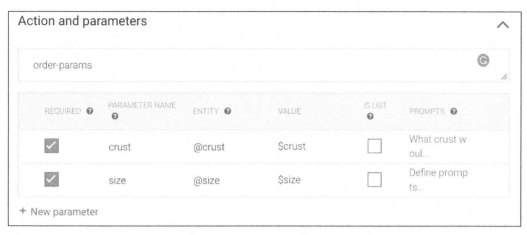

Figure 9.11: Required parameters for the order intent

For each parameter, we need to specify some prompts that the agent will use to ask the user for the information. *Figure 9.12* below shows some example prompts for the size parameter. You may choose to configure your phrasings for the prompts:

Figure 9.12: Prompt options for the size parameter

The last step in configuring the intent is configuring a response once the information is collected. This configuration is done in the **Responses** section and is shown in *Figure 9.13*:

Figure 9.13: Response configuration for the order intent

Note the use of $size.original and $crust.original in the response text. It uses the original terms used by the user while ordering when it repeats the order back. Finally, note that we set this intent as the end of the conversation as we have obtained all the information we needed to get. Our bot is ready to be trained and tested. Hit the blue **Save** button at the top of the page after you have configured the training phrases, action and parameters, and the responses. There is another section at the bottom called fulfilment. This allows connecting the intent with a web service to complete the intent. The bot can be tested using the right side. Note that though we configured only text, Dialogflow enables both text and voice interfaces. While we demonstrate the text interface here, you are encouraged to try the voice interface as well:

Figure 9.14: An example of dialog showing the response processing and the variable being set

Cloud-based solutions have made it quite easy to build task-oriented conversational agents for general uses. However, building an agent for a specialized domain like medical uses may require custom builds. Let's look at options for specific parts of such a system:

- **Intent identification**: The simplest way to identify intent is to treat it as a classification problem. Given an utterance or input text, the model needs to classify it into several intents. Standard RNN-based architectures, like those seen in earlier chapters, can be used and adapted for this task.

- **Slot tagging**: Tagging slots used in a sentence to correspond to inputs can be treated as a sequence classification problem. This is similar to the approach used in the second chapter, where named entities were tagged in a sequence of text. Bi-directional RNN models are quite effective in this part.

Different models can be developed for these parts, or they can be combined in one end-to-end model with a dialog manager. Dialog state tracking systems can be built by using a set of rules generated by experts or by using CRFs (see *Chapter 2*, *Understanding Sentiment in Natural Language with BiLSTMs*, for a detailed explanation). Recent approaches include a Neural Belief Tracker proposed by Mrkšić et al. in 2017 in their paper titled *Neural Belief Tracker: Data-Driven Dialogue State Tracking*. This system takes three inputs:

1. The last system output
2. The last user utterance
3. A slot-value pair from the possible candidates for slots

These three inputs are combined through the content model and semantic decoding model and fed to a binary decision (softmax) layer to produce a final output. Deep reinforcement learning is being used to optimize the dialog policy overall.

In the NLG part, the most common approach is to define a set of templates that can be dynamically populated. This approach was shown in the preceding figure *Figure 9.13*. Neural methods, such as semantically controlled LSTM, as proposed by Wen et al. in their paper *Semantically Conditioned LSTM-based Natural Language Generation for Spoken Dialogue Systems* in 2015, are being actively researched.

Now, let's move on to another interesting area of conversational agents – question-answering and machine reading comprehension.

Question-answering and MRC conversational agents

Bots can be trained to answer questions based on information contained in a **knowledge base (KB)**. This setting is called the question-answering setting. Another related area is **machine reading comprehension** or **MRC**. In MRC, questions need to be answered with respect to a set of passages or documents provided with the query. Both of these areas are seeing a lot of startup activity and innovation. A very large number of business use cases can be enabled with both of these types of conversational agents. Passing the financial report to a bot and answering questions such as the increase in revenue given the financial report would be an example of MRC. Organizations have large digital caches of information, with new information pouring in every day. Building such agents empowers knowledge workers to process and parse large amounts of information quickly. Startups like Pryon are delivering conversational AI agents that merge, ingest, and adapt a myriad of structured and unstructured data into unified knowledge domains that end users can ask natural language questions as a way to discover information.

KBs typically consist of subject-predicate-object triples. The subject and object are entities, while the predicate indicates a relationship between them. The KB can be represented as a knowledge graph, where objects and subjects are nodes connected by predicate edges. A big challenge is the maintenance of such knowledge bases and graphs in real life. Most deep NLP approaches are focused on determining whether a given subject-predicate-object triplet is true or not. The problem is reduced to a binary classification through this reformulation. There are several approaches, including the use of BERT models, which can solve the classification problem. The key here is to learn an embedding of the KB and then frame queries on top of this embedding. Dat Nguyen's survey paper, titled *A survey of embedding models of entities and relationships for knowledge graph completion*, provides an excellent overview of various topics for a deeper dive. We focus on MRC for the rest of this section now.

MRC is a challenging task as the objective is to answer any set of questions about a given set of passages or documents. These passages are not known in advance and may be of variable length. The most common research dataset used for evaluating models is the **Stanford Question Answering Dataset** or **SQuAD**, as it is commonly called. The dataset has 100,000 questions for different Wikipedia articles. The objective of the model is to output the span of text from the article that answers the question. A more challenging dataset has been published by Microsoft based on Bing queries. This dataset is called the **MAchine Reading COmprehension** or **MARCO** dataset. This dataset has over 1 million anonymized questions, with over 8.8 million passages extracted from over 3.5 million documents. Some of the questions in this dataset may not be answerable based on the passages, which is not the case with the SQuAD dataset, which makes this a challenging dataset. The second challenging aspect of MARCO as compared to SQuAD is that MARCO requires the generation of an answer by combining information from multiple passages, whereas SQuAD requires marking the span from the given passage.

BERT and its variants such as *ALBERT: A Lite BERT for Self-supervised Learning of Language Representations* published at ICLR 2020 form the basis of most competitive baselines today. BERT architecture is well suited to this task as it allows passing in two pieces of input text separated by a [SEP] token. The BERT paper evaluated their language model on a number of tasks, including performance on the SQuAD task. Question tokens formed the first part of the pair, and the passage/document formed the second part of the pair. The output tokens corresponding to the second part, the passage, are scored to represent whether the token represents the start of the span or the end of the span.

A high-level depiction of the architecture is shown in *Figure 9.15*:

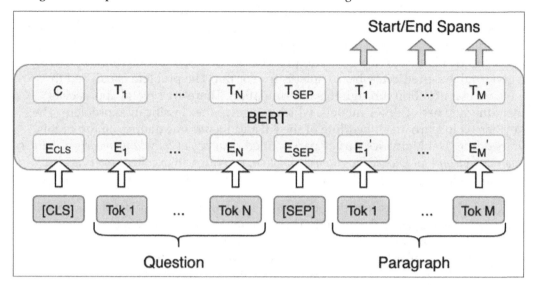

Figure 9.15: BERT fine-tuning approach for SQuAD question answering

A multi-modal aspect of question answering is Visual QA, which was briefly introduced in *Chapter 7, Multi-modal Networks and Image Captioning with ResNets and Transformer*. Analogous architectures to the one proposed for image captioning, which can take images as well as text tokens, are used for solving this challenge.

The setting for QA above is called single turn because the user presents a question with a passage from where the question needs to be answered. However, people have conversations with a back and forth dialog. Such a setting is called multi-turn dialog. A follow-up question may have context from a previous question or answer in the conversation. One of the challenges in a multi-turn dialog is coreference resolution. Consider the following dialog:

Person: Can you tell me the balance in my account #XYZ?

Bot: Your balance is $NNN.

Person: Can you transfer $MM to account #ABC from *that* account?

"that" in the second instruction refers to account #XYZ, which was mentioned in the first question from the person. This is called coreference resolution. In a multi-turn conversation, resolving references could be quite complicated based on the distance between the references. Several strides have been made in this area with respect to general conversation bots, which we'll cover next.

General conversational agents

Seq2seq models provide the best inspiration for learning multi-turn general conversations. A useful mental model is that of machine translation. Similar to the machine translation problem, the response to the previous question can be thought of as a translation of that input into a different language – the response. Encoding more context into a conversation can be achieved by passing in a sliding window of the previous conversation turns instead of just the last question/statement. The term open-domain is often used to describe bots in this area as the domain of the conversation is not fixed. The bot should be able to discuss a wide variety of topics. There are several issues that are their own research topics.

Lack of personality or blandness is one such problem. The dialog is very dry. As an example, we have seen the use of a temperature hyperparameter to adjust the predictability of the response in previous chapters. Conversational agents have a high propensity to generate "I don't know" responses due to a lack of specificity in the dialog. A variety of techniques, including GANs, can be used to address this. The *Personalizing Dialogue Agents* paper authored by Zhang et al. from Facebook outlines some of the approaches used to address this problem.

Two recent examples that highlight the state of the art of writing human-like comments come from Google and Facebook. Google published a paper titled *Towards a Human-like Open-Domain Chatbot*, with a chatbot named Meena with over 2.6 billion parameters. The core model is a seq2seq model using an **Evolved Transformer** (ET) block for encoding and decoding. The model architecture has one ET block in the encoder and 13 ET block in the decoder. ET block was discovered through **neural architecture search** (NAS) on top of the Transformer architecture. A new human evaluation metric called **Sensibleness and Specificity Average** (SSA) was proposed in the paper. The current literature has a variety of different metrics being proposed for the evaluation of such open-domain chatbots with little standardization.

Another example of an open-domain chatbot is described by Facebook on `https://ai.facebook.com/blog/state-of-the-art-open-source-chatbot/`. This paper builds on several years of research and combines the work on personalization, empathy, and KBs into a blended model called BlenderBot. Similar to Google's research, different datasets and benchmarks are used to train this chatbot. The code for the bot has been shared on `https://parl.ai/projects/recipes/`. ParlAI, by Facebook research, provides several models for chatbots through `https://github.com/facebookresearch/ParlAI`.

This is a very hot area of active research with a lot of action happening in it. Comprehensive coverage of this topic would take a book of its own. Hopefully, you have learned many techniques in this book that can be combined to build amazing conversational agents. Let's wrap up.

Summary

We discussed the various types of conversational agents, such as task-oriented, question-answering, machine reading comprehension, and general chit-chat bots. Building a conversational AI system is a very challenging task with many layers, and it is an area of active research and development. The material covered earlier in the book can also help in building various parts of chatbots.

Epilogue

First, let me congratulate you on reaching the end of the book. I hope this book helped you get a grounding in advanced NLP models. The main challenge facing a book such as this is that it will likely be obsolete by the time it reaches the press. The key thing is that new developments are based on past developments; for example, the Evolved Transformer is based on the Transformer architecture. Knowledge of all the models presented in the book will give you a solid foundation and significantly cut down the amount of time you need to spend to understand a new development. A set of influential and important papers for each chapter have also been made available in the GitHub repository. I am excited to see what you will discover and build next!

10

Installation and Setup Instructions for Code

Instructions for setting up an environment for the code in the book are provided in this chapter. These instructions:

- Have been tested on macOS 10.15 and Ubuntu 18.04.3 LTS. You may have to translate these instructions for Windows.

- Only cover the CPU version of TensorFlow. For the latest GPU installation instructions, please follow `https://www.tensorflow.org/install/gpu`. Please note that the use of a GPU is highly recommended. It will cut down the training times of complex models from days to hours.

The installation uses Anaconda and `pip`. It is assumed that Anaconda is set up and ready to go on your machine. Note that we use some new and some uncommon packages. These packages may not be available through `conda`. We will use `pip` in such cases.

 Notes:

- On macOS: `conda` 49.2, `pip` 20.3.1
- On Ubuntu: `conda` 4.6.11, `pip` 20.0.2

GitHub location

The code for this book is located in the following public GitHub repository:

```
https://github.com/PacktPublishing/Advanced-Natural-Language-Processing-
with-TensorFlow-2
```

Please clone this repository to access all the code for the book. Please note that seminal papers for each of the chapters are included in the GitHub repository inside each chapter's directory.

Now, the common steps to set up the conda environment are explained below:

- **Step 1**: Create a new conda environment with Python 3.7.5:

```
$ conda create -n tf24nlp python==3.7.5
```

  The environment is named tf24nlp but feel free to use your own name and make sure you use that in the following steps. I like to prefix my environment names with the version of TensorFlow being used and I suffix a "g" if that environment has a GPU version of the library. As you can probably infer, we are going to use TensorFlow 2.4.

- **Step 2**: Activate the environment and install the following packages:

```
$ conda activate tf24nlp
(tf24nlp) $ conda install pandas==1.0.1 numpy==1.18.1
```

  This installs the NumPy and pandas libraries in our newly created environment.

- **Step 3**: Install TensorFlow 2.4. To do this, we will need to use pip. As of the time of writing, the conda distribution of TensorFlow was still at 2.0. TensorFlow has been moving quite fast. In general, conda distributions are a little behind the latest versions available:

```
(tf24nlp) $ pip install tensorflow==2.4
```

  Please note that these instructions are for the CPU version of TensorFlow. For GPU installation instructions, please refer to https://www.tensorflow.org/install/gpu.

- **Step 4**: Install Jupyter Notebook – feel free to install the latest version:

```
(tf24nlp) $ conda install Jupyter
```

The rest of the installation instructions are about specific libraries used in specific chapters. If you have trouble installing through Jupyter Notebook, you can install them from the command line.

Specific instructions for each of the chapters are given as follows.

Chapter 1 installation instructions

No specific instructions are required for this chapter, as the code for this chapter is run on Google Colab, at colab.research.google.com.

Chapter 2 installation instructions

The tfds package needs to be installed:

```
(tf24nlp) $ pip install tensorflow_datasets==3.2.1
```

We use tfds in most of the chapters going forward.

Chapter 3 installation instructions

1. Install matplotlib via the following command:

```
(tf24nlp) $ conda install matplotlib==3.1.3
```

A newer version may work as well.

2. Install the TensorFlow Addons package for Viterbi decoding:

```
(tf24nlp) $ pip install tensorflow_addons==0.11.2
```

Note that this package is not available through conda.

Chapter 4 installation instructions

This chapter requires the installation of sklearn:

```
(tf24nlp) $ conda install scikit-learn==0.23.1
```

Hugging Face's Transformers library needs to be installed as well:

```
(tf24nlp) $ pip install transformers==3.0.2
```

Chapter 5 installation instructions

None required.

Chapter 6 installation instructions

A library that will be used to compute ROUGE scores needs to be installed:

```
(tf24nlp) $ pip install rouge_score
```

Chapter 7 installation instructions

We require the Pillow library for processing images. This library is the friendly version of the Python Imaging Library. It can be installed like so:

```
(tf24nlp) conda install pillow==7.2.0
```

TQDM is a nice utility to display progress bars while executing long loops:

```
(tf24nlp) $ conda install tqdm==4.47.0
```

Chapter 8 installation instructions

Snorkel needs to be installed. At the time of writing, the version of Snorkel installed was 0.9.5. Note that this version of Snorkel uses older versions of pandas and TensorBoard. You should be able to safely ignore any warnings about mismatched versions for the purposes of the code in this book. However, if you continue to face conflicts in your environment, then I suggest creating a separate Snorkel-specific conda environment.

Run the labeling functions in that environment and store the outputs as a separate CSV file. TensorFlow training can be run by switching back to the tf24nlp environment and loading the labeled data in:

```
(tf24nlp) $ pip install snorkel==0.9.5
```

We'll also use BeautifulSoup for parsing HTML tags out of the text:

```
(tf24nlp) $ conda install beautifulsoup4==4.9
```

There is an optional section in the chapter that involves plotting word clouds. This requires the following package to be installed:

```
(tf24nlp) $ pip install wordcloud==1.8
```

Note that this chapter also uses NLTK, which we installed in the first chapter.

Chapter 9 installation instructions

None.

Share your experience

Thank you for taking the time to read this book. If you enjoyed this book, help others to find it. Leave a review at https://www.amazon.com/dp/1800200935.

Other Books You May Enjoy

If you enjoyed this book, you may be interested in these other books by Packt:

Deep Learning with TensorFlow 2 and Keras - Second Edition
Antonio Gulli
Amita Kapoor
Sujit Pal

ISBN: 978-1-83882-341-2

- Build machine learning and deep learning systems with TensorFlow 2 and the Keras API

- Use Regression analysis, the most popular approach to machine learning

- Understand ConvNets (convolutional neural networks) and how they are essential for deep learning systems such as image classifiers

- Use GANs (generative adversarial networks) to create new data that fits with existing patterns

- Discover RNNs (recurrent neural networks) that can process sequences of input intelligently, using one part of a sequence to correctly interpret another

- Apply deep learning to natural human language and interpret natural language texts to produce an appropriate response

- Train your models on the cloud and put TF to work in real environments

- Explore how Google tools can automate simple ML workflows without the need for complex modeling

Transformers for Natural Language Processing
Denis Rothman

ISBN: 978-1-80056-579-1

- Use the latest pre-trained transformer models
- Grasp the workings of the original Transformer, GPT-2, BERT, T5, and other transformer models
- Create language understanding Python programs using concepts that outperform classical deep learning models
- Use a variety of NLP platforms, including Hugging Face, Trax, and AllenNLP
- Apply Python, TensorFlow, and Keras programs to sentiment analysis, text summarization, speech recognition, machine translations, and more
- Measure productivity of key transformers to define their scope, potential, and limits, in production

Index

A

abstractive summaries
examples 186, 187
**Adaptive Moment Estimation
(Adam Optimizer) 119**
Attention mechanism 123
Audio-Visual Speech Recognition (AVSR) 228

B

Bahdanau Attention architecture 126
Bahdanau attention layer 197-199
Batch Normalization (BatchNorm) 245
beam search 171, 180
used, for decoding penalties 218-220
used, for improving text
summarization 214-217
BERT-based transfer learning 123
attention model 125, 127
encoder-decoder networks 123, 124
transformer model 128, 130
BERT fine-tuning approach
for SQuAD question answering 341, 342
**bidirectional encoder representations from
transformers (BERT) model 131-133**
custom layers, building 142-147
normalization 133-139
sequences 135
tokenization 133-139
**Bi-directional Long Short-Term Memory
(BiLSTM) 25, 47**
**Bilingual Evaluation Understudy
(BLEU) 221, 280**
BiLSTM baseline model 295
data tokenization 296, 297

data, vectorizing 296, 297
training, on weakly supervised data from
Snorkel 322-324
used, for training 297-300
BiLSTM model 65-69
building 83-86
bottleneck design 244
Byte Pair Encoding (BPE) 26, 117, 132

C

captions
generating 274-280
**cloud-based solutions, for building task-x
task-oriented conversational agents**
intent identification 339
slot tagging 339
Common Objects in Context (COCO)
URL 235
conda environment
setting up 346
Conditional Random Fields (CRFs)
working 87, 89
**Consensus-Based Image Description
Evaluation (CIDEr) 280**
constructor
parameters 195, 196
context-free vectorization 36
Continuous Bag-of-Words 41
Continuous Skip-gram 41
conversational agents
overview 328-338
conversational AI applications 330
conversation, with bot
example 331

I

image captioning 232-234
  MS-COCO dataset, using for 235-238
  performance, improving 281, 282
image feature extraction
  performing, with ResNet50 245-249
image processing
  with CNNs 239
  with ResNet50 239
IMDb sentiment analysis
  improving, with weakly supervised labels 290
  performing, with GloVe embeddings 110
IMDb training data
  loading 112-114
inner workings, of weak supervision
  with labeling functions 288-290
In-Other-Begin (IOB) 77
Inverse Document Frequency 37

K

knowledge base (KB) 340

L

labeled data
  collecting 3
  development environment setup, for collection
    of 4-6
labeling functions 288
  iterating on 304-306
language models (LM) 128
  training cost 172
layer normalization 174
learning rate annealing 159
learning rate decay 159
  implementing, as custom callback 159-164
learning rate warmup 160
lemma 32
lemmatization 31-33
longest common subsequence (LCS) 222
Long-Short Term Memory (LSTM) 49
  cell value 50
  forget gate 50

  input gate 50
  output gate 50
Long Short-Term Memory (LSTM)
    networks 50, 51
LSTM model
  with embeddings 62-65

M

Machine Learning (ML) project 2
MAchine Reading COmprehension
    database (MARCO) 341
masked language model (MLM)
    objective 131, 224
Max pooling 241
Metric for Evaluation of Translation with
    Explicit Ordering (METEOR) 221
morphology 32
MRC conversational agents 340, 341
MS-COCO dataset
  used, for image captioning 235-238
Multi-Head Attention block 130
multi-modal deep learning 228
  language tasks 229-231
  vision 229-231
multi-task learning 108, 109

N

Naïve-Bayes (NB) 306
Naïve-Bayes (NB) model
  used, for finding keywords 306-313
Named Entity Recognition (NER) 72-74
  GMB dataset 74, 75
  using, with BiLSTM 89
  using, with CRFs 89, 90
natural language generation (NLG) 340
Natural Language Processing (NLP) 229
natural language understanding (NLU) 46
natural language understanding (NLU)
    module 328
NER datasets
  URL 73
News Aggregator dataset 151
normalization 55

W